Television and Society

Television and Society

An inquest and agenda for improvement

Harry J. Skornia

McGraw-Hill Book Company

New York   London   Sydney   Toronto

3 4 5 6 7 8 9 - MU - 9 8

Contents

1   Introduction: The Problem   7
2   The Business Corporation as a Controller in
    Broadcasting   17
3   Leadership: The Managers and the Networks   39
4   The Problem of Regulation   69
5   The Hidden Economics of Broadcasting   88
6   Ratings and Mass Values   120
7   The Effects of Television and Radio: Some Burning
    Questions   143
8   The United States and Its Image Abroad: Broadcast-
    ing and International Relations   181
9   An Agenda for Change: Some Proposals and
    Recommendations   202

Appendices

A. Edward R. Murrow Address to the Radio and Tele-
    vision News Directors Association Convention,
    October 15, 1958   227
B. Excerpts from *Congressional Record,* June 9, 1934   239
C. Message "To All Law Enforcement Officials," May
    1, 1958, by J. Edgar Hoover   244
D. Walter Lippmann, "The Problem of Television,"
    from The New York *Herald Tribune,* October 27,
    1959   246

Acknowledgments

Adequate acknowledgments for materials, information, and contacts useful in the preparation of this book would run to several thousands. Several hundred books, volumes of official hearings, and copies of testimony and speeches by government officials and industry representatives, along with other original source materials, were used. Participation in some two hundred national and international conferences provided many materials. The individual letters from patient officials of foreign broadcast organizations alone run to several hundreds. I have tried to give due and full credit for all specific quotations and information, although the extent to which the ideas of others have shaped my own is difficult to assess. For all this aid and encouragement from friends and associates deep thanks are due. Any errors or omissions are unintentional, and deeply to be regretted.

Yet a few more specific credits are due: to my wife Lorene, whose faith never wavered during the several years this book was in preparation; to Jack Kitson, former student and loyal aide, who spent many hours in editing earlier drafts and providing and securing from others useful suggestions; to editor Chester Johnson for patient and invaluable stylistic and organizational contributions; to William G. Harley, my successor as President of the National Association of Educational Broadcasters; Robert L. Shayon, of *Saturday Review;* Al Preiss, of *Telefilm* magazine; and Frank Orme, of the National Association for Better Radio and Television—to these and a few others who have been generously helpful in very specific ways, deep and special thanks.

Harry J. Skornia
September, 1964

Television and Society

1

Introduction: The Problem

For over forty years broadcasting in the United States has been carried on principally as a business, conducted purely for profit, by corporation-trained leaders with a sales and business orientation.

Today satellite broadcasting is a reality. Color television with its vastly increased impact and expense is rapidly replacing black and white. As television enters this new stage, it is important to examine how well its leadership, structure, and philosophy—dating in their essentials from the Harding, Coolidge, and Hoover administrations—meet present needs.

Has the United States found the proper institutional framework and control mechanisms for the essential communications functions which television and radio must provide if democracy is to prevail? Are vast and powerful business corporations, which centralize control each year in fewer hands, the best trustees for the nation's radio and television communications systems?

In Canada, where broadcasting was at first wholly commercial, a coexisting national public-service network was found to be essential. It was added thirty years ago. In Great Britain, the validity of the continued existence of a noncommercial monopoly in television was studied by several distinguished commissions. Britain now has a commercially based television service which is nearly ten years old, coexisting with the noncommercial BBC. Following World War II, the structures of broadcasting in Germany, Austria, Italy, and Japan were drastically changed. Decentralization, imposed by the Western occupation powers, has replaced the corporate-state mechanisms of the earlier totalitarian era. In the late forties wholly new types of structures came into existence, often with the help of United States consultants. In most countries mixed systems, involving public service, education, and other variants in reasonable balance, now prevail. The dangers of leaving these instruments under the control of any one social, political, economic, or religious group have been clearly identified in many national and international studies.

It is not here implied that there is anything inherently wrong with a commercial system as *one* of *several* balanced systems in a nation. But there is increasing evidence that current structures and practices, as the *dominant* ones, are inadequate to ensure maximum over-all public service as contrasted to sales and advertising service. Coexisting systems and balancing uses of television and radio—including a publicly owned network, educational and subscription combinations, and other variants—need to be considered if the imbalances which have been demonstrated by the present system are to be redressed.

Any adequate plan of action must be based on an analysis of the problems to be corrected. Therefore, although the most essential portion of this study is the recommendations to which it leads, early sections provide an examination of what appear to be persistent, recurring, and critical weaknesses in our broadcasting.

The approach taken here may well be a prejudiced one. It represents a very specific and critical point of view, evolved after many years of study and work with many national and international broadcast systems and organizations. This analysis and critique does not claim to present a balanced picture of United States broadcasting any more than a medical diagnosis can take the time to list all the parts of the body which are functioning properly. The author invites correction and the participation and contributions of other men of goodwill. In a democratic system responsible expert and public criticism is the best instrument available to achieve improvement. This book is intended as a step in this direction.

Nearly forty years of the present broadcasting system has conditioned a generation of citizens to find it normal. Most people find it difficult to think of other kinds of broadcast systems and uses. Recent discussions in particular have painted an oversimplified, polarized picture in which freedom, or what we now have, is contrasted with public control, which is characterized as big government, socialism, censorship. An imaginative, flexible approach recognizes that many alternatives and variations between these two extremes are possible.

Since some of the current practices are so serious in their implications, some of the measures which will be suggested will no doubt seem to be drastic or radical. The need to break out of present frames of reference in thinking of possible new uses and controls for television and radio can hardly be exaggerated.

The structure we now have has been shaped principally by industry itself in *ad hoc, fait accompli* stages. However honest the individuals involved may be, members of the broadcast industry as presently constituted cannot assess the overall role of what they have come to think of as *their* instruments. They are too close to the parts to see the whole of the problem. Born and nurtured in a corporate and sales-based environment, they cannot fail to have blind spots and prejudices. No institution has the perspective to criticize itself adequately; outside consultants with different perspectives must be used.

In his address at the Alfred I. Du Pont Awards Foundation Dinner, in New York, March 26, 1962, Hugh Carleton Greene (now Sir Hugh), director general of the British Broadcasting Corporation, told of a ninety-minute film which the BBC had recently produced. It examined television in many places: in Europe, the United States, Africa, Asia, and Latin America. Then Mr. Greene said: "The main impression [caught by the film] was of the way in which television is being misused—of the way, it would not be too harsh to say, in which broadcasters are betraying their responsibilities."

In most discussions and analyses of broadcasting in the United States, it has been generally assumed that the flaws of our present system are inevitable characteristics of the medium and that competition, as practiced under the present system, is good. The present analysis does not take these premises for granted.

How the present system of radio and television came about in the United States is little understood, and is less discussed. In most nations national commissions of various types studied the problems of broadcasting and made considered decisions on the basis of a great deal of evidence, carefully weighed. In the United States no such studies have ever taken place. Furthermore, congressional action has been influenced by unbelievably effective industry lobby pressures.

There was not even a quorum present in the House when the Communications Act of 1934, on which all present regulation and practices are based, was rushed through, essentially reenacting the 1927 Act. The 1927 Act itself was based on inadequate understanding and study and was intended only as an *ad hoc* and temporary measure.

The present broadcast system, therefore, is neither accidental nor natural. It was carefully shaped and nurtured by individuals and corporations whose credentials and biases will later be examined. It is what it is now because this form of broadcasting is most profitable to those who control it, not because it serves the public interest better than, or even as well as, any of a number of alternatives might. But it is not inevitable or necessarily permanent. It can be changed whenever the citizens of the United States and their leaders decide that a change is needed.

Broadcasting and Government Regulation in a Free Society, a pamphlet published in 1959 by the Center for the Study of Democratic Institutions, listed sample shortcomings of our present system as seen by James L. Fly, a former chairman of the Federal Communications Commission. Some of these included "excessive use of film under guise of network operation; permitting excessive control by dominant advertisers especially over discussion programs and news programs and analysts; lack of courage in dealing with ugly public issues; yielding to hysteria in black-listing outstanding program participants under guise of tenuous loyalty charges . . . and excessive concentration of station interests."

To these could be added a score or more of others: payola, quiz-rigging, and various other types of rigging; the failure of stations and networks to keep promises made in order to secure stations and monopolies; the exodus of creative talent from broadcasting; the increased incidence of collusion and other practices forbidden by antitrust and other regulatory statutes; distortion and concealment of facts regarding public costs of "free TV"; censorship and the withholding of controversial news favorable to interests, such as labor or conservation, inimical to big business; and opposition to frequencies for educational radio and television. Such practices will be examined in some detail in later pages of this study.

Several other questions will be raised as well. Broadcasting, when it began, produced its own programs. It was therefore then exempt from common-carrier status. Now that broadcasting is essentially (as David Sarnoff once said), "only a pipeline" for films and programs and sales messages, and for news from tickers of the large news syndicates, is that exemption still justified? Or should television and radio now be regulated wholly or partially as common carriers? All three television networks are scheduling more and more old films even in prime time; they are, in effect, functioning as "retail outlets" for the products of parent and other corporations. How should they be controlled?

Another question revolves around the stake which present broadcast owners have in continued armaments, cold-war tensions, and defense contracts. In view of the fact that RCA, CBS, Westinghouse, General Electric, and scores of other broadcast firms receive from 10 to 40 per cent of their income from government contracts related to defense efforts, how wholeheartedly and sincerely can they be expected to press for genuine and lasting peace? How much recognition do United States broadcasters give to the fact, stated in the UNESCO preamble, that wars begin in the minds of men? How peace-oriented is United States broadcasting?

How well does United States broadcasting measure up in the international area? There have been reports reflecting pride in how many United States programs are being shown in the rest of the world and how large a proportion of foreign systems are now either partly owned or partly controlled by United States networks and other United States firms. But we also read and hear quite different things. We read, for example, the story of the pressure tactics used by foreign branches of United States firms to cause commercial television to be intro-

duced in England over the objections of large segments of both
political parties, and without the British public's having any
real opportunity to participate in the decision. United States
broadcasters, advertising agencies, and trade journals have taken
considerable pride in such "successes." Should the United States
public share the pride of United States broadcasters in such
accomplishments? Or is the image of America which is now
going into all parts of the world something more than United
States *broadcasters'* business? Many thoughtful Americans are
disturbed about increased references to "cheap American" films;
they do not like to have the United States equated with cheap-
ness and vulgarity.

Foreign friends and visitors have asked some searching
questions. Many underdeveloped nations clamor for agricul-
tural, medical, and educational instruction, which television
could provide; must they huddle night after night around television sets watching United States westerns and crime and adventure series? Are such series justified, however profitable
they may be? Are these profits the criteria now needed? The
New York speech of Hugh Carleton Greene, referred to earlier,
contained these carefully chosen words: "Looking at the world
as a whole, one cannot help feeling that a great opportunity is
being lost—and I hope you will not think that I am abusing
your hospitality in saying so. The leadership of the Western
world is today in American hands. . . . One cannot help won-
dering whether the good that has been done by programme
after programme of foreign aid is in danger of being undone
by the image of America as it appears . . . on the television
screens of the world. . . ." Mr. Greene reminded us that "In
countries of Asia, Africa and Latin America there are thousands
of young idealistic people who want more from television than
the ideals of Tombstone and Dead Man's Gulch. If we in the
West fail to help these people to make better use of television,
they can turn for their ideals elsewhere." "If I have said more
than is becoming in a guest," Mr. Greene continued, "I can
only plead the hope that frankness may be excused among
friends."

A great Canadian, Brock Chisholm, has asked us similar
questions about United States broadcasting. Dr. Chisholm
was director general of the World Health Organization from
1948 to 1953; more recently he has been president of the World

Federation for Mental Health. Like Mr. Greene, he has dared to ask us some embarrassing questions on our own soil. In his Bampton Lectures at Columbia University in 1957 (later published in book form) he asked, as a citizen of Africa might ask, "why Americans allow this to happen, because those films do more harm than a hundred Voices of America could do good. They almost completely, or more than completely, neutralize much of the true educational work that is being done about North America in our part of the world. Yet when we ask why such films are sent to us, there isn't any answer that makes sense. The only answer apparently is to make money, and we just cannot be convinced that the United States needs money so badly that it would blacken its own reputation in the eyes of hundreds of millions of people to earn a few dollars." [1]

As new nations of colored peoples emerge in Asia and Africa, we ask what our national administration is doing in the civil rights area. For this will tell them much about the contempt or respect in which we hold them. But we should also ask: What is United States *broadcasting* doing in this crucial area? What is the effect of exports to Asia and Africa of westerns based on Indian-killing, or of programs in which Negroes are shown principally as comic characters, or as qualified only for menial tasks? What is the effect on new nations and starving natives of pictures of American life abounding in violence, materialism, luxury, and waste? These are not problems to be left to the broadcasters. They are problems involving our whole nation and the respect or disrespect in which Americans are held around the world. How much can the Voice of America do, when far more of this material goes into a country in a month than the Voice of America can voice in a year?

At home we read and hear much about the deplorable state of mental and physical health, the crisis in education, the rise of juvenile delinquency, and other social problems; when the role of television is discussed in relation to these problems, most industry spokesmen disclaim any connection between them. However, the evidence to the contrary continues to mount in the records of distinguished psychiatrists, prison superintendents, mental-health clinics, veterans' hospitals, and juvenile courts, and in hundreds of research studies in Europe and Asia. Such evidence, and conclusions to be drawn from it, will be found in a later chapter devoted entirely to this problem.

Much has been said and heard about the threat of censorship. Regulation has been stoutly resisted by industry because this would, it is claimed, constitute censorship. To what extent is there justification for the claim by Newton Minow, former Federal Communications Commission chairman, that industry, more than government, is now blocking the "free flow" of information essential to the survival of the United States? To what extent have ·industry and corporation values pushed all others aside? With single corporations often controlling networks and stations, patents, set manufacture, transmitter types and prices, programs, and commercials, how much more than lip notice do labor, education, religion, intellectuals, artists, and other vital segments of our society receive? What is industry's attitude toward these groups? How does the exclusion of such groups and points of view affect what is thought of as the national image, not only in television and radio but also in our daily life?

It should perhaps not be too surprising if the single administration which broadcasting has had in the United States since the early 1920s has preserved a *status quo* more complete than that found in virtually any other field of endeavor. How has it been able to do this? During these same years political structure and practice in the United States at both the state and national levels have had to make several drastic changes to meet changing conditions. It is difficult to find any such basic changes in the approach to broadcasting. When new blood has been introduced into leadership positions, it seems not to have survived—corporately acceptable types, however, persist. People who were yesterday executives at ABC are today officers of CBS and tomorrow will be at NBC, and in the agencies. Most are merchandisers and salesmen. Are these the leaders the nation needs in broadcasting? How is the nation to get a different kind of leadership to balance the views of the Sarnoffs, Paleys, Goldensons, Taishoffs, however excellent as businessmen they may be? How capable are representatives of the old regime of providing the flexibility, change, and public-service leadership the nation needs today?

The profits of a few stations, which are owned by an ever-smaller group of large owners, have risen sharply in recent years. The profits of smaller and independent stations have declined. There is little or no opportunity for new-station entry in most markets. How long can a system which breeds such trends be tolerated? The tactics with which newcomers are excluded deserve attention. Flagrant misrepresentation is becoming more common. Are such trends not perhaps dangerous enough to deserve careful attention?

In such a context, the role of government regulation of television and radio becomes a far more basic question than a mere difference of opinion between broadcasters and government. It is a matter affecting the entire national welfare. It is every citizen's business.

The recent shift [from government to industry] of the balance of power in broadcasting has been too little noted. The tactic of industry has been to conceal this trend, warning instead of the dangers of encroachments by government. Those who note developing imbalances which may jeopardize essential freedoms or the structure of democracy, regardless of whether they come from government or other sources such as corporations, have an obligation to point them out. Such imbalances and pressures are becoming more numerous. It is especially incumbent upon educators and other honest critics, who have no vested interests in either industry or government, to participate in necessary criticism and planning.

The long-term goal for television and radio is not greater restriction, but greater freedom. The objective is the liberation of broadcasting from the chains, taboos, and anachronistic practices which bind it, keeping it from realizing its full potential.

A great deal of the current difficulty which the broadcast industry has brought into being is traceable to its "mass" concept. Technically, immediate feedback provision could have been built into the United States broadcast system from the outset. It would have cost more, and it would have reduced the channels for the one-way flow we now know as broadcasting. But it was possible. Some rating agencies and pay-television systems already use electronic devices whereby viewers can push buttons and send immediate reactions and answers to raters miles away. Many educational stations in the United States and many foreign systems exemplify non-mass media. Such systems need to be explored as national alternatives to the present stifling mass-media obsession.

Our atomic and electronic age requires faster decision making and better policy guidance to elected representatives than present practices make possible. Two-way flow is needed to replace the authoritarian imposition of attitudes and values manufactured by the business community. Instantaneous voting possibilities via federal, satellite-based, and other types of systems and facilities remain to be explored.

The occasional fine program on television provides a glimpse of what television could be, but a sense of eventlessness and sameness prevails most of the time. A change in *kind* of broadcasting, not just in amount or degree, or in the mix, needs to be explored. The sales roles of these media need now to be restricted to their proper, limited role.

Television should clarify life and experience, enrich rather than vulgarize, and create conditions in the minds of men which will lead to peace instead of war, to brotherhood instead of hatred and bitterness. In no other instruments or natural resources does the nation have such natural means for releasing individual talents and for discovering and developing the new ideas and new types of leadership which America and the world now need. What is needed can be done.

2

The Business Corporation as a
Controller in Broadcasting

In all nations the birth of broadcasting raised the problem of control. In most nations distinguished commissions made careful studies of TV broadcasting before it was decided what kinds of organizations were needed. The basic question was: How could broadcasting be operated and controlled so that it would serve *all* the diverse elements of a nation's life without becoming more subservient to one aspect (e.g., business, labor, religion) than to others, and without neglecting the over-all *public* interest in favor of private interests?

In some nations broadcasting was entrusted to religious, labor, or professional groups. In some it was entrusted to government, either as a special department or attached to a ministry, such as education. In others it was turned over to specially created nonprofit corporations.

In the United States the decision was made to turn radio, and later television, over to free enterprise. How compatible and reconcilable with the *public* or over-all national interest are those practices which a business corporation *must* observe in a competitive environment?

Before examining the conflicts of interest which have developed between the public and (increasingly favored) private interests, four brief examples might be cited of the general incompatibility.

In the early history of the Ford Motor Company, when Henry Ford decided that prices of Ford cars could be reduced, a Ford stockholder by the name of John F. Dodge took exception to this generous impulse. In the suit which followed, the Michigan Supreme Court upheld Mr. Dodge's position regarding the role of the business corporation. The court held that the business corporation, created to operate for profit, must serve its stockholders first and the public only secondarily—the corporation interest, rather than the public, must be favored whenever profits may be affected. "A business corporation is organized and carried on *primarily for the profit of the stockholders.* The powers of the directors are to be employed for that end." A corporation's charitable or public-interest expenditures must advance the long-range prospects of profit making. To quote the court again: "The discretion of directors is to be exercised [only] in the choice of means to attain that end and *does not extend to a change in the end itself.*" [1] Therefore, a corporation created to operate for profit, regardless of any desire to serve "public interest first" by its officials, must serve its *owners* and *stockholders* first, returning to them as large a profit as possible. Many corporations have been able to reconcile these two interests satisfactorily; how well broadcast corporations have done so will become clearer as the record is examined.

A second source of conflict is found in the position of the corporation with regard to labor. Management and labor are natural rivals for a share in the profits of the enterprise involved. If the corporation is to survive and serve its *owners* well, it must and does oppose labor's claims and pressures every day of its life. How it can do that and yet be fair to labor and the *public* is one of the important social problems of our age. The present broadcast structure has provided no satisfactory solution to it—the two groups appear to be inimical. If the corporation were to give labor good program time and favorable news coverage, its position at the bargaining table would weaken. The corporation, as most managers see its role, cannot afford to do this. Therefore, it is inappropriate and naïve to expect the business corporation to be *able* to synthesize and represent the public's interests when they conflict with its own profit interests.

A third reason for the inability of the corporation to represent the over-all public interest is to be found in its internal organization. The larger TV business corporations are typically monolithic in structure. This is one of the advantages claimed for such corporations: that they are capable of making decisions more quickly than more bureaucratic or democratic organizations. Their greater efficiency in industrial areas is undoubted. It is one of the sources of the nation's might. The question arises, however, whether it is not ironic for such totalitarian organizations to be expected to be bulwarks of democracy.

The fourth aspect of this problem can be found in any of the recent annual reports of such firms as CBS, ABC-Paramount, or RCA. The CBS Annual Report for 1961, for instance, contains a discussion entitled "Industrial and Military Electronics," in which CBS contracts with the military are described. The RCA Annual Report for 1961 reports that 38 per cent of RCA's income for the year, or $582,012,000, came from United States government contracts. Recent ABC-Paramount annual reports note the new projects undertaken by the firm in the national defense effort, including participation in nuclear tests in the Pacific area. It appears that the greater the world tension, the more intense the cold war, the greater the space race, and the more numerous the world crises, the greater will be the profits of such corporations. How honestly or strongly *can* their TV broadcasting be expected to press for peaceful or disarmament activities? These are serious questions which require careful consideration.

These brief examples illustrate the nature of the interests and problems involved. And it would appear that in order to resolve such conflicts, the corporations have sought to *change the public's interests and tastes to conform to the corporation's sense of values.* Therein lies the danger—it constitutes a very real and special problem.

Perhaps never before in history have the most powerful channels to the people been so completely controlled by so small a segment of the national life. Since government itself has no equivalent channels with which to talk back, and since labor, religion, and other parts of our culture have no equivalent voices, the citizens have an image which is almost wholly dictated by sales-, advertising-, and business-oriented custodians. Is the picture which they provide accurate, objective, complete, and democratic? There is mounting evidence that it is not.

This situation is all the more serious because magazines, films, phonograph records, and radio stations are now largely controlled by the same kinds of corporations that control TV. Press empires and other types of monopolies have been widely discussed in past years. Less generally discussed is the extent to which television and radio stations, especially the networks, are only branches of larger corporations in which broadcasting is only one of many integrated activities. Most newspapers and even press empires in the United States were founded by individuals instead of corporations. They were established by journalists or crusaders—good or bad, radical or conservative—who felt that they had a sacred mission. Publishers generally wished to reveal truth, oppose evil and injustice, and promote the general welfare as they saw it; rarely was their motive principally profit seeking. The operators and controllers of most broadcast empires, however, usually had other businesses. RCA and the Sarnoffs were engaged primarily in equipment manufacture; so were General Electric, Westinghouse, Philco-Ford, and a score of others. The Paley family was engaged in cigar manufacturing. Leonard Goldenson was engaged in the movie business before his firm purchased ABC. The secondary position (except for profits) which broadcasting played in their over-all corporate interests is apparent. Stations owned by newspapers have been viewed usually as subsidiaries. Stations operated by equipment manufacturers, such as RCA, General Electric, and Westinghouse, are most unlikely to serve the public interest when this conflicts with their profit interest. It must be recognized that the roots of commercial broadcasting, especially those of the networks, are anchored to big business. We must first examine this matrix in order to understand the overall problem—and to glimpse the key to its possible solution.

In Britain the British Broadcasting Company was originally a stock company, owned by manufacturers of broadcast equipment. It was, however, realized that a service as important as broadcasting should provide the best possible programs—regardless of profit; this *company* was, therefore, dissolved in 1926, and a new nonprofit, public corporation, the British Broadcasting Corporation, was established in its place. The new corporation excluded any manufacturer of broadcast equipment. Such dual roles as those of RCA in the United States were deemed to be conflicts of interest which could not be tolerated in broadcasting.

Such distinguished social scientists as Paul Lazarsfeld pointed out many years ago that it should not be surprising that broadcasting in the United States represents primarily the interests of big business—he who pays the piper calls the tune. The people of the United States accept the present system because they are unaware of the alternatives. The corporation has come to exert the same kind of domination of thinking and behavior, in many respects, that the Church exercised during the Middle Ages. Hence, it is no surprise that we do not analyze what is happening to the standards and mores of the TV world. An example of this is to be found in the acceptance of quiz fixing, payola, and other such practices. True, such practices were natural to business, but they were not generally accepted by the national community. With time, however, the sense of shock and outrage passed. These corporate practices, like commercials, soon were accepted by the wider community, thus setting the style for the whole nation.

In international relations also, corporation policy finds little challenge. Industrial investments in the Middle East, Cuba, and elsewhere have become interests which the entire nation is called upon to protect—in recent Telstar negotiations, AT&T signed agreements with nations who had expected the United States government to be the signator.

United States networks and film companies show no hesitancy in exporting any films or television programs which will return a profit, regardless of the adverse effect which some of these exports have on the United States image abroad. The extent to which the profit interests of such corporations fail to coincide with our national interests is becoming obvious.

Another problem arises with the growth of "corporate citizenship." A foreign employee of a United States hotel chain or oil corporation may find his status dependent on his job with the foreign branch of that corporation—he is likely to identify more closely with the corporation than with his own nation. If he achieves an outstanding record with the firm, he may be invited to move to the United States and may even become a United States citizen—or he may be transferred to branches or offices in other parts of the world, changing nationality as needed, while retaining his "corporate citizenship."

A parallel development is to be noted domestically. Many corporations seek to develop in United States citizens a greater loyalty to corporations, under the term "free enterprise," than to the government. Utility companies, particularly, have sought to portray the government as being antagonistic to the people's interests, rights, and liberties. Considerable success seems to have been achieved in this effort through the mass media, in spite of the obvious fact that an adult citizen has a vote in government, whereas only the large stockholders have an effective vote in corporations and small stockholders almost none at all. True, corporations do go through the motions of conducting elections at their annual meetings. But this ritual is now largely conducted for show. The president and directors usually renominate themselves; when one of these men dies or the board needs enlarging, only someone with a philosophy consistent with their own is appointed. This is essentially the procedure followed in deciding who runs RCA, NBC, CBS, and ABC-Paramount, or Westinghouse, Hearst, Knight, Storer, and other groups which control most of our broadcasting. The dynastic corps of managers so elected remains in control year after year. The advantage which this system has over the manpower of government, whose personnel is subject to change as a result of popular elections, accounts for the frequent defeat of government agencies in consent-degree cases which extend over long periods of time, often spanning more than one national administration.

In the past, the corporate economy was only one part of society; business corporations have, however, raised their economic umbrella over the whole of the diverse elements which make up our nation. If people speak of the United States as having a good year, they are likely not to mean in desegregation, education, health, welfare, or agriculture but in industrial production and profits. These have become the nation's criteria of success, national health, and prosperity. In recent years critics of the corporation have suggested the need to curb certain corporate trends. If corporations are to behave like governments in their external relations, should they not be required to practice republican forms of management? At least in broadcasting should not fair labor practices and other characteristics of democracy be required? If the nation's electronic communications systems are to *serve* democracy, should they not also *exemplify* or *practice* democracy?

During the quiz and payola scandals, when victims had to be found promptly in order to give the impression of a spontaneous and voluntary housecleaning and in order to prevent more stringent government action, the networks spent little time on employee hearings or fair trials. The sudden dismissals of employees who protested their innocence and claimed to be doing only what they were ordered to do may seem to be the corporation's own business—but many recent studies have reminded us that the internal procedures of a large organization may tell more about it than all of its official statements.

The Constitution of the United States had nothing to say about democracy within labor unions and corporations—neither existed at the time the Constitution was written. Legal provisions have since been enacted to ensure democratic elections and open books for labor unions. No comparable provisions have yet been enacted regarding the corporation.

One way in which corporations have sought to silence criticism which accuses them of not being democratic is by selling stock widely enough so a considerable number of stockholders may be cited as the corporation's constituency. In this way the Paley family has broadened the ownership base of CBS, while still retaining management control of officers and policies. Similarly, numbers of people are used in rating statistics and "popularity quotients" as proof of operation in the public interest.

When the Bell Telephone Company engaged in widespread distribution of stocks in the 1930s, it was less interested in securing the additional dollars which it could have secured with less expense from larger sources than it was in securing the proprietary interest and support of large numbers of people who can be cited as the company's real owners. Each stockholder, it has been found, tends to identify with the corporation in which he holds even a small amount of stock. As "co-owners," stockholders often become lobbyists for "their" company, opponents of regulation, and members of the corporation *we* family. As a stockholder the individual becomes a willing receiver of public relations releases and other reports, appeals, and explanations which can conveniently be attached to stockholder reports. A mailing list of such large numbers of friendly citizens is in itself of no small value to a corporation, even if it does not need their dollars.

Broadly based stock ownership also enables corporations to

speak before Congress on behalf of and "in the name of" millions of stockholders, identifying them as "the public." This corporation practice also deserves scrutiny. For besides confusing the issue of who are "the people," or what *is* the public interest, it also confuses and bypasses the regular, legitimate channels of government and real public influence.

With what type of people do corporate leaders surround themselves? What kind of behavior ensures that employees will get ahead? How are dissenters and independent thinkers treated? Many of these questions have been discussed by William H. Whyte in *The Organization Man,* and by Martin Mayer in his description of advertising agencies, *Madison Avenue, U.S.A.* Many a station or network employee, as a member of a company-controlled retirement plan, has held his tongue rather than speak out too bluntly or forget company discipline. It would be strange indeed if the business corporation, which by nature favors conformity and opposes dissent in its own organization and philosophy, should by some superhuman or super-corporate miracle favor dissent, controversy, and independent thinking so far as broadcasting programs are concerned. The ability to lead such a double life is beyond the power of most corporations.

Richard Hofstadter, in *Social Darwinism in American Thought,* tells how Darwin's theory of the survival of the fittest was eagerly adopted and interpreted by large American corporations: If the small and the weak were swallowed or destroyed, it was not the fault of the stronger and larger firm—it was God's will, the law of evolution. John D. Rockefeller even explained at a Sunday School picnic that the ruthless competition found in American business, killing off the weak or the too humane, was "merely the working out of the law of nature, and a law of God." [2] Such tactics may well be acceptable in industrial corporations or in businesses dealing with goods. How acceptable are they in the communications system of a democracy or in the realm of ideas?

Another relevant aspect of the value system of corporations is the emphasis placed on short-range profits and on tangibles as opposed to intangibles. By these standards factories are investments, but hospitals and schools are expenses since they produce no money. One contributes to antidelinquency or mental-health drives in order to cause a reduction in one's own tax assessment rather than in the suffering of others. In fact, certain humanitarian tendencies, when exhibited by a corporation, are interpreted as signs of softness. The business ethic is "practical," i.e., hard-boiled. Decisions must make not only sense but also dollars. These tendencies may very well be essential in business corporations—but are they the best ones in the realm of ideas and communications?

Indeed, social problems created by industry are made to appear as natural social problems, which must be solved at *public* expense. Such are the problems of water and air pollution, delinquency, and slums which grow up around factories. In such an environment it is not surprising that networks and broadcasters should deny responsibility for alleged adverse effects of television programs—they consider these as social problems rather than as problems caused in whole or in part by them.

The Federal Trade Commission from 1928 through 1931 investigated the pressures of corporations on the schools. The "businesslike" respect in which corporations feel justified in purging textbooks and the schools of anti-industry or pro-government materials is well described in Jack Levin's book *Power Ethics*.[3] One of the ways which industry found useful for keeping schools and teachers friendly to them was explained in some of the exhibits presented. One speaker outlined in a speech to the National Electric Light Association in 1924 how teachers, who are usually in need of summer jobs, could be employed during the summer in order to indoctrinate them and make them friendly to privately owned utility companies. A second way of shaping education is found in the pressure brought to bear to keep out of textbooks any material critical of free enterprise or private utilities, or favorable to public ownership of utilities. For example, Merlin H. Aylesworth, then director of the National Electric Light Association, coordinated the efforts of the utilities to set up a textbook committee to keep material unfriendly to the utilities out of school textbooks, particularly those of the lower grades. In this effort the utilities and Mr. Aylesworth were joined by officials of AT&T, the Illinois Bell Telephone Company, the National Association of Manufacturers, and other well-meaning guardians of the public interest. Most of these groups are still keeping a watchful eye out for material favorable to the TVA, rural electrification, cooperatives, and other publicly owned or nonprofit projects.

Another corporate practice in the realm of ideas and education is illustrated by the story of radio, as found in most textbooks. Lawrence Lessing, in *Man of High Fidelity*,[4] describes how successful the steady pressure of AT&T, RCA, and a few other large corporations has been in securing in most textbooks recognition of Lee De Forest as the "father of radio." They have succeeded in pushing aside claims of rival Edwin H. Armstrong, who was kept in court by RCA and by Mr. De Forest for most of the latter years of his life. During much of his life he also had to fight off their efforts to discredit his inventions. Mr. Armstrong, as a distinguished inventor, was for many years not mentioned in RCA publications. Their readers and subscribers had little opportunity to know of him and his work.

Such pressures are today being extended from the older media to the new: to films, educational television and radio programs, and visuals of various types which are often supplied at no charge to both commercial and educational stations, to the schools, and to church and civic groups.

The corporations also affect educational policy by their employment practices. They not only determine the type of students who get jobs, but they eventually affect what qualities schools will cultivate. This is not to say that this is a deliberate intention of the corporations. Nevertheless, by special grants, which make possible the addition of chairs or entire departments, industries and foundations, no less than the federal government, can determine what schools will teach or emphasize. This is particularly true for schools which need financial help. Much of the character of public as well as private education has been determined by the act of giving or withholding assistance to education by specific corporations or trade associations.

For many years industry called for more practical and vocational subjects in the schools—and curricula were developed which trained rather than educated young people. More recently, however, industry has discovered that well-educated, rather than merely trained, individuals are more adaptable for the rapid changes brought about by automation. Therefore, having influenced the public schools and colleges to move in vocational directions, large corporations like GE and AT&T more recently began to set up their *own* educational training programs for employees and executives. Most such programs emphasize a return to the humanities and liberal arts. Such programs are in a sense similar to parochial education as compared with public education. Whether such a parallel educational system, operated by industry itself with budgets almost as high as those of the public schools, is or is not in the public interest is not the main point here. What is relevant is that, in addition to the constant educating and conditioning carried out by industry through the mass media, a regular system of private education exists outside the formal public educational structure of the nation. Its existence and well-financed operation has wide influence on both public education and the popular value systems. Obviously, this coexisting educational system competes for both teachers and funds with the public and private institutions of the nation.

Another means of influencing education locally is the practice by large national corporations of encouraging the managers of their local branches to be as active as possible in local affairs; the dues and expenses of such employees are generally paid by the company. And among the positions they are often encouraged to accept is that of membership on school boards. Studies have indicated how frequently board members for both local systems and colleges and universities come from the commercial and financial classes, even though the groups they represent are often only a very small proportion of the total population. This situation is traceable in part to the greater access to mass media which these individuals have, through ownership of stations or sponsorship of programs by their companies.

Perhaps more disquieting and revealing are the corporation's activities in the field of government and politics. The large corporation has the power to mount great pressure as a lobby; it thus exerts great control over decision makers within government agencies, in the Senate, and in the House of Representatives. Since industry controls most of the television and radio outlets which politicians need for reaching the people, few politicians will risk defying or offending them.

How a corporation may bring to bear its many powers and resources is clearly illustrated in the antitrust suit filed by the U.S. Department of Justice in 1949 in an effort to force AT&T to divest itself of Western Electric. The three volumes of testimony taken in 1958 before the Antitrust Subcommittee of the

House Committee of the Judiciary, under the chairmanship of the New York Representative, Emanuel Celler,[5] provide a quite different picture than that usually held by the public of government versus the largest corporation in the world. The methods employed by AT&T and the support it received provide a sobering lesson in corporate power as compared with that of the federal government.

Among salient disclosures brought out in the hearings were the following:

1. The Department of Defense provided AT&T with copies of all the information it gave to the Department of Justice, treating AT&T as if it were actually a department of the United States government. Both the Defense Department, headed by Charles Wilson, and the Federal Communications Commission, headed by George McConnaughey, opposed the suit of the Department of Justice and exerted their influence on behalf of AT&T. It was the United States government which was divided, not AT&T.

2. With its continuity of staffing and its excellent attorneys and officials, AT&T was able to outman, outmaneuver, and outwit government officials at each turn; also, in the change of national administrations, government personnel changed. AT&T was able to assign one of its top attorneys to the full-time opposition of each staff member of the Department of Justice.

3. The usual suspicion of payola was involved: A government employee was fired for buying stock in companies involved in the litigation, but only *after* the outcome of the suit was determined. No corporation personnel were dismissed for their part in the same practices.

4. The "friendliness" of television, radio, and most of the press to AT&T was so great that there seems to have been virtually no news coverage of this case, which was one of the most important antitrust suits the government has ever undertaken and, in effect, lost. The government of the United States found itself unable to protect the public interest against the efforts of well-organized, financially powerful corporations.

There is abundant evidence [6] to prove that broadcast regulation written in 1927 and 1934 was shaped under pressures from corporations with heavy financial interests in broadcasting. In later years this trend has only been intensified. The regulations adopted were frequently not enforced. The 1927 Radio Act directed the Federal Radio Commission to refuse licenses to firms found guilty of unlawful monopoly. However, RCA, found guilty in 1931 of violating the antitrust laws, did not lose its licenses. A dozen other large corporations, convicted of similar violations, are still licensed—and are still broadcasting.

Constant industry pressure through and on Congress has kept both budget and staff of the Federal Communications Commission small. Consequently the Commission has generally found itself unable to translate its studies into regulatory standards; in fact, many of the existing regulations, and hence many technical problems surrounding UHF and FM, are traceable to the Commission's reliance on industry-loaned engineers. Once these standards are set, those industries are able to blame the government for the problems engendered.

Lawrence P. Lessing, in the November, 1949, issue of *Fortune* magazine,[7] described TV pressure on the Federal Communications Commission to set standards which ignored the problems of channel interference and "overlap." RCA and its allies, he noted, were in haste to capture the postwar market.

These examples illustrate the tactics used by broadcasting corporations opposing FCC regulations, i.e., regulatory powers delegated by Congress itself. Since congressmen and senators need access to television to be elected, and since many are owners or part-owners of broadcast properties, their most vigorous efforts in broadcasting seem to have been exerted on behalf of stations and networks. The "errand boy" role of congressmen in broadcast matters has been noted more and more through the years. Just what kind of action may be expected from Congress in the future?

With no deliberately vicious intent, corporate leaders honestly tend to equate the public interest with corporate interest—hence Charles Wilson's classic statement that what was good for General Motors was good for the public. Making sure that the public identifies its interests with those of the corporation requires powerful public relations effort. *Television Age* magazine in 1957 carried an article, "TV and the Corporate Challenge," [8] which pointed out how essential it is for America's big corporations to reach people with their story, communicating through television the corporation's ideas and friendly image to customers, shareholders, and the general public *—and which described television's effectiveness in reaching decision makers in government, not only top officials but also the staff members of the various agencies and congressmen who prepare recommendations and reports. In this endeavor, certain types of "commercials" are of particular importance. This use of television is often forgotten in studies of business pressures on government —and it is usually denied by the network officials. The extent to which most of the larger corporations now use television and radio "commercials" for public relations and policy formation illustrates the imperceptible growth of corporate control of media content. For example, President Ralph Cordiner of General Electric, in the *Television Age* article cited earlier, pointed out that since citizens fear size when they do not understand it, "on the GE Theatre we talk about the General Electric Company as a warm human organization making contributions to the country as a whole." [9] Companies such as United States Steel have few items to sell to the consumer directly. Yet they use television as a consumer medium. Their sales messages on television try to create a favorable impression of United States Steel. Such impressions are useful to large firms at times of labor strikes, price increases, or threats of government interference.

The favorable position of the United States corporation in the minds of most citizens has been achieved as a result of industry's control of the electronic mass media. The interests of business have come to be identified with the public interest: the corporation identifies itself with the total national, or even international interest, and the federal government is made to look like a special-interest or pressure group. That a propagation of this concept is in the public interest seems, at the least, open to challenge.

Another corporate practice which is equally incompatible with public-interest broadcasting is secrecy: the opposite of communication. Although open books and free access are recommended for labor, education, courtrooms, the Congress, and the Federal Communications Commission and such other

* In an address to the Second National Conference on Educational Broadcasting in Chicago, Nov. 29, 1937, William S. Paley, then president of CBS, declared: "We sell time to sponsors solely for the advertising of their goods. We do not sell time for propaganda. . . . The sole exception we make to this policy is the sale of time to political parties during an actual election campaign."

agencies, secrecy is considered indispensable by most broad-casting corporations. An editorial in *Broadcasting* on the re-port of former FCC member Robert F. Jones for the Senate Commerce Committee noted that Mr. Jones would "confiscate" that station's secret financial data.[10] This was seen as a danger to be avoided at all costs. Secrecy as a procedure is not new to corporate behavior; what *is* new is the concept that corpora-tions valuing secrecy so highly should be good custodians of communications for a "free and open" democracy.

As corporate practices go, it is only a short step from secrecy to "rigging." The care that goes into this selective presentation of facts is very great indeed.

Annual reports of large corporations generally appear to be straightforward statements of income, expenses, profits, and dividends. For example, in the annual reports of AT&T, profits usually appear very modest since expenses are usually high. Costs and expenses for phone equipment, for example, are high. The fact that they are paid to Western Electric, which is owned by AT&T, does not occur to many readers of annual reports.

In the 1956 hearings before the Senate Committee on Inter-state and Foreign Commerce, NBC President Robert Sarnoff explained dramatically how great were NBC's losses in the first years of television operation. Losses from 1947 through 1954, he said, amounted to a cumulative loss of 4 million dollars. Con-siderable probing was needed before Mr. Sarnoff admitted that during the same period the profits of NBC's owner RCA were very handsome indeed, as consumers turned from their radios and rushed to buy TV sets. Other examples of selective re-porting might be found in such areas as NBC's listed expenses for equipment. Since most such equipment is usually purchased from RCA, the use of list prices gives impressions different from those which actual cost reports would provide.

When quiz rigging and payola were publicly revealed, net-work officials insisted that they were only isolated cases. While Robert Sarnoff and Robert Kintner were signing full-page ads in the nation's press, protesting that NBC was not responsible for the dishonesty of a few selfish individuals, RCA and other recording companies were agreeing to Federal Trade Commis-sion consent decrees outlawing various payola practices in the promotion and broadcast of phonograph records.

Consistent with the use of secrecy and rigging is the use which the corporation makes of research. Corporation research appears in many respects to be a means of delaying change or preventing progress. As University of Toronto Professor Marshall McLuhan, widely known consultant to industry, has observed, though the top budget item in big industry is research, this research is directed not to the acceleration of change but to its control. The tendency of larger corporations to buy up and bury patents which would make obsolete their most profitable products or services illustrates this practice. In such cases the public's need or interest is likely to have to take second place to that of the business corporation. Why should a company publicize or promote an invention, idea, or national policy that may put it out of business, or even reduce its profits? In such an environment, research comes to have a special meaning. Those research results which lead to profits for the corporation will be adopted and accepted. Research that would redound to the public's interests, but not to the industry's, is likely to be suppressed. Thus, "research" preserves the *status quo*. The reasons why RCA opposed FM development, patents on which it did not control, and why the large corporations, which secured early VHF monopolies, opposed UHF television are obvious: increased competition and decreased profits. This position dramatizes the basic conflict of interests which characterizes the United States commercial broadcast system.

"Competition" is a word that now applies only in a very special sense to corporate broadcasting. Most businessmen hate real competition. Competitors help reduce profits. General Motors prefers having Chevrolet, for example, produce five or six "wholly different cars," to having five or six different firms produce an equal number of models. Most corporations experiencing competition seek to replace it with something better. Although this new practice is still called competition, it reduces the term to meaninglessness. Edward H. Carr in *The New Society* [11] has described the transformation of competition into agreements and understandings in which price-fixing, wage-fixing, and other such practices are completely accepted. Such price-fixing is now labeled fair-trade practice. Observers of AT&T and RCA will note how competition between the two was historically solved by their agreeing to stay out of certain activities and to engage in others. The agreement does not mention how each will proceed against any outsider who seeks to disrupt this arrangement.

One of the best illustrations of this "competition" is found in the recent indictment of General Electric and Westinghouse, both of which own and operate broadcast stations. The manner in which identical bids were received from these and other firms demonstrates the new concept in action. The extent to which one of the nation's greatest industrial scandals has been passed over in relative silence by television and radio also illustrates one of the consequences of overlapping ownership of communications media. To say that these practices (described in John Fuller's book *The Gentlemen Conspirators* [12]) are isolated instances is to overlook an overwhelming accumulation of contrary evidence. Especially notable is the similarity between the denials of responsibility by these corporation executives and the declaration of the television executives that they were unaware of the malpractices going on under *their* jurisdiction.

Television, while reporting lawlessness by individuals and unions, does not dare expose corporate collusion and conspiracy. The public is, therefore, unprepared for such disclosures when they do appear. Even after cases of antitrust law violation by large firms are reported in some areas of the press, many broadcast stations, as the faithful branches of such firms, naturally do not report them. This is not conducive to any very great faith in broadcasting's freedom as "press" or its function as the public's watchdog.

Another characteristic of corporations, reflected faithfully in their broadcasting subsidiaries, is a preoccupation with bigness, power, and as much monopoly as possible. Probably all the national networks already are too big, too rich, and too smug for efficiency. Even Eric Sevareid of CBS, the biggest of the television networks, pointed out on a "Press and the People" program in 1959 that bigness breeds weakness and timidity. In the information field, the bigger one becomes, the less courageous one can afford to be. Yet each year the assembled affiliates of the three networks hear statements from their respective executives calling urgently for increased growth and additional income.

Rarely mentioned is the extent to which featherbedding and nepotism come to prevail at the executive level. Examples of family domination can be found in the lists of officers of networks like NBC, or in publications such as *Broadcasting* and *Television* magazines. Since these corporations control so much of the press, it is not surprising that this type of featherbedding is largely unreported.

Many of the specific corporations and leaders now prominent in broadcasting have been militantly anti-labor. It is notable that the Congress Cigar Company, in which CBS Board Chairman William S. Paley was at that time a young executive, moved many of its operations from Chicago to Philadelphia, giving labor difficulties as one of the main reasons for the move. The relentless labor difficulties besetting many of the electrical and equipment manufacturers, which own large blocks of stations, are also a part of labor history.   And probably no single group has more militantly fought labor union efforts than the broadcast-owning newspaper chains and magazine publishers. Such corporations cannot put behind them their life-and-death struggle against labor—it is only natural that labor interests will receive short shrift from the corporations' opinion-making media.

It is naïve and romantic to expect a corporation to have either a heart or a soul in the struggle for profits and survival— RCA, for example, born out of intercorporate warfare among such firms as General Electric, Westinghouse, and Marconi, had to learn rough in-fighting early.   During these early years many bitter lessons were taught RCA.   It should not be surprising that in relations with others RCA should show similar ruthlessness. Does this qualify them to be the custodians of television and radio in our democracy?

One of the reasons for the dominant positions of RCA and CBS in so many fields is the consummate skillfulness of David Sarnoff, William Paley, and the remarkably qualified individuals (by business standards) with whom they have surrounded themselves.   RCA emerged from its early corporate struggles with a capable legal staff and some skill in aggressive tactics, and this should not be held against it.   It does, however, raise the question of how it qualifies RCA to provide the imaginative, democratic public service which is expected from RCA's subsidiary, NBC.   RCA was victorious over CBS in its struggle to secure adoption of its own color-television system.   But democratic tactics were not used; corporation tactics prevailed.

It is understandable, then, why network top executives have so little time for broadcast or program matters.   Whether a given policy or program is in the public interest is a question far down on their agenda; making these decisions would be a waste of their unique management talents.

In launching RCA's new electronic data-processing branch in late 1961, David Sarnoff called it RCA's newest important business. He also reported that RCA had profits of 35.1 million dollars in 1960, and a net profit of 23.8 million dollars during the first nine months of 1961. He predicted an overall industry rate of sales for color television in 1962 of around 200 million dollars. Since RCA tubes are used in virtually all United States color sets, profits from this source have been rising in recent years. In February of 1962 W. Walter Watts, group executive vice-president of RCA, told stockholders that color-television production would soon push RCA's manufacturing business into the billions of dollars. NBC can advertise and promote the sale of RCA transmitter and receiver equipment, phonograph records, and many other items. And it can itself use enormous quantities of all such products. RCA, being a diversified corporation, buys from itself.

RCA's patent controls enable it to receive royalties on sets which other manufacturers produce. By the high prices charged for transmitter facilities which it manufactures, RCA can control to a great extent access to the broadcasting business. By keeping out low-cost equipment and approaches, RCA can control to a large extent the kind of individuals or firms who may enter the broadcasting field; certainly, small and poor companies and individuals cannot. The diversity of ownership allowed under present regulations has been rendered virtually impossible by the RCA type of monopoly.

In many cases educational stations cannot be built because of the lack of funds. RCA's attitude toward education in this and other respects deserves mention.

On October 28, 1959, John Burns, who was then president of RCA, unveiled an exciting plan for nationwide educational television. He estimated that the annual cost would be 2.5 billion dollars—13 per cent of the 19 billion then being spent on education. The educators to whom he spoke, the National Association of Educational Broadcasters, were urged to raise the money. Several conferences with Mr. Burns and other RCA officials followed. RCA was invited to make an initial contribution in order to launch this project—it declined. There seems to have been no further activity in this area by Mr. Burns's successor, Elmer W. Engstrom, or by other RCA leaders.

CBS holdings, although smaller than those of RCA, are also surprisingly diverse. During late 1961 a newsletter from Frank Stanton, president of CBS, Inc., was distributed to CBS employees. It was helpful in explaining what the "Inc." includes. In the twenty-four years of its history, CBS interests have expanded considerably. As Dr. Stanton pointed out: "CBS has grown from a radio network of sixteen stations to a company that is active in radio, television, phonograph records, electronics, research and other related activities. It operates a world-wide news organization; both a radio and a television network; seven AM radio and seven FM radio stations; it has interests in television-set-making foreign firms, in picture tubes, phonographs and phonograph records; it distributes television programming overseas (more than 80,000 half hours in forty-five countries); it produces animation for television; it licenses products from books to games; it markets home entertainment programs with encyclopedias and film projectors; and it develops microminiature components for space satellites." The complexity of CBS activities raises the same problems as those raised by RCA. Already noted is the stake that CBS, like RCA, has in military electronics, through its Industrial and Military Electronics Division.

The problem of the regulation and control of broadcasting is not the narrow problem that it seems to be. It is not a simple matter of station-government relations. It is to a large extent the complex problems of the corporations' economic role in society. Broadcasting is only one of their many interests.

In a discussion with the Federal Communications Commission in February of 1962, Oliver Treyz, who was then vice-president in charge of ABC-TV, explained that ABC-TV programs were decided upon by an advisory board. He admitted, however, that he personally had to agree to a program before it could be broadcast. Moments later he conceded further that if ABC-Paramount President Leonard H. Goldenson wished to participate in the decision, Mr. Goldenson's vote alone, even against all others, would determine what would happen. Such is the way in which the corporation decides what the people are to have—their freedom of choice is limited not by government, but by the corporations themselves. Individuals now come into more contact with corporations than they do with government. People find themselves and their behavior increasingly controlled by corporations. The Constitution was designed to protect the individual only against *official* wielders of power, since corporations were then no threat. However, corporate controllers are so powerful today that the public should be protected against them. One of the requirements of democratic, dynamic government is a recognition of the need to change continually the amount and kind of government activity needed, in order to keep in balance the changing powers developed by different parts of the social, economic, and political complex. It is obvious that piecemeal efforts to solve the nation's broadcasting problems are futile unless the real power centers, rather than merely the implementers, are controlled.

N. R. Danielian, in his monumental study of the telephone business, suggests one approach: "The solution of this problem in the case of AT&T is relatively simple. The Congress can simply write into the Communications Act the provision that interstate telephone companies cannot engage, directly or indirectly, in any business other than communications and services incidental thereto . . . There is clear authority in the Congress to remedy this situation." [13]

A similar provision, drafted to apply to RCA-NBC, CBS, and ABC-Paramount, would be equally simple. Divestiture of all nonbroadcast activities, by networks at least, is essential if they are to be freed from the pressure of corporate interests. Network-owning firms should be free to decide whether to devote their full time and effort to broadcasting, as the nation deserves, or to other activities.

Second, safeguards similar to those introduced to ensure democracy in trade unions (such as open books and open elections) should be introduced if broadcast firms desire to be accorded freedom from more stringent regulation. Firms which desire secrecy could retain it, but they should not be licensed to broadcast, and vice versa.

Adam Smith is often quoted by free-enterprise spokesmen to justify present corporate practices. It is too often forgotten that he himself warned against entrusting the total public interest to business interests! "The proposal of any new law or regulation of commerce which comes from this order [business interest], ought always to be listened to with great precaution. . . . It comes from an order of men whose interest is never the same with that of the public, who have generally an interest to deceive and even to oppress the public and who accordingly have upon many occasions both deceived and oppressed it." [14]

Some economists have suggested that many of the problems now observed in broadcasting and corporations are evidences that the corporation is a sick institution. Is it possible that there is a size, a power, and a role beyond which corporations cannot go without getting into problems they cannot themselves solve without outside help? Should not corporations be eager to find that help and to honor those limitations which will ensure the survival of our democracy?

The steps urged here grow not out of enmity for capitalism and democracy but out of profound concern for their survival. And until a broad approach to the broadcasting problem of the nation is undertaken, there is little that can be done to correct the ailments of broadcasting in the United States.

Leadership: The Managers and the Networks

Even in a structure as depersonalized and monolithic as the broadcasting corporation, men (somewhere) make the decisions. Who these men are and the credentials and values they bring to the making of these decisions are the subject of this chapter.

Probably no other industry is now led by men whose careers are such excellent examples of the Horatio Alger story. David Sarnoff and Sol Taishoff were both poor immigrants of sturdy Jewish stock from Minsk, Russia. Both Mr. Sarnoff and Mr. Taishoff started in communications as telegraph operators. William S. Paley's family came from Kiev, Russia. The resourcefulness shown by Samuel Paley, William's father, and by his brother Jacob, in setting up the Congress Cigar Company and the La Palina Cigar Company, both of which were later incorporated into the Consolidated Cigar Company, illustrates the way in which industrial empires were built by ambitious, hard-working immigrants. Only ABC-Paramount President Leonard Goldenson, among the top four leaders in United States broadcasting, is a member of a profession. The son of a tradesman father who also had an interest in movie theaters, Mr. Goldenson holds a law degree from Harvard.

The senior leader in United States broadcasting is RCA Board Chairman David Sarnoff. Born in Uzlian, Minsk, Russia, in 1891 the future brigadier general David Sarnoff came to the United States, virtually penniless, at the age of nine. His brilliant and distinguished career has been the subject of enough articles and brief biographies so that it need not be reviewed here. In addition to the role now being played in broadcast leadership by Mr. Sarnoff and his sons, Mr. Sarnoff's younger brother, Irving, was, until his death, active in such radio and television parts and sales firms as Sterling Radio and Electric Company, George L. Patterson, Inc., and Bruno–New York, Inc. Most of David Sarnoff's interests and prophecies seem to have revolved around devices rather than uses: the radio music box, electronic devices for medicine, and vest-pocket communications devices illustrate the miracles he has accurately forecast.

David Sarnoff's sons, as they become older and more experienced, are gradually assuming various responsibilities in NBC and RCA from their father. Robert Sarnoff is now NBC board chairman. A younger son, Thomas, is an NBC executive on the Pacific Coast. A third son has not yet been heard from in broadcasting affairs.

Sol Taishoff—whose family owns and publishes *Broadcasting, Television,* and other trade magazines—was also born in Minsk; he was brought to the United States in 1906 at the age of two. *Broadcasting* magazine is referred to in its promotional materials as "mirror and mentor of radio and television progress since 1931." Since the power and policy-making role exercised by Mr. Taishoff's publications are considerable, it is essential to include him among the leaders who have shaped broadcasting through the years.

In addition to the broadcasting publications which he owns, Mr. Taishoff publishes *Food-Drug-Cosmetics Reports* and has active interests in the DeSales Realty Company, the Jolar Corporation, and the Mycalex Corporation of America. The Mycalex Corporation, of which he is vice-president, manufactures electronic and electrical insulation materials, components and products of bonded mica, ceramo-plastics and synthetic mica, telemetering switches and plates, miniature and subminiature UHF and transistor sockets, and printed circuit bases. This gives Mr. Taishoff an interest in television and radio parts manufacturing. Mycalex president, chairman, and treasurer is Jerome Taishoff, Sol Taishoff's elder brother.

The Taishoff interests, like those of the Sarnoffs, are welded by strong family ties. Of principal officers in *Television* Magazine Corporation, Sol Taishoff is listed as president, B. T. Taishoff as treasurer, and H. H. Tash (Tash being the maiden name of Mrs. Sol Taishoff) as secretary. Assistant publisher is Lawrence B. Taishoff.

Although one branch of the Paley family came from Minsk, as did the Sarnoff and Taishoff families, the parents of William S. Paley came to the United States from Kiev. Mr. Paley himself was born in Chicago in 1901.

The Federal Communications Commission's *Report on Chain Broadcasting* of 1941 describes how the Paley family gained control of CBS. To quote from this report:

> The organization which later became the Columbia Broadcasting System was incorporated in New York on January 27, 1927, under the name of United Independent Broadcasters, Inc. . . . In November 1927 Jerome H. Louchheim, Isaac D. Levy, and Leon Levy acquired a controlling stock interest in United and controlled the network until September 1928, when William S. Paley and his family purchased 50.3 per cent of the stock. . . . As of the time of the committee hearings, William S. Paley and his family hold about 16 per cent of the class A stock and about 54 per cent of all the stock of CBS. Since there are 7 directors elected by each class of stock, the cumulative voting of the class A stock together with the non-cumulative voting of the class B stock gives the Paley family the power to elect a majority of the entire board of directors of 14 even against the holders of the other 67 per cent of the CBS stock.[1]

This control situation seems not to have changed greatly since then. The Paley family has been able to sell several additional millions of dollars' worth of CBS stock while still retaining control of the corporation. However, considerable interests in CBS are still held by the Levy family, which is related to the Paley family. Leon Levy held 183,561 shares in December, 1962. Mr. Paley's own holdings by the mid-fifties were down to only about 12 per cent of CBS stocks, although these were still adequate to ensure management control. In early January, 1963, he held 797,580 shares direct and 144,383 shares through a holding company. Later in 1963, Mr. Paley sold 75,000 shares worth $3,675,-000, retaining 866,000 shares worth $44,382,500. Mr. Paley's father, Samuel, continued as president of the Congress Cigar Company until his retirement in 1931. Samuel also served as a director of CBS during this time and subsequently. It is important to remember that most of the funds used to purchase CBS, and the executive experience which controls it, came from cigar manufacturing. Frank Stanton and Leonard Goldenson, presidents of CBS and ABC-Paramount, respectively, did not enter the broadcast business until much later. Long before they were active in broadcasting, David Sarnoff, William S. Paley, and Sol Taishoff had shaped broadcasting in the United States as no other men have done.

Under present conditions there is little likelihood that either the Sarnoffs, Taishoffs, or Paleys and Levys will be replaced by other or very different owner-controllers. When Mr. Paley and Ed Sullivan celebrated their birthdays together on September 28, 1961, Mr. Paley reportedly extended Mr. Sullivan's contract for thirty years. This would take Mr. Sullivan up to his ninety-ninth birthday. There is apparently every intention on the part of present controllers of the two largest networks and the largest trade publications to retain their control for some time to come.

Leonard Goldenson, born in Pennsylvania in 1905, is president of ABC-Paramount. Like Frank Stanton of CBS, he is a relative newcomer to the small and select circle of controllers of the networks of the nation. He is a self-made millionaire of boundless energy and ambition. Most of his experience has been in the movie business, and he has made no secret of his belief that television is a part of show business. In spite of his degree in law, his practical orientation to television indicates that he is a merchant of mass entertainment rather than a professional in the usual sense of the word.

Such are the principal individuals who control United States broadcasting, the men who decree what Americans see and hear over the broadcast media. Enormous stamina, dedication to work, and realism characterize all these leaders. As executives they are unquestionably among the most efficient and most distinguished corporation leaders this nation has produced. But contrast their background, education, and interests with those of the founders of early newspapers, and compare the two traditions represented. In most cases the Benjamin Franklins, Horace Greeleys, Peter Zengers, and Joseph Pulitzers were crusaders consumed with ambitions which could not be described as primarily financial. Broadcasting, on the other hand, seems to have attracted entrepreneurial individuals interested principally in profits.

The array of top leaders in broadcasting would contain greater diversity if educational broadcasting had been able to develop parallel to commercial service, as it started out to do. Unfortunately, thanks in no small measure to the opposition of the leaders discussed here, educational broadcasting was harassed and reduced almost to nonexistence during the early period when it might have provided a significant counterweight to sales uses.

Instead of including religious, educational, artistic, literary, and other types of professionals, the top niches in United States broadcasting leadership are almost completely dominated by technicians, tradesmen, salesmen, and other types of businessmen, who were born in poverty and hardship and are interested in making up for their early years.

Routine operational decisions are made at the next level of the corporate hierarchy by the principal salaried officials. At this level the slightly different structure of the three networks becomes evident. The president of CBS is Frank Stanton, who holds a Ph.D. in psychology from Ohio State University. However, Dr. Stanton is president of all CBS interests, not merely of those parts of CBS engaged in broadcasting. At NBC, President Robert Kintner has less scope. He frequently shares various responsibilities with NBC Board Chairman Robert Sarnoff; this raises some question about the roles of chairman of the board and president. It is not entirely clear where decisions are made in NBC's upper echelon, with its sixteen or more treasurers and its many vice-presidents. Considerable leeway for *ad hoc* decisions by the Sarnoffs seems evident, and many of the decisions appear to be made rather suddenly. The tradition of sudden firings in broadcasting is undoubtedly traceable quite largely to such decision-making arrangements.

Mr. Kintner, before entering broadcasting, was a partner with Joseph Alsop in a distinguished reporter combination. He, James Hagerty, and Thomas W. Moore, mentioned below, are among the few journalists to be found in high administrative posts at the networks.

At ABC-Paramount, the vice-president in charge of ABC-TV is Thomas W. Moore. Mr. Moore brings to his position training in journalism at the University of Missouri and experience with both CBS Films and ABC. But the suddenness and vigor with which Mr. Goldenson sometimes acts suggest that Mr.

Moore's position may be less secure than that of either Mr. Kintner or Dr. Stanton. In spite of the fact that he is theoretically
responsible only to Mr. Goldenson, Mr. Moore appears to be
operationally more nearly on a level with CBS-TV President
James T. Aubrey.* What authority Mr. Moore has over ABC-TV
News, headed by Elmer W. Lower, for example, is not clear.
When James C. Hagerty, now vice-president in charge of corporate relations, headed ABC News, he said that ABC News was
responsible only to Mr. Goldenson. Mr. Goldenson's dismissals
of Mr. Kintner, now of NBC, and Mr. Treyz, now of Warner
Brothers, illustrates the suddenness with which roles and names
may change. Dr. Stanton's dismissal of Louis Cowan as president
of CBS-TV at the time of the quiz-rigging disclosures is an example of the scapegoat role which second-level people must be
prepared to assume.

To a striking extent the top twenty-five or thirty operational
executives in broadcasting seem to be engaged in a game of
musical chairs. In different years their names can be found in
different organizations and in different capacities. These men
are essentially interchangeable; their identities seem little more
important than those of viewers. Even at the highest operational
levels this has been common corporate practice for years. When
Pat Weaver left NBC, he soon was employed to direct the 100-
million-dollar international television project of the McCann-
Erickson Agency. Oliver Treyz, dismissed from ABC-TV, moved
over to Warner Brothers, from which ABC-TV continues to take
eight or so hours a week of films, programmed largely by Mr.
Treyz. ABC's Thomas W. Moore moved to ABC from CBS when
James Aubrey went from ABC to CBS to replace Mr. Louis
Cowan, when the latter was dismissed by Dr. Stanton. Robert
Kintner, dismissed by Mr. Goldenson from ABC, soon showed up
across the table from new ABC executives, representing NBC.
The crossover traffic in executives among Benton and Bowles, J.
Walter Thompson, Young and Rubicam, and other advertising
agencies; Screen Gems, Four Star, Warner Brothers, Paramount,
and other film companies; several trade publications and associations; and the three networks, is regular and steady at most
executive levels. The McDermotts, Doziers, McAvitys, Werners,
Levys, Robinsons, Hausmans, and a score of others, all capable
executives, can work equally well for any one of the networks or
broadcast-related agencies. The qualities which ensure success

* Resigned suddenly Sunday, February 28, 1965.

for these executives include a capacity for hard work, loyalty to whichever firm or individual they happen to be working for, a warm personality, aggressive salesmanship, and a realistic, down-to-earth concept of the role of broadcasting as an instrument of commerce and entertainment. If there were a government network, many of these people could move into it with equal ease, just as Edward R. Murrow was able to move into the United States Information Agency directorship from CBS. In early 1962 one count revealed that six CBS vice-presidents had come from NBC, and even more of NBC's and CBS's top executives had come from ABC. In this situation, the competition is at least controlled or of a special kind. Whether agencies or networks have the responsibility for quiz shows and other programs, virtually all their successful executives have been schooled by Messrs. Paley, Sarnoff, Goldenson, or Taishoff or all four.

It is difficult to overemphasize the influence of broadcast leaders on the daily life and values of every American. The top leadership of the networks, particularly, is in a position of great responsibility. These men are not merely supervising their employees or operations, nor are they merely entertaining the nation. They are educating the nation by what they offer, by what they say, and by what they do. Probably few United States Presidents have had as profound and pervasive effects on the nation as these broadcast leaders have, however inconspicuous their powers have been.

Most of the controllers of television and radio today, it must be remembered, did not invent these instruments—they exploited them. Alexander Graham Bell ended up, within a few years of his invention, with a tiny share of the telephone company's stock, and with a listing as "electrician" in the company directory. The same fate was suffered by many radio and television inventors as men with capital took over. When present controllers boast of the accomplishments of these miracle instruments, as they frequently do, listeners must distinguish between the innate powers of the media and those functions which controllers define and prescribe as well as prevent. Almost all present leaders represent families and firms which, by brute force of dollars usually earned in other pursuits, were able to secure *control* of these media from a diversity of smaller owners. What might now be available if different types of people and firms had gained or been able to retain control of these media? Today's leaders see themselves as businessmen; why should they be expected to be sociologists or

professionals?   Protestations that broadcasting does not contribute to delinquency, mental illness, physical unfitness, citizen
passivity, the school crisis, and other social problems indicate
that even today leadership seems unaware of the massive social
effects of broadcast programs.

The way in which the nation's tastes, values, and votes can
be determined by what the Sarnoffs, Paleys, Goldensons, Stantons,
Kintners, Moores, and Taishoffs allow or encourage is a new
phenomenon.   We need to recognize it more clearly.   We need to
know how this power is wielded, and to what ends.   It is greater
in many respects than that of government itself.   Certainly, as
noted in Chapter 7, it is more powerful in many respects than
formal education in the lifelong conditioning it provides.

Through the years broadcasting leaders have resisted government regulation, preferring the *status quo*.   This attitude, of
course, is not new to corporate leaders.

Edward R. Murrow told the Radio and Television News
Directors' Association in November of 1958:

> I cannot believe that radio and television or the corpora-
> tions that finance the programs, are serving well or truly
> their viewers or listeners, or themselves. . . . The top man-
> agement of the networks, with a few notable exceptions,
> has been trained in advertising, research, sales, or show
> business. . . . It is not easy for the same small group of
> men to decide whether to buy a new station for millions of
> dollars, build a new building, alter the rate card, buy a new
> Western, sell a soap opera, decide what defensive line to
> take in connection with the latest Congressional inquiry,
> how much money to spend on promoting a new program,
> what additions or deletions should be made in the existing
> covey or clutch of vice-presidents, and at the same time
> . . . to give mature, thoughtful consideration to the mani-
> fold problems that confront those who are charged with the
> responsibility for news and public affairs.

Speaking of malpractices which had recently been revealed,
Mr. Murrow concluded:

> The responsibility can be easily placed, in spite of all the
> mouthings about giving the public what it wants.   It rests
> on big business, and on big television, and it rests at the
> top.[2]

Lord Reith, the first director general of the BBC, whose attitudes shaped British broadcasting in its first thirty years, often

spoke of the awesome responsibilities of broadcast leadership.   In his autobiography, *Broadcast over Britain,* he said:

> I think it will be admitted by all, that to have exploited so great a scientific invention for the purpose and pursuit of "entertainment" alone would have been a prostitution of its powers and an insult to the character and intelligence of the people. . . . I wonder if it is realized how much was left to us [the leaders], in policy, in judgement and in enterprise, and how different the state of affairs might have been today had we been content with mediocrity.[3]

Herbert Hoover repeatedly expressed his concern over the public responsibilities which broadcasters assume in conducting a service "so greatly affecting the cultural progress of our people," as he described it.   What kind of record has United States leadership established in meeting the public responsibilities referred to by all those quoted above?   Let us see.

By the mid-fifties, certain groups had begun to protest the continued televising of wrestling.   It was becoming obvious to even the most naïve that wrestling matches were either rigged or staged.   That they were listed as "sports" instead of drama would in itself represent a type of rigging.   Critics also began to call attention to the obviously canned applause used on many programs and to the long time required in rehearsal to achieve the desired spontaneity in question-and-answer programs in the presidential campaign, and in such others as the Nixon-Checkers program.

Numerous newspapers in the United States in August and September of 1959 reported the indictment of former Mutual Broadcasting System officials Alexander L. Guterma, Hal Roach, Jr., and Garland L. Culpepper, Jr., for failing to register as foreign agents of the Dominican Republic, whose propaganda they agreed to broadcast as news on Mutual news and personality programs.   This was part of a $750,000 contract.   The remaining management of Mutual promptly disclaimed responsibility for this malpractice and indicated shock at such tactics, practiced by a few guilty individuals in the network.   The contract was quickly canceled, though not until after trial runs (with Mutual network reporters broadcasting make-believe news reports to show how the system would work) convinced the Dominican dictator that Mutual could deliver the service promised.

Then the quiz scandal broke.   After first denying that quiz rigging existed, network executives denied that they knew about it, then claimed that only a few wicked employees were to blame, and fired them.

Critics asked: However busy the leaders were, how could quiz rigging be such a surprise and shock to them? Did they really fail to know about it? Or was quiz rigging so similar to usual corporate and broadcast industry practices that it faded into the rest of the scenery and therefore escaped notice?

In 1956 a contestant on the "Big Surprise" program protested that it was rigged. The Federal Trade Commission asked the network if this was true; the network's representative denied the charge. The *New York World-Telegram and Sun* did a series of articles hinting that there was rigging. *Time, Look,* and other publications also indicated that something was wrong. A Revlon vice-president told CBS in early 1958 that "The Challenge" was rigged. Still, it appears, Mr. Paley and Dr. Stanton did not know. It took the explosion caused by Edward Hilgemeier's story to the *New York Post* in the summer of 1959, over two years after most observers called attention to quiz rigging, to bring the networks to admit that there *was* rigging of quiz shows.

While rigging was going on at NBC, Master of Ceremonies Jack Barry was telling the loyal audiences of "Twenty-one" that "at no time has any contestant ever [etc., etc.] . . . We have not betrayed your trust in us. We never will." What role did top executives at NBC play in such announcements? If there was no suspicion of rigging, critics asked, why such disclaimers?

When Dr. Stanton was confronted with inescapable evidence of rigging, he conceded that he could not deny that he had had an inkling of such practices. But, he insisted, an inkling is very different from the solid evidence needed before one takes action.

Robert Kintner, NBC president, told the press that NBC got "its first established evidence" of quiz-show rigging only through the Washington hearings. Many industry leaders swore that they knew nothing of what had gone on. New York District Attorney Frank Hogan told reporters in November of 1959 that about one hundred of the two hundred witnesses who testified in September, 1958, before the New York grand jury (investigating possible quiz rigging) had obviously lied. Since a large percentage of these people were network and agency officials and sponsors, the record is not one of which broadcast leaders can be proud.

In October of 1959, the president of the National Association of Broadcasters declared that the industry had proved, "in its four decades of service, it can clean its own house when necessary." Many believed that the evidence led to the opposite conclusion. Housecleanings seemed always to have been delayed until they were forced from the outside. How enthusiastically would an industry clean up a condition it had itself created and tolerated because it was so profitable?

By some odd logic, quiz contestants, rather than their teachers, were made to appear to be the villains. It was suggested that those contestants who were "helped" should give back their ill-gotten gains. Some did. There is no evidence that either the sponsors, who made millions, or the networks, who did likewise, gave back *their* earnings.

United States programs, sent to other countries, carried rigging with them. Miss Leonora Millington, who won over $10,000 on "Twenty-one" in Britain, imported from NBC, admitted being told from which groups of questions hers would come. Some British writers objected to this type of import from the United States. Was there not some way, they asked, in which this epidemic of dishonesty, made in America, could be kept from spreading to other nations?

What did network leaders *finally* do about the quiz scandals? Very little. NBC on December 27, 1959, announced formation of a committee of five prominent citizens to review NBC policies and standards. How active this committee is today is not known.

CBS, with heavy publicity coverage, announced the abolition of all big-money quiz shows, rehearsed "unrehearsed" programs, canned applause, and related rigging. As soon as the furor blew over, canned applause, game shows, and most of the other outlawed practices were back on CBS, but with no publicity releases or fanfare.

In a rush to quiet those who threatened tighter regulation, both networks announced an increase in news and public-affairs programs. A few blunt observers accused the networks of putting on such public-service shows to get the government off their backs so they could return to their old practices as quickly as possible. As for the threatened government crackdown, loyal friends of the networks in Congress limited government efforts largely to outlawing *quiz* rigging and deceit as the industry defined it. The *symptoms* were treated. The structure out of which the practices so naturally grew remained relatively undisturbed. Business as usual again prevailed. Was it true, as the *St. Louis Post-Dispatch* and other newspapers quoted industry spokesman Louis

Hausman, that "the worst you can condemn the networks for is carelessness"?

How should corporation leaders react to accusations of malpractice within their industry? Should a leader set an example of honesty for his staff and followers; or should he show them how to handle the problem in the corporate way? The strain on staff members' respect for their boss, and his for them, can be very great when either falls short of expectations. What was the ultimate effect on staff respect of the way their leaders handled the quiz problem? This history must decide. However, the glimpses backstage provided by the quiz scandal and subsequent payola, plugola, and other malpractice exposures have revealed a few previously unnoticed facts about present broadcast leadership.

In network broadcasting, leadership does not mingle much with staff, and seems hardly to notice what staffs are doing. Contacts usually are in the form of orders or memos. Most of the contacts that the leader has are with others of his kind. The corporate value system prevails, relatively undisturbed by other value systems or concerns. A peculiar *esprit de corps* flourishes in such circumstances.

John Steinbeck, in *The Wayward Bus,* described a comparable situation. "He was never alone," Mr. Steinbeck wrote of one of his characters, Mr. Pritchard. "His business was conducted by groups of men who worked alike, and even looked alike. His lunches were with men like himself who joined together in clubs so that no foreign element or idea could enter. . . . Wherever he went he was not one man but a unit in a club, in a lodge, in a church, in a political party." [4] A better description of United States broadcast leadership would be difficult to find.

Being part of big business, broadcast leadership is traditionally conservative. It is conservative both in wanting to preserve the *status quo* in broadcasting and in its political orientation. Mark Ethridge, chairman of the board of the Louisville *Courier-Journal* and *Times,* and former president of the National Association of Broadcasters, pointed out in a 1961 interview that: "In the last election the press was 65 per cent for Nixon for President: . . . there is nothing mysterious about the 65 per cent being for Nixon: those newspapers are run by big businessmen; their sympathies are with the Republican Party." [5]

This is also true for television and radio leadership. *Broadcasting* magazine, December 4, 1961, gave the results of a report on the political contributions by officials of networks and advertising agencies, as compiled by the AFL-CIO Committee on Political Education (COPE). *Broadcasting* said: "The report shows that Republican candidates received $13,000 from CBS executives. CBS Board Chairman William S. Paley is said to have donated $7,500; President Frank Stanton and his wife, a total of $3,000; and board members Ralph F. Colin and Joseph A. W. Iglehart, $1,000 and $500 respectively. COPE was unable to find contributions from officials of ABC or NBC."

Broadcast leaders have trade-union problems. They find unions troublesome. And they pay high corporation taxes. There is little likelihood that the stations or networks they control will press editorially for higher corporation taxes, even if the public interest would be served by such a step. Nor will employees report union activities favorably when they know that the boss would disapprove.

Broadcast leaders who hope to get ahead in their company must protect the corporate interest even against the public interest. Officials who become too generous with the corporation's money, or who begin to favor the public interest over the profit interests of the corporation, are promptly brought to book.

Nevertheless, under the present system the networks and large station groups must *pretend* to be democratic and devoted to the public interest, rather than to the interests of Westinghouse, RCA, GE, Hearst, or any of the other corporate complexes which own and operate them. Somewhat self-consciously, they seek to give the impression that, with reference to *programs,* the *people* decide. It would hardly serve their interests to admit that an unorganized mass audience has no mechanism for mutual decision making.

As noted earlier, the executives of the networks and agencies are highly interchangeable. Senator Thomas J. Dodd observed in the June, 1961, Hearings of the United States Senate Subcommittee to Investigate Juvenile Delinquency that all three of the then presidents of the three networks—Kintner, Aubrey, and Treyz—"were high officials of the American Broadcasting Company in the embryonic development of ABC's concept of how to entice the viewing audience, . . . a concept which emphasized crime, violence and sex. These three men eventually became the operating heads of our giant networks." [6] Not much real competition can be expected among networks operated by such similarly schooled executives.

The pattern of the type of individuals found desirable as network executives had of course been set years before. The first president of NBC was Merlin H. Aylesworth. He can be taken as an example of the type of executive favored by Messrs. Sarnoff, Paley, Goldenson, and Stanton. Mr. Aylesworth moved to NBC from the National Electric Light Association. The Federal Trade Commission a few years earlier had investigated the NELA and found that it had conspired to deceive the public through propaganda on behalf of the privately owned utilities. Some of the methods used by Mr. Aylesworth, as noted in the previous chapter, included the purging of textbooks of materials favorable to public ownership of power or critical of private utilities.

The business orientation of later leaders is just as clear. If David Sarnoff's first commercial love was technology and equipment manufacturing, that of William S. Paley was cigar manufacturing. His ambition to acquire control of a broadcasting network grew out of his realization of the effectiveness of radio in selling cigars manufactured by the Paley-owned Congress and La Palina Cigar Companies. Mr. Paley surrounded himself with capable men. In 1928 he hired a former Federal Radio Commission member, Sam Pickard. He realized that individuals who knew government procedures would make excellent "defense officials" for CBS. Since that time a good many former commissioners and other government agency employees have found positions in industry.

Still closely identified with the cigar business, Mr. Paley sought distinguished, well-educated individuals to give CBS prestige and leadership. Eschewing any public role for himself, he needed an effective speaker and spokesman for CBS. He found one in Frank Stanton, undoubtedly the most academically distinguished of upper-echelon commercial-network officials. This is in striking contrast, of course, to the situation in the broadcast systems of most other countries, where intellectuals, philosophers, historians, poets, artists, professors, journalists, and other professional leaders occupy many of the highest positions. Dr. Stanton's attractive personality and academic degree have been advantageous in commanding respect for CBS in hearings and testimony through the years. His public-relations value to CBS has been very great.

Dr. Stanton's major interests as a psychology student were comparing impressions received through the ears with those received through the eyes and measuring audience interest in programs by various methods. He might justly be considered as the father of the present rating systems. As CBS president since 1946, he is senior to all in network leadership except David Sarnoff and William Paley. But, by the time he became CBS president, NBC had been operating for twenty years and CBS for eighteen. The patterns were already set. Dr. Stanton did not go to CBS to alter the corporate structure but to protect it and improve its image. This he has done, and done well.

The attitudes of CBS toward the reservation of channels for educational radio and television and toward requests to CBS for grants and assistance in developing educational media research programs have been largely negative, except for modest grants in very recent years (now that educational broadcasting appears inevitable). Wherever the interests of educational applicants conflicted with CBS, they were opposed by CBS.

Although it is the goal of all the networks to earn profits, actual policy guidelines are difficult to find because so many decisions are made off the record. The major pronouncements of broadcast executives are often contradictory. Thus, when network heads have been asked in hearings why they surrendered program control to sponsors and agencies, they have usually declared that the networks *have* control. When they are asked why, then, they produced rigged quiz shows, or practiced payola or plugola, they have generally replied that *they* did not but outsiders or a few dishonest employees did.

In most of his speeches, William S. Paley has said in essence, as he did in his address of November 29, 1937, in Chicago: "We must never have an editorial page." On the other hand, Dr. Stanton, in some of his most impassioned speeches, has called for the right to editorialize. "I appear at this hearing in favor of the right of radio broadcast licensees to editorialize," he said on March 1, 1948, to the Federal Communications Commission. The problem of reconciling the statements of Mr. Paley and Dr. Stanton is often considerable. A number of newsmen at CBS who have dared to editorialize, only to be dismissed, seem to confirm the belief that Mr. Paley's views generally prevail.

After Hugh M. Beville, in charge of research at NBC, had defended ratings before the Federal Communications Commission, he was reminded that David Sarnoff had condemned them, saying they did not mean what they say or say what they mean. Mr. Beville's remark that his boss was entitled to his own opinion precipitated understandable laughter.

Robert Sarnoff has contradicted himself regarding ratings. On the one hand, he has frequently denied that ratings carry as much weight as critics claim; ratings, he has said, are only one factor in NBC program decisions. But on the other hand, when asked why shows are dropped, he most frequently quotes ratings as the only or main reason. When he was asked in early 1957 why "Ding Dong School" was dropped, he said that it was because the kids had quit watching. "Its ratings had dropped to nothing." When asked if specials were on the way out, since more regular programs were filling NBC's schedules, Mr. Sarnoff said: "No. Ratings on the one-shots . . . are running well ahead of the first two years."

During the quiz scandals, NBC President Robert Kintner faced the difficult problem of indicating that NBC was really in charge and yet did not know what was going on. *Time* magazine on November 16, 1959, quoted him as finally explaining that "the ultimate responsibility is ours, but the ultimate power has to be the sponsor's because without him you couldn't afford to run the network."

David Sarnoff's often-quoted remark that: "We're in the same situation as a plumber laying a pipe. We're not responsible for what goes through the pipe," also contrasts sharply with both Robert Sarnoff's early 1962 statement: "I think we are masters of our own house," and with Dr. Stanton's 1959 declaration that: "It is we and we alone who decide not only what is to appear on the CBS-TV Network, but how it is to appear."

The consistent and favorable picture which the American public has of networks and broadcasters in the United States is high tribute to superb public-relations skills. In their 1955 statements opposing pay television,[7] NBC and CBS were confronted with the need to protect their position and high profits while appearing to defend the interests of the viewer. Dr. Stanton declared that the industry had been able to provide the American public with the best radio and television service in the world. In the 1958 Hearings before the House Committee on Interstate and Foreign Commerce, he added that pay television would "simply restrict to the carriage trade programs of a quality now enjoyed without charge by everybody." He further commented that "the consequences of pay television will be a real misfortune for the American people. Viewers will have to pay for what they now receive free."

With the excellent staff David Sarnoff had at his disposal to prepare his presentation, he struck the people's note even more strongly. In his June 6, 1955, text he said: "It would be tragic for this Commission to authorize pay television to cripple this great democratic medium for the free dissemination of ideas, education and entertainment to all the people of America. My earnest plea to the Federal Communications Commission is: 'Keep American radio and television broadcasting free to the public.'"

Harry S. Ashmore, in his comments in *Television,* a 1961 Fund for the Republic brochure including an interview with Jack Gould, said:

> Partly because of the temper of the times, partly through the conscious efforts of their skilled fuglemen in the advertising agencies, the proprietors and managers of American broadcasting have managed to reduce one of the most urgent contemporary issues to a polar exercise in black and white, as oversimplified as the character of a television cowboy. We are told, and most of us seem to believe, that our choice is between what we are now seeing on television and government censorship, accompanied by subversion of the free enterprise system, and violation of our democratic principles.[8]

One of the more remarkable characteristics of present industry leaders is the obsolescence of the economic concepts they quote as relevant today: that production is still the nation's greatest problem; that there is real competition in the old sense of the word; that network broadcasting is a risky and insecure business; that corporation policies are determined by stockholders, democratically; that government regulation always reduces freedom; that enterprise is free; that it is still possible for the little man to compete favorably with established companies; and so on. Perhaps this should not be surprising since most of the network and trade publication leaders have been in control since 1931 or before. The power of the mass media to declare a self-serving, long outdated version of economics to be the correct one has very serious implications. It countermands and mocks education and modern-day economics. More than that, it contributes to a hardening of our economic system at a time when it needs to be flexible.

Repeatedly, broadcast leaders speak of their "enormous investments and enormous expenditures." Public investment, some twenty times greater, is not mentioned. The risks they take are proclaimed. The extent to which these risks are increasingly passed on to society in recent years is not noted. Although the facts are wholly different from the fictions still being repeated, the power of broadcast leadership and of the megaphones they control is sufficient to perpetuate them into a century in which they are no longer applicable. The clichés and postulates which are quoted as today's gospel are the economic and intellectual currency of an earlier age. They date from political administrations appropriate thirty years ago when the industrial empires of what might be called Paley and Family, Taishoff and Taishoff, or Sarnoff and Sons were rising on the American scene.

In some cases representatives of the business community themselves, as well as of broadcasting, seem a bit impatient with the old-line pronouncements. In 1959 the vice-president and general counsel of the Ford Motor Company, William T. Gossett, warned corporation colleagues: "Self-serving pleas will do us no good. Negativism, always being against change, expressions of fear and alarm, distrust of the motives of everyone else, predictions of ruin that never comes; all these have been thought of in the past as clichés of business—not, I think, without reason." [9]

One of the more obvious anachronisms of network leadership, however, is its repeated warnings that television is still a young and delicate industry. Tampering with it, we are told, might destroy it before it can become sturdy and strong. These remarks were perhaps appropriate in the early days of broadcasting or television. They seem out of place several billions of dollars and ten years later. Frank Stanton's speech "TV Today," in January of 1958, after CBS had enjoyed profits of many millions, spoke of the "delicacy, the vulnerability of its profit structure." Robert Sarnoff, the previous October, after one of RCA-NBC's most dramatically profitable years, had called for "caution in tampering with the delicate mechanism of the broadcasting structure." Even in January of 1962 Dr. Stanton was quoted in the trade press as saying: "We tend to forget that it [television] is an infant medium of communication and that it must be allowed its growing pains." A spokesman of the print media, who noted the tremendous competition which television was giving to newspapers and magazines, commented: "Some kid!"

Broadcast leaders also blame the people for most of the

problems of broadcasting. Programs have to be lowbrow, people are told, because public tastes and interests are low. If education, parents, the government, intellectuals, and critics would do their job better, broadcasting would soon be fine. And the public has accepted the blame for the ills of broadcasting; it has done very little to protest against the practices of the industry in general. It is not in a position to do so: like small stockholders in a large corporation, it is not organized to do more than passively tolerate the system—unless it acts through government. The government is the public's only instrument of organized regulation and defense in such cases.

There are other types of rigging that are equally characteristic of broadcast management. In the case of shows dropped because "the public does not want them," how accurate are such allegations? A graduate student of the author's studying program trends, in 1959 predicted that "Playhouse 90" was scheduled for the skids. How could he tell? It began to be moved around in the schedule. Programs that management wants to keep are stubbornly held in the same spot. Mr. Paley insisted that the Philharmonic be kept at the same time Sunday afternoons for years, so it might develop an audience. "Playhouse 90" was tried on a biweekly basis. Then, it was alternated on Thursdays with "The Big Party." Then it was eased out under the heading, "special." When it was dropped, after being given "the treatment," what were the reasons given? In *The Saturday Evening Post* of October 28, 1961, John Bartlow Martin says: "Today, asked why *Playhouse 90* went off the air, Aubrey says, 'Basically because the public lost interest in it completely.' And Stanton, 'Because the audience turned its back on it. The fatigue factor. Television wears out ideas and men faster than anything.' " [10]

It is well known that, using such tactics as this, there is no difficulty in getting poor ratings for a show one wants to drop. Network officials then can quote the ratings they have achieved as the reason for dropping the program involved. Such is one use of ratings by network leadership. Another tactic used to get rid of a program, so it can be replaced by a cheaper or more profitable one, is that of reporting that the program lost money. Since the network's books are secret, no one can dispute such a statement. This practice is common in both the television and film worlds. Usually when a network spokesman speaks of a film as not having made money, he does not mean that it *lost* money. He only means that if he had done something else he might have made more money. Since the highest possible profits are his goal, the conclusion is obvious.

Sometimes networks claim that out of a sense of deep responsibility they have carried a program which was not popular with the public. Thus, the Khrushchev broadcast of 1957 was reported to have been unpopular with viewers. Not reported was the fact that only 105 CBS affiliates carried it, whereas 220 carried the Ed Sullivan program the same day. The people in 115 communities were *not allowed* to vote for the Khrushchev broadcast.

In Philadelphia a few years ago NBC boasted of keeping two fine programs, "Lifetime Unlimited" and "Opinion," on the air despite low ratings. Not reported was the fact that these serious programs were aired after midnight, when ratings are bound to be negligible. Nineteen fine NBC programs were offered in the Philadelphia area between 12:30 A.M. and 7:00 A.M. Some critics referred to these as public-service programs for night watchmen; others noted their sleep-teaching possibilities.

Many stations schedule religious programs at the lowest-audience times of the day, usually at the time that church services are held on Sunday mornings. Since most religious-program viewers are also churchgoers, as many studies have revealed, and since such people cannot be in two places at once, it is easy to prove by ratings that there is no significant audience for religious broadcasts.

There are two other techniques which should be noted in a discussion of the practices permitted by broadcast leadership. For years monitors have noted the skill with which many network newscasts unobtrusively crowd more commercials into them than the industry code permits. When the Federal Trade Commission condemned Regimen and other reducing-product ads as misleading, CBS and NBC stations in several areas continued to carry them for several weeks, apparently until normal contract expiration.

In the 1962 network hearings Hyman Goldin of the Federal Communications Commission reviewed profit figures for the networks. Profits appeared to be very adequate. Apparently caught off guard, the industry was unable to contradict them before a number of them were reported in the press. By the next day, however, NBC-TV Executive Vice-president Walter D. Scott, using the same figures, was able to show that after-tax profits for the three television networks really dropped from 20.8 million dollars in 1956 to 16.1 million dollars in 1960. The ability to "interpret" profit figures properly appears to be one of the most important qualifications a network executive must have.

In many such cases, broadcast leaders may with justice protest that they have no villainous intentions. As has been pointed out, certain practices in the corporate environment become part of the very fiber of broadcast leaders. These are *not* conscious evasions or deliberate rigging, but simply the way things are done, the unconscious standards which characterize the usual broadcast leadership. The practices and ethics of the networks are passed on to the stations, but the stations are almost powerless against the networks should they want to oppose them. Network leaders claim that if left in charge without government regulation, they can serve the nation, democracy, education, and the people best. The *Report on Chain Broadcasting* commented on this position as early as 1941 when it stated: "Solicitude for the smaller stations is not easy to reconcile with the NBC and CBS policy of tying up the best possible stations in a city and refusing their programs to the smaller stations. The contention comes with little grace, too, from network organizations whose restrictive practices have tended to prevent the rise of new networks which might supply these less-favored stations with programs." [11]

Through various types of controls, including the power of withholding or withdrawing affiliation contracts from stations which show an inclination to become too independent, the networks exercise life-and-death control over the television stations of the United States. Even more important, talent or programs which are under exclusive contracts to one network will not be available to areas of the country which that network may not or does not serve. Networks alone decide which stations may affiliate with them. The similarity of this practice to that of patent controls, which many of the mother corporations exert, is obvious. Thus, industrial corporation practices, designed to apply to products, come to control programming, which comprises ideas. Therein lie the sources of many of the concerns expressed here.

Edward H. Carr has pointed out in *The New Society* that the real choice in our society today is no longer one "between monopoly and competition, but rather between monopoly and what economists call 'oligopoly' . . . that fig-leaf which serves to temper the shock of monopoly to a prudish public and to evade ill-conceived anti-trust laws . . . the system by which two or three powerful groups flourish side by side in the same field on the basis of written or unwritten price-fixing and market-pooling agreements." [12]   Mr. Carr's statement is a good description of NBC's and CBS's many years of coexistence. Litigation or the threat of it is also used to discourage outsiders from entering the broadcast business. It is not unusual for a participant in hearings to pay $100,000 or more for the chance to compete for a station application. Large existing station groups, by contesting applications, even unsuccessfully, very often are able to prevent the entry of new licensees.

Throughout broadcasting's history, network and trade association leaders have warned that each successive step by government to regulate them would destroy them. These "wolf! wolf!" tactics have usually included warnings that the American way of life was at stake. In 1946 NBC spokesmen warned that the American system was being jeopardized by the chain broadcasting regulations which were then adopted. President Miller of the National Association of Broadcasters called the Federal Communications Commission's Blue Book "dangerous, subtle poison." The FCC members were called "violators of the first amendment . . . stooges for the Communists . . . obfuscators . . . guileful men . . . and astigmatic perverters of society." The 1958 Barrow report was referred to as "efforts to pound the networks into small pieces." In a 1937 address to a group of educational broadcasters in Chicago, William S. Paley set the pattern for coping with critics: "He who attacks the fundamentals of the American [broadcasting] system attacks democracy itself." [13]

The arguments used by present television-radio management against regulation reveal how perfectly present network broadcast leaders are big industry's faithful sons. Arthur Schlesinger, Jr., has noted this dilemma:

> They are in precisely the position that responsible business-men were in twenty-five years ago when they wanted, for example, to treat their workers better but could not afford to do so because of the "competitive situation." Thus many employers disliked sweatshops and child labor but knew that raising wages and improving working conditions would increase their costs and thereby handicap them as against their more callous competitors. Private initiative was impotent to deal with this situation. . . . There was only one answer—public action to establish and enforce standards through the industry. Finally the Wages and Hours Act required all employers in interstate commerce to meet cer-

tain specifications and thus abolished the economic risks of decency.[14]

Is it not time for the government, on behalf of the public, to take similar steps regarding broadcasting? Replying to claims that government reduces freedom, Barbara Ward reminded readers of the January 27, 1962, issue of *Saturday Review* that government regulation often brings *more* freedom. "To give the most obvious instance," she noted, "a ban on child labor reduces the 'freedom' of a few industrialists, while increasing the freedom of a lot of children." [15]

The broadcast industry has often staved off government action with good promises. The industry's codes can be called *voluntary* self-regulation only by the greatest stretch of the imagination. The 1952 NAB Television Code, for example, was adopted only a few months ahead of threatened congressional investigation.

Dr. Stanton's promised ban after the quiz scandals broke, of big-money quiz shows, canned applause, the appearance of "spontaneous" interviews (really rehearsed), and all other forms of program deceit (and quiet reappearance of many of these practices) has already been discussed. Meanwhile, the promises and bans had held threats of regulation at bay long enough to enable industry's friends in government to draft and pass legislation which left the basic structure of the network-agency-sponsor complex undisturbed.

Meyer Weinberg, in *TV and America,* recalls that "In presenting incomplete results of a poll [on what the people thought of the industry] to an industry group in New York, CBS President Stanton stated that more results would be released later. . . . CBS, however, failed to keep its promise to release these results." [16] In the spring of 1960, at a time when criticism was in the air, CBS announced that "Playhouse 90" would be kept on for the entire season. By October the project was abandoned, after providing excellent favorable publicity regarding CBS's fine, unselfish attitude toward creative drama.

In 1954 Dr. Stanton spoke for increased CBS emphasis on live as opposed to filmed programs. In testimony before a Senate subcommittee on June 18, 1954, he said: "It is the live quality, the sense of seeing the actual event . . . which is the real magic of television." Three years later the percentage of film on WCBS-TV and other CBS stations was far higher than ever before.

In 1934 [17] Mr. Paley testified in opposition to the proposal to allocate certain frequencies to education. In his testimony Mr. Paley showed how the commercial stations and networks could and would serve the needs of education. He pointed out that only some 30 per cent of CBS's time was commercial. Almost 70 per cent was reserved for such public services as education. Congressmen listening took this as a promise that CBS would continue to provide education with the facilities it needed. The less than 5 per cent of CBS time which is now devoted to bona fide noncommercial educational programs and granted to educational institutions indicates how well a promise which helped prevent education from getting its own allocations has been kept.

Former Federal Communications Commission Chairman Newton Minow, who had perhaps read some of the unkept promises of broadcast leaders during the last thirty years and compared them with facts, said in an address before the Commonwealth Club in San Francisco, December 22, 1961:

> Nothing in this country—nothing—is more important than freedom of expression. . . . But freedom of speech should not be confused with freedom to make promises in order to secure a TV license and then freedom to break those promises in order to exploit that license. Freedom of speech does not mean freedom to propose a carefully spelled out plan of balanced programming, accommodating both the majority and the minority of viewers in an area; and then freedom to toss balance overboard and rush off in frantic pursuit of higher ratings and higher profits. Freedom of speech does not mean freedom to fool the people.

Frank Stanton's impassioned appeal to the FCC for the right of broadcasters to editorialize has been noted earlier, but some of the specifics of his promise made at that time deserve review. He said: "In the event we are given the right to editorialize on the air, we expect that the primary responsibility for preparing CBS editorials would be placed with a special editorial staff, disassociated from the regular news department . . . we decided that a period of time similar to that used for our own editorials would provide the most satisfactory balance of opposing views. This would amount to a radio counterpart of a 'letters-to-the-editor' column in a newspaper . . ." [18]

That, then, was CBS would do if "unchained" to editorialize. The change Dr. Stanton requested in Federal Communications Commission rules was approved. How has this service been developed? The editorial staff Dr. Stanton promised seems not to exist. Most of the editorials CBS has broadcast since 1949, when this rule was revised, seem to have been only disguised efforts to serve its own rather than the public interest, viz., they were against pay television and equal time requirements for political broadcasts, and in favor of other issues in which CBS itself has heavy financial stakes. The vital problems of the nation and world seem to have been covered very little by CBS network editorializing. Many CBS newsmen who did editorialize, even when they clearly labeled their remarks as their opinions, are no longer with CBS. "Letters to the Editor" columns are permanent features of newspapers. How many thousands of such minority views, opposing CBS positions, has CBS by now broadcast?

CBS is of course not the only offender in such practices. LeRoy Collins, former president of the National Association of Broadcasters, on January 31, 1961, did not hesitate to tell a Senate subcommittee: "We assert with assurance that if the Congress shall repeal the equal opportunity requirements of Section 315, broadcasters will be faithful to their public responsibilities and continue to meet their obligations for fair treatment of candidates and differing points of view." (Section 315 is the FCC provision that "if any licensee shall permit any person who is a legally qualified candidate for any public office to use a broadcasting station, he shall afford equal opportunities to all other such candidates for that office. . . .")

It is not known how Mr. Collins could promise what broadcasters would do, when the networks were still generally refusing to allow the NAB, a voluntary association, even to preview their programs and when only 32 per cent of the nation's radio stations and only a little over half of the television stations subscribed to the NAB Code. The record shows that the nation's stations have plainly flouted the NAB, its promises, and its code whenever they wished.

A more recent promise of the NAB, which it should soon be time to check on, was announced December 1, 1961, also by Mr. Collins. Speaking to the Louisville, Kentucky, Advertising Club and Better Business Bureau, he said: "It is not enough that the broadcasting business . . . be able to assure itself it is not a contributor to the delinquent behavior of American youth. It is our responsibility—and we intend to discharge it—to help get to the root of the real causes of juvenile anti-social behavior and then help carry that story to the American people and assist them in treating those causes." These illustrations could be multi-plied indefinitely.

The networks use several other procedures to ward off in-terference or criticism. One is to give people information, but to provide it in such confused, complicated form that it cannot be understood.

Another approach guaranteed to slow down a hearing or cause critics or examiners to doze, and possibly miss a few flaws or slipups, is the reading of long lists of large numbers, together with interpretive comment and the presentation of charts pre-pared at great time and expense. For a government agency to brush them aside would be denounced as censorship.

Certain words, too, are more effective than others for warding off incursions into the broadcast industry's freedoms. Freedom, itself, is one such word. The people must be left free—unless, of course, they should want to try pay television, or see certain programs which network stations decide not to carry.

The *challenge* is also a useful tactic. Robert Sarnoff has said that he doesn't think "anyone has proved that bad television is harmful." This verges, of course, on doubletalk. Bad, thus understood, does not necessarily mean harmful. Reassurance is effective, too. This is usually couched in platitudes. Like any propaganda instrument, it requires repetition. Dr. Stanton, in his Benjamin Franklin lecture at the University of Pennsylvania, December 7, 1961, referred to above, told his respectful listeners that "the medium will change because there is a constant, slow but inevitable upward movement in the standards and interests and capacities of a free people." Since both democracy and educa-tion are based on the premise that improvement is not inevitable but comes only from planned upward effort, his reassuring state-ment is questionable. In fact, Dr. Stanton's words on this occasion seem to be quite contrary to his usual position. He has often been quoted as saying that since television is a mass medium, it can never be perfect. Paul Goodman explained this point of view in an interview with Studs Terkel over Chicago's fine arts station, WFMT, April 13, 1962. A network executive once asked Mr. Goodman to do a critical piece about television for a new maga-zine being set up by the industry to criticize itself. Mr. Good-man quoted him as saying: "We here at the Network think that if we put out a magazine of self-criticism, then everybody will see we are on the up-and-up."

Later when Mr. Goodman began to sketch his suggestions for

ways to improve television, he was interrupted. As Mr. Goodman reports: "The TV executive began acting very nervous and after a while his hair stood up. 'Goodman,' he complained, 'you don't get the idea at all: what I want you to do is to write an article saying that TV is lousy but that it is inevitably so; and since it is inevitably so, nothing can be done. All *you* want is to show how we can *improve* the medium. If I printed your article I would be fired immediately!' " [19]

Two additional tactics have been developed for coping with critics of the networks. John P. Warwick, of Warwick and Legler, has been quoted as saying: "Tampering with TV programming can derail the economy." [20] Mr. Paley and others have said that an attack on United States broadcasting is an attack on the American way of life. Critics are generally treated as un-American, or as communists or saboteurs of the United States economy or the democratic way of life. Efforts to restrict the export of some of those television films which might blacken the American image abroad have been denounced in this way. Network and agency spokesmen have warned that this could upset the United States balance-of-payments position, and cause great economic hardship in the United States.

One of the most effective tactics, however, is to remind critics, the public, and regulatory agencies of the enormous generosity of the networks. Reports in *TV Age* and other trade publications in September of 1962 told of the public-service "contributions" of some $91,864,669 worth of "free" time by the 541 stations listed for the April-to-June period. This compared favorably with the "donations" of earlier years. The reasons for this amazing "giveaway" by United States broadcasting are cited. Not cited is the fact that this is what stations *promised* to do, not as a gift, but as an *obligation,* before they could get a license. This is the only *royalty* they paid on this use of a public resource. Individual broadcast leaders may be very generous. Many have contributed generously to charities. But when broadcasting *corporations* insist how generous they are, one should accept what they say with caution. Generosity is not a characteristic of such business corporations.

Much can be learned, too, about broadcasting leaders by looking at their staffs and noting the morale which prevails. As in other large corporations, retirement benefits are intended partly to keep employees loyal—an employee usually receives no retirement benefits unless he has been with the company ten years or more. Yet firings are sudden and total; there can be no sense of security at either the executive or the occupational level. John Cogley [21] has documented the sordid record of the networks in blacklisting many innocent performers and writers, in many cases with no proof or hearings.* Many quiz-show employees and disc jockeys who were fired during the quiz and payola scandals claimed that they were only doing what they had been told, encouraged, and even trained, taught, and hired to do. This ruthless personnel tradition contrasts with that found in most large foreign broadcast systems, like the BBC or the French Broadcasting System, as well as with the morale and practices found in the better large newspaper and magazine organizations in the United States, or other old, established publishing firms employing professional personnel.

Many professionals find network and agency employment inhospitable. A professional journalist, for instance, likes to practice his profession with all the integrity he can muster. The experiences of Don Hollenbeck, Cecil Brown, Edward P. Morgan, Howard K. Smith, Edward R. Murrow, and several others from CBS alone, seem to indicate that in many respects they have had considerably less freedom than they would have liked. In many cases, of course, even newsmen become so conditioned that they are no longer aware of the respects in which they are subservient. They accept the smaller amounts of prime time allotted to news, as compared, for example, with the time devoted to westerns or commercials, the smaller budget and staff available for news as compared with entertainment, and certain taboos ("you don't *need* to show that he was killed in a Ford"). How different this balance might be under another kind of broadcast system, or another kind of management, rarely occurs to people who work in broadcasting. Too often they allow management and sales to decide what constitutes news, leaving it in the hands of what one newsman called, "jazzed-up newscasters, fender-benders, sensationalists, alarmists, carnival barkers, and others whose approach to broadcast news is frenzied and irresponsible."

The situation of writers in television, as described by Rod Serling, Paddy Chayevsky, and a dozen or so others who have detailed the nature of the taboos imposed on them, further illustrates the plight of the few intellectuals and artists still left in the broadcast field. Professional standards are not yet as respected

* While this book was in production, John Henry Faulk's *Fear on Trial* (New York, 1964) brought the documentation up to date.

in broadcasting as they are in the newspaper or magazine fields. In 1956 a spokesman for a film company was quoted as saying: "The nine to twenty-four age group wants action, horror, rock and roll. . . . We are supplying action and exploitable product. . . . We are flexible. If they want us to make pictures in a sewer and they'll make money, we'll do it."

The preoccupation of broadcast leaders with ratings is symptomatic of the way they equate quantity with quality. Peter Levathes, president of Twentieth Century-Fox, was quoted October 21, 1959, as asking: "Who is to say that if . . . millions tune in a western, that show isn't good? . . . Quality on TV is what a great number of people like and enjoy. We fail in our aim when viewing drops. That can be our only guide." [22] To those who remember that Hitler had a higher rating than anyone else in Germany, such values are likely to arouse misgivings.

By standards such as this, excellence is likely to be judged by the expense incurred, the amount of hardware used, and the number of people involved. Thus, the major networks repeat proudly that they spent over two million dollars to cover the Khrushchev visit to the United States. But James Reston and a score of other newsmen pointed out that there were so many newsmen and cameras present that they got in the way and changed the course of events, possibly of history. John Crosby declared that it was impossible to get a coherent quote, and the reporter from the London *Times* placed the blame for the "chaos which prevailed," as he called it, on the very network clutter which CBS and NBC boasted so much about. What television made of what was expected to be a fairly cool, dignified, and controlled visit by a chief of state should be kept in mind in evaluating such requests as that for the right to broadcast from courtrooms.

The standards of the broadcast industry are totalitarian in their implications: when quantity is equated with quality there ceases to be a distinction between individuals and masses.

Under such conditions, it is no surprise that programs are juggled with impunity, like ping-pong balls. Films are bought according to availability, cost, discounts, and other quantitative rather than qualitative factors: virtually by the gross, the ton, or the "warehouseful." Concern for content, sentiment, or effects on people have no place in decision making of this type. ABC-TV in 1959 announced it was juggling programs to compete with CBS and NBC programs in order to get the highest ratings for as many nights as possible. Shortly after he went to

NBC, network President Robert Kintner made short shrift of "Wide Wide World," "Omnibus," and such live dramatic shows as "Kraft Theatre." He said this was necessary to catch up with CBS. Such decisions make program quality, as compared with ratings, virtually irrelevant. To think of polling the people or even considering what the people might really want is equally out of the question. What people can expect from television is narrowed to what is most profitable, and, as if this were not frightening enough, the prevailing system excludes and opposes alternatives such as educational broadcasting, pay television, a federal system, or new networks.

Such is the record of broadcast industry leadership. From even this superficial survey it would appear to be not what democracy needs. It is true that there *are* courageous leaders in both the broadcast industry and other businesses in the United States. There are courageous sponsors who believe business should promote controversy and diversity. There are concerned newsmen who wonder if our nation can survive present press repressions and distortions, and who know how much better a job they could do if the gatekeepers, their bosses, had different values and did not limit journalistic freedoms by mercantile standards. But most broadcast leaders believe they are merely engaged in business. The fact is that it is they who determine the flow of the life blood of democracy: they determine what we respect, admire, ignore, or have access to, in this nation.

Moreover, given the dynastic ownership and control of the network corporations, there is little hope for a change in the kind of leadership—only in the degree. Unless the *system* is changed, the progeny of present families and corporations will control the broadcasting our children and grandchildren will have. This would not be fatal if only one of several coequal broadcast services of the nation were controlled by them. But such is not the case. They seek also, on the assumption that only profits are involved, to stamp out alternative services which might compete with them. Yet these alternatives might well prove to be their salvation as well as the nation's, in keeping democracy and capitalism alive. If the United States is to profit from *all* the potentials of broadcasting, the medium must be made as easily available to the surgeon, the labor leader, the minority politician, the educator, and the philosopher as it is to the salesman.

4

The Problem of Regulation

The regulatory structure which controls broadcasting in the United States would be a farce if it were not so tragic in its failure to protect the interests of the public.

The Wireless Ship Act was passed in 1910. It applied only to the use of radio by ships. The Radio Act of 1912, the first law for the control of radio in general, made the Secretary of Commerce and Labor, as the cabinet post was then constituted, responsible for licensing radio stations and operators. But no criteria for rejection of applications were established. In fact, the courts ruled that the Secretary, Herbert Hoover, had no authority or right to deny applications. The result quickly became a chaos of overlapping station signals which prevailed from about 1917 until the 1927 Radio Act was passed. This interference of broadcast signals with each other dramatized the need for some sort of traffic control.

During the Wilson administration there were numerous government efforts in the direction of government ownership and operation of communications. On July 8, 1918, Secretary of Navy Josephus Daniels, using many of the arguments earlier advanced by Samuel Morse, called for government ownership and operation of wireless communications facilities. He was supported by Postmaster General A. S. Burleson. With the change to a Republican administration, the watchword was free enterprise. Opposition to government ownership, operation, and regulation was the order of the day. The mobilization of business efforts against government encroachments was powerful and effective.

Annual National Radio Conferences called by Secretary of Commerce Herbert Hoover, each year from 1922 through 1925, resulted in requests by the new broadcasting industry for regulation. Recommendations were made by these conferences regarding the form such regulation might take, but no concrete steps were taken. In 1926 President Coolidge asked the Congress to remedy the increasingly untenable broadcast interference situation. The Dill-White Radio Act of 1927 was the result. It created the Federal Radio Commission (FRC), a five-member board with certain regulatory powers. However, Congress failed to appropriate adequate funds for its operation and created the FRC as an *ad hoc* Commission, for only one year; it retained this nebulous status until 1929. So sensitive was the Commission to lobby pressures that although the 1927 Act directed the FRC to refuse licenses to individuals or firms found guilty of unlawful monopoly, it failed to do so. It is not surprising that the Splawn Committee, set up to advise President Franklin Delano Roosevelt on broadcasting, urged wholly new legislation and the creation of a far more effective regulatory mechanism.

On February 26, 1934, President Roosevelt sent a message to Congress requesting the creation of a Federal Communications Commission to include the functions of the Federal Radio Commission in addition to those functions and controls over telephony and telegraphy which were then vested in the Interstate Commerce Commission. The next day companion bills, obviously drafted earlier in conference with the President or his advisers, were introduced by Senator Clarence C. Dill, Democrat from Washington, and Representative Sam Rayburn, Democrat from Texas. Powerful lobby pressures soon ended this hopeful new approach.

To the disappointment and frustration of various members of the House on June 9, 1934, the old Radio Law of 1927 was rammed through (with few changes) as the new Communications Act. (See Appendix B, transcript of debate from the *Congressional Record*.) Whereas most other Western nations created special commissions to study the uses and control of broadcasting, the

United States passed the Act—without a quorum or roll call—just as if it were voting on new street signs.

Variety and numerous writers of that time reported the efforts of the National Association of Broadcasters to stem the tide of threatened regulation. The NAB wrote to all senators, begging them "not to destroy the whole structure of broadcasting" by such restrictions as the original, tough Dill Bill, S.2910, as it was first introduced in the Senate. The bill finally passed was essentially the House bill, written by Sam Rayburn. How it came to be substituted for the earlier, rougher Senate bill is a lobbyist's success story which deserves to be traced in greater detail than is possible here.

The Wagner-Hatfield amendment, offered on the Senate floor on May 15, 1934, proposed to reserve 25 per cent of the broadcast spectrum for noncommercial use. It was opposed by Senator Dill. His proposed alternative solution was to require commercial stations to give a specified percentage of their time to education and religion. Mr. Paley of CBS, in his speech (referred to earlier) before the Federal Communications Commission October 17, 1934, virtually promised that not over 30 per cent of CBS time would ever be sold and that the balance would be available for education and other public services. Such a promise seemed to make educational stations unnecessary.

Network broadcasting was still young and television had not yet been born when the regulatory provisions now controlling broadcasting were passed. NBC and CBS made clear the precarious nature of their existence, and the need for freedom from controls if they were to survive. No restriction whatever was placed on networks in either the 1927 Act or the 1934 Act. But the change in attitude which occurred after industry pressure was organized represents more than the change between national administrations. It is a virtually complete reversal of the views expressed in resolutions growing out of Herbert Hoover's first Radio Conference in 1922, which urged that radio be viewed as a public utility and as such be regulated and controlled by the federal government in the public interest.

Since the 1927 Radio Act and the 1934 Communications Act, there have been a score of reports, investigations, and proposed bills intended to bring about the reorganization frustrated in 1934. In 1939, President Roosevelt, realizing how unsatisfactory the 1934 Act was, wrote the chairmen of both the Senate and House Interstate Commerce Committees. He said that "new legislation is necessary to effectuate a satisfactory reorganization of the Commission." But the subsequent Wheeler Bill and other measures, introduced that same year, failed to pass. The 1927–1934 structure stands today in all its anachronistic glory, as a tribute to the power of the networks and other large industry-owned stations to prevent effective regulation. In fact, the changes brought about by later legislation, notably in 1946 and 1952, have most often hampered the Federal Communications Commission and limited its powers.

Appointment of Newton N. Minow to the chairmanship of the Federal Communications Commission, under the Kennedy administration, suggested that government finally intended to meet its regulatory responsibility. More recent developments have not borne this out. At one of his first press conferences Mr. Kennedy was asked if he favored any significant changes in the basic structure of broadcasting. He replied that he did not, thereby clearly limiting the *kind* of changes which Mr. Minow and his successor, E. William Henry, could expect to bring about. Earlier, in late 1959 under the Eisenhower administration, John C. Doerfer, then chairman of the FCC, warned the industry that if it did not survive the loss of public confidence, precipitated by quiz scandals, payola, and other malpractices, it would have no one to blame but itself. He reminded industry leaders that they had had every reasonable opportunity to develop the structure and practices needed to realize the high promise implicit in the potential of broadcast devices. He mentioned the great patience of the Congress, the Federal Communications Commission, and the courts in past years. But he also warned that unless industry really cleaned its own house, increased regulation would be inevitable.

These and scores of other warnings have failed to frighten broadcast leaders, or to make them more cooperative. In testimony before the Federal Communications Commission, when it was becoming obvious that some limitation on industry and freedom was inevitable, NBC's Robert Sarnoff was asked what kind of bill or legislation would help curb malpractices and improve service to the public. His reply was simple: no bill. Instead, every instrument in industry's arsenal was rolled up as artillery to defend the *status quo.*

Yet the pressure has continued to mount. Extensive investigations and studies by several presidential commissions, Federal Communications Commission study committees, and House and

Senate committees have shown that the present broadcasting situation in the United States is too far deteriorated to be allowed to continue. Yet the action and changes called for in study after study never come. The volumes gather dust on the shelves of congressmen and senators favorable to industry or holding shares in the many corporations whose profits would be affected. Most studies blame both the Congress and the FCC for the present situation. And most, like the report of Attorney General Rogers to President Dwight D. Eisenhower in 1960, call for new legislation needed to give the regulatory agencies more power to control increasingly dangerous trends.

As noted earlier, the difference between total public interest and industry interest would perhaps be better understood if we visualized how fully the total *public* interest would be represented if stations and networks were *all* controlled by labor unions, or perhaps by predominantly religious groups, as in Holland, instead of by business or commercial firms. There would unquestionably be competition if one network were controlled by the AFL and another by the Teamsters. Or competition would exist if one station or network were controlled by the Catholics, another by the Methodists, and others by other religious groups. But this would all be competition *of the same kind.* However sincerely a labor union, a religious group, education, advertising, or any other one group may seek to represent the whole interest of society, it cannot. For it is itself only a part of the whole. Its interests are competitive with, as well as different from, those of other groups which make up the whole. Regulation, to date, and emphasis on self-regulation, have failed to recognize this basic problem or provide for the diversity and balance needed. Certainly, in the minimally-financed educational broadcast stations of the nation, most of them busy with narrower, specifically-educational tasks, no such adequate balance is to be found.

One democracy after another has concluded that government, when democratic, is a more reliable guardian and representative of the whole public welfare than any single type of institution. Yet, since the organs of mass media are almost 100 per cent dominated by large corporations, who thereby control the picture we have of what "controls" and "freedoms" mean, we do not perceive our true situation.

The term "public" has largely been preempted by *private* corporations. Their power is so great that the public comes to identify with industry as *we,* viewing government as *they.* This blurs the concept of regulation by confusing which forces are public and which are private.   The freedom of industry to discredit government is accepted; the fact that government has no equivalent weapons, and no advertising budget with which to reply, is rarely pointed out.   The *Congressional Record* is hardly a match for the modern media controlled by industry.

In the area of programs the broadcast industry asks that government keep its hands off; the assertion is that this decision must be left to the people.   The fact that the people have been unable to control impure foods or drugs or any other such products, except through government mechanism, is forgotten and concealed.   Herbert Hoover in 1925 made it clear that when he spoke of freedom in radio he referred to the listener and his freedom to hear all available facts on all essential problems.   Only secondarily was he interested in the broadcaster's freedom.   And by the latter he meant the broadcaster's freedom to meet the public's needs—not his own, his firm's or his segment of society's. Yet regulation in the United States has failed to provide a policy statement of what electronic communications must do in terms of the *public's* needs and rights.   The fact that in recent years so large a proportion of legislation has been devoted to protection of property and of the rights of broadcasters, rather than to protection of the consumers, reveals the power of the broadcast industry to define regulation and effect legislation on their own terms. Broadcasting serves the corporate community rather than the public at large.

Fortunately, strength attracts attention.   Although the over-all operation of the electronic mass media gives the impression of free access, the sheer accumulation of self-seeking and protective measures is beginning to attract notice. Requests for legislation to outlaw pay TV; requests for favorable tax laws and tax deductions; requests for laws to eliminate the need to grant time to any except the two large political parties—these and similar steps raise questions about whose interests recent broadcast legislation serves.

At present who is really regulating whom?   The power and speed with which the broadcast industry can manufacture public opinion and alert its friends in Congress and the administration to electoral and other consequences of noncooperation with the broadcast industry are beginning to provide strong evidence of government by pressure groups, minuscule in numbers but great in power.   And all too many of the pressure groups seem controlled by threads running back to the corporations which control the broadcast industry. Are the names of thousands of people on petitions circulated by television stations, in response to the station's or network's presentation of only *their* version of a problem, really public opinion or democracy at work? Or are such efforts a version of public opinion manufactured by broadcast media? Are they as rigged as quizzes? The broadcast industry protests that regulation would curtail its freedom, but what is this freedom if not the license to shape opinion to suit its own ends, to create wants and appetites, which thus control what choices people shall have? It is finally becoming clear that regulation must be seen in far broader than merely economic terms.

Regulatory commissions are, of course, a comparatively new and experimental development in federal government. The purpose of such commissions initially was to protect the consuming public and to foster private competition through government regulation.

It was assumed that through regulation a balance would be maintained between private and public interests. The imbalance which Galbraith and other recent economists have noted suggests that this assumption may well be wrong. It was also assumed that regulation would favor competition as opposed to monopoly. The fact that the opposite has occurred suggests that this assumption, too, was wrong. No equivalently powerful broadcasting system has risen to balance that of the advertising-based, industry-owned and -controlled system. Instead, the monopoly of the latter increases, and the firms in control become fewer and bigger. Belief in spontaneous or automatic countervailing power no longer seems justified. There is no one left who is big enough to provide such countervailing power except government.

Over thirty years ago Supreme Court Justice Felix Frankfurter questioned the regulatory concept now still in effect. He declared that not only were regulatory agencies not protecting the public; they were actually operating to defeat those purposes.

In part, the failure of regulatory agencies can be attributed, as the distinguished historian Bruce Catton and others have pointed out, to an ossification and senility which set in after the first few years. More pertinent, however, is the manner in which regulators associate with the managers of the industries regulated, so that they soon come to identify with these people and defend them against outsiders. Meanwhile, the regulated industry brings pressure to bear on the individuals who make up the regulatory agency; eventually it pretty well controls them. With its control of mass-media channels, the broadcast industry can subtly or directly belittle and otherwise discredit people it dislikes. It can promise lush jobs, following expiration of the regulator's appointment, provided that while he is in office he does not estrange important segments of the industry. Regulatory agencies have tended to promote monopoly instead of competition, and to defend the regulated industry better than they have defended the public. Studies of the Interstate Commerce Commission (ICC) clearly revealed how it has come to protect railroads against trucking interests, instead of protecting the people against railroads; between trucking carriers, the large have been favored over the small. The Federal Maritime Board was found by the Supreme Court to have suppressed rather than promoted competition. The Civil Aeronautics Board (CAB), by promoting large carriers against possible newcomers, has established a record of refusing licenses to smaller applicants and new applicants. It has been called the best friend the big twelve airlines ever had. In its first twenty years of operation, the CAB did not certify a single new applicant. The large lines became bigger, competition became less, and monopoly became greater. The record of the FCC is no different.

"Self-regulation," as it has come to be called, fills the vacuum created by the failure of the Federal Communications Commission. The broadcast industry itself—through its own trade association (the National Association of Broadcasters), the networks, and the trade press—claims to be self-regulating. The NAB, for example, has developed and administers codes for both radio and television. But only some 30 per cent of radio stations even pretend to subscribe to the radio code, and there are flagrant violations of the television code even by the stations claiming to subscribe to it. Self-regulation is ineffective—except to keep official regulation at bay. LeRoy Collins, former Governor of Florida, and one of the finest leaders the industry has had, was probably hired by the NAB as its president because of the respect he enjoyed and his potential as a "Secretary of Defense" against the FCC and government in general rather than because of his knowledge of broadcasting. Certainly, a large part of his responsibility involved coordinating industry pressures against government or public threats. The limitations of self-regulation are obvious. The *Christian Science Monitor* several years ago asked if the policing of television by the industry was not something like expecting distillers or liquor stores to provide liquor regulation. Industry has never written very stringent curbs on its own practices any more than unions have generally devised adequate regulations governing their operations. American business has insisted traditionally that it can regulate itself. In 1929 the National City Bank and the nation's largest financial institutions resisted government efforts to limit credit buying in the stock market, denouncing them as attempts to meddle with their freedoms. The 1929 crash proved the government right and these financial interests wrong. More important, it revealed the extent to which industry's freedoms, whether in banking or broadcasting, are of vital national concern and not merely the business of the industry concerned.

Where self-regulatory codes have worked they have been based on stringent educational and professional standards, such as those of the medical profession, where entry is based on specific credentials and disciplines and on the assumption that there are many things that a member of the profession will not do for money.

No clause in the self-regulation code of the broadcast industry sets forth even minimum qualifications of managers in any truly professional or ethical terms. Nor are there any guarantees that newsmen and other professionals shall not be overruled by sponsors, managers, salesmen, or disc jockeys in the fulfillment of their professional duties. Nor does the code provide that a station shall not overcharge, misrepresent its profit balance, or discriminate against labor, cooperatives, public ownership, or other movements and groups which now suffer from denial of free and equal access to the mass media.

The industry itself recognizes that self-regulation will not work except at certain times and in certain limited circumstances. In most cases government regulation has come in response to requests by industry instead of requests by the general public. When foreign competition has become a problem, industry has called for regulation of imports in the form of tariffs. When disasters, blizzards, or droughts have struck, banking, agriculture, and industry have turned to the government for the kind of help and efforts which in better times would be called meddling or limiting their freedoms. When large firms in broadcasting in the 1920s found the signals of their stations being interfered with by small stations, they called for regulation.

As if the failure of the broadcast industry to regulate itself and its resistance to effective government regulation were not bad enough, the preconceptions on which the existing regulations are based have been proved false or obsolete by the growth of the industry. When regulatory legislation for broadcasting was written in the 1920s, it was intended to prevent the building of industrial empires on publicly-owned frequencies. Yet NBC and CBS have been in the broadcast business since the outset; and they have annually grown more dominant, since 1926 and 1927, respectively. Licenses were to be granted only for "limited periods of time." Three-year broadcast licenses lose their meaning when the richest stations are controlled by the same firms for thirty years or more. Regulation in the early days, based on economic and political theories of the time which are no longer applicable, was designed to control isolated, competitive stations, licensed to enterprising individuals, representing hundreds of different businesses. There were no networks. Stations produced their own programs.

Perhaps one of the aspects of broadcast regulation most in need of review is that which excludes broadcasting from common-carrier status. The fact that the terminology of the Communications Act, especially such terminology as the "public interest, convenience, or necessity," is taken from the utilities field, reveals how radio and television were thought of in franchised utility terms. However, they were excluded from common-carrier classification because, it was asserted, unlike trucks, trains, and telephone and telegraph services (in which what is delivered or sent is beyond the control of the facilities operator), the licensee station was itself the creator of, and directly responsible for, the content or material sent over its facilities. Recent developments, however, raise the question of whether broadcasting has not in recent years come to behave like a common carrier and therefore to qualify for common-carrier status. Common carriers must make and keep various kinds of detailed reports, follow prescribed accounting procedures, open their books for inspection when requested, and be subject to rate regulation. No wonder big broadcasting firms resist common-carrier classification.

Abdication of responsibility by licensees to networks, to advertising agencies, to package agencies, to sponsors, and so on, through a maze of overlapping obligations, indicates that the original requirements responsible for providing exemption from common-carrier status for broadcasting no longer prevail, except in those few independent stations which do create what they broadcast. There are a number of these, especially FM stations, which provide their own discussions, have their own reporters and news departments, and themselves write or produce the only commercials heard on the station. To apply common-carrier status to such stations would be inappropriate. But most stations, which merely plug in to the network, or play back on their projectors or turntables syndicated materials which are often as much of a surprise to station personnel as to viewers or listeners, seem to be common carriers as much as trucks which deliver packages without responsibility for their contents. Alternative provisions, with station management left free to decide which kind of station or utility it wishes to operate, might well be designed. They could perhaps be given the choice of engaging in broadcasting or in some other activity, such as set manufacturing, but not in both. Broadcasting deserves the primary and exclusive attention of those who engage in it. Corporations which remain in broadcasting might be given the additional option of meeting the same sort of standards, with regard to public disclosure and democratic election of officers, as trade unions or public or semipublic agencies, if they do not wish to be treated as regulated utilities; alternatively, if they choose to operate as monopoly utilities, they should be subject to appropriate profit-rate and accounting controls. To ask freedom from either the need to operate democratically or the regulation imposed on groups which do not so operate is to ask for more license than can be granted to any single institution.

In 1926 in Britain, the Crawford Committee insisted that no company or body organized along trade or business lines and run for profit should be allowed to operate broadcast stations or networks. How would similar provisions work in the United States, where the public watches NBC programs from an RCA-owned network, received on RCA receivers showing NBC talent, produced with RCA cameras and microphones, using RCA films and recordings, and transmitted over station transmitters purchased from RCA?

Licensees should *not* have the right to prevent the media from realizing their full potential, or to prevent access to them for free and full discussion of all aspects of national life, including broadcasting itself. Nor should broadcasters be immune to public scrutiny which might reveal the degree to which they were excluding other possible operators, thus using the media for private instead of public benefit.

The inadequacies of the FCC go deeper than the outdated preconceptions already discussed. In effect, the FCC does not even have the sole responsibility for allocating and controlling the frequency spectrum. The Interdepartmental Radio Advisory Committee (IRAC) controls much of it, on behalf of the military and other services. It even licenses the FCC, whenever the latter needs access to frequencies. In effect the FCC administers that part of the spectrum that is left over after the military, the Department of Commerce, and other such services have the space they want. The Telecommunications Coordinating Committee (TCC), still another agency advisory to the President, is supposed to reconcile differences and conflicts between the FCC and the IRAC. But overlaps with the Federal Trade Commission (FTC) and the constant problems raised by the FCC's many other bosses—the President, the Congress, the Bureau of the Budget, the Civil Service Commission, the military, the courts, and the Department of Justice—make the present situation an administrative monstrosity.

The Telecommunications Coordinating Committee was at one time made up of representatives of the State, Commerce, Treasury, and Defense Departments. When the Defense Department was split, the military were given three representatives— Army, Navy, and Air Force—instead of only one. This representation, favoring military interests, is quite different from that carefully planned civilian balance that existed when the TCC was created in 1946.

The FCC is hamstrung, moreover, by a staff far smaller than that of any of the networks, and by salary ceilings so low that securing good-quality people is increasingly difficult. The FCC is further harassed by the power of the broadcasters to publicize what the Commission does, or else to keep its activities from the public. If the networks wish, the Commission has no access to the people except via the print media. And since many of the newspapers and magazines of the nation are owned by the same individuals and firms who control the nation's most important radio and television stations, there is very little real alternative here. More important still, the FCC can deal only with comparatively irrelevant details; it is forbidden by law from controlling ownership, policy, or program content.

The networks and the National Association of Broadcasters

fairly successfully keep the FCC too weak to hurt big firms, but strong enough to keep out newcomers or interlopers. It is capable of regulating the weak but not the strong. Harassed by congressional investigations which have been instituted each time it shows promise of toughness, the FCC has compiled a record of contradictions and inconsistency which few agencies in any nation can match.

In many cases commissioners have used their appointments to the Commission as steppingstones to industry positions. Many former commissioners moved to network jobs upon leaving government service. In other cases appointments have been political payoffs of one kind or another. Robert E. Lee, a friend of the late Senator McCarthy, and Robert Bartley, nephew of the late Sam Rayburn, are two recent illustrations of this basis of selection.

Mr. Bartley has made clear through the years that he is opposed to strong control by the FCC, though he has done as conscientious a job as most. Robert E. Lee, who has also proved to be one of the FCC's better members, declared when he was appointed that he did not believe in government regulation. Former FCC Chairman George G. McConnaughey made clear that he believed in "as few controls as possible." John C. Doerfer stated that the concentration of ownership and control of the biggest and best stations in the hands of a few big corporations like RCA, CBS, Storer, GE, and Westinghouse did not frighten him. "Somebody has to be dominant," he said. The FCC has been kept ineffective by the appointment of friends of the industry and men who do not believe in regulation itself. The assumption has been that individuals favoring strong regulation would not receive Senate confirmation. Such has been the record to date.

All the weaknesses of the FCC are traceable to the act which created it, or to subsequent amendments. Built into both are safeguards engineered by a powerful, pressure-group industry, and jealous provisions on the part of Congress reserving for itself, against the power of the President, the final decisions regarding what is to happen in broadcasting. Many congressmen see the FCC as an arm of the Congress in the constant seesaw of power between the executive and legislative branches of government; they have no difficulty in frustrating FCC efforts directed against friends or benefactors of the Congress or congressmen. Candidates coming up for Senate approval to the

FCC are asked whether they view their agency as a "creature of Congress." Knowing how easy it is for the Senate to refuse to confirm a commissioner whom the networks or other friends of the Congress object to, most candidates know how to answer this question.

The FCC's budget is controlled by both the Congress and the Bureau of the Budget; lobby pressure by the broadcast industry sees to it that this budget is kept down; yet appropriations below the FCC's estimates of its needs can cripple its operations. FCC Commissioner Rosel Hyde in 1959 pointed out the organization's complete inability to carry out its responsibilities with the 1,100 people it then had on its staff. He also referred to the way in which budget and staff requests to the Bureau of the Budget, justified and supported with meticulous care, traditionally suffer percentage cuts—which are wholly unrealistic if the FCC is to be expected to do more than rubber-stamp the decisions of the most powerful figures in the industry and their friends in Congress.

In the last few years the FCC has had to review and approve some two and a half to three million radio authorizations. It must do this with a staff numbering from 1,100 to 1,300 employees, of which one-fourth are in the field, and with appropriations of some 12 million dollars, of which over 80 per cent go for personal services. The FCC's year-end statement for 1962 noted that radio authorizations by the end of the year totaled over 3.8 million, 400,000 more than there were in 1961. This includes over 1,050,000 radio stations, over 2,500,000 commercial radio operator licenses, and 246,000 amateur-operator permits. In 1959, for which fuller reports are available, the FCC received 600,000 applications of all kinds. Over one and a half million pieces of mail were received and sent. The plethora of radio, television, telegraph, and telephone authorizations which the FCC must process—from walkie-talkie, taxi, FM, multiplex, and facsimile companies to the most powerful corporation-owned station complex—leaves it little time for study or policy making. There are some 4,800 radio and television station licenses alone, one-third of which come up for renewal every year. There are some 4,000 common-carrier aircraft and 40,000 private aircraft stations. Police radio stations number over 12,000; highway maintenance stations total nearly 2,500. Special emergency services of the Red Cross, Civil Defense, and beach patrols; ambulance, physician, veterinarian, school-bus, and a large number of other services in radio; microwave and other operations by common carriers—these are some of the problems with which the FCC must cope daily. And broadcasting is only *one* of the FCC's responsibilities in communications.

A single investigation, such as that of AT&T in 1939, often costs the United States government $150,000 or more, besides tying up entire staffs. Sometimes the costs mount toward the million-dollar mark, as the legal resources of corporations for fighting off regulation by lobby and legal efforts are increased. Since industry is in a position to outbid government for talent and since, through lobby pressure, it can keep FCC budgets low enough to be ineffectual, and since corporations can match the dollars of such agencies as the FCC (up to ten or more to one) in litigation, the dead end of present approaches begins to be obvious.

The activities of the FCC are further hampered by fiascos such as the so-called "AVCO Rule," adopted several years ago, as large monopoly groups and newspaper interests began to acquire more and more of ·the most desirable stations. This was named for the Aviation Corporation of America, which proposed to buy the Powell Crosley, WLW interests in Cincinnati. Under the AVCO rule the Commission would ask for competitive bids for such broadcast properties and would then consider which bidder, as the new licensee, would by Commission criteria best serve the public interest. During a sixty-day period any interested potential purchasers could apply and bid. The FCC would then make the grant to the applicant which seemed to promise best service of the public interest. In 1949 this provision was changed, and an amendment passed by Congress in 1952 stated that in acting on transfers of station ownership ". . . the Commission may not consider whether the public interest, convenience and necessity might be served by the transfer, assignment or disposal to a person, other than the proposed licensee." This incredible provision effectively obliterates the value of the selectivity process applied to original licenses. For if one individual cannot get a station because of a bad record, he can usually have a "clean" dummy friend secure one and then transfer it to him. As Robert E. Lee has pointed out, anyone legally, financially, and technically qualified, regardless of all the other aspects of qualification (criminal record, morality, business ethics), and regardless of other potential candidates, cannot be denied the privilege of station ownership and. operation.

This, however, is only one such chain on the FCC. Such provisions as the McFarland Bill prevent the FCC from discriminating against licensees because of business affiliation. The FCC is thereby blocked from preventing ownership of stations by large newspaper chains or other large single firms.

Another provision which has effectively hampered Commission operation is that which until 1961 prevented Commissioners, who must make Commission decisions, from consulting with the Commission's own professional staff members: e.g., general counsel, chief accountant, or chief engineer. This provision effectively deprived the Commission of access to the know-how available in its staff for the preparation of decisions. The examiner in any hearing or case was explicitly forbidden to consult with *anyone,* including FCC staff, unless *all* interested parties were allowed to participate in the consultation. Such was the bill approved by both houses of Congress July 2, 1952, and signed into law July 14, 1952. It prevailed through the formative years of television until 1961.

When this legislation, which was designed to paralyze the FCC, was first proposed in April, 1951, FCC Chairman Wayne Coy warned how severely it would handicap the FCC. Commissioners would be able to reach their decisions only by themselves reading the hearings and perusing the exhibits—a process involving the reading of hundreds of thousands of pages. This provision condemned FCC members to making decisions based on insufficient knowledge. They were then criticized by industry and critics for their poorly considered decisions and ineffectual efforts. Thus, the FCC was kept from being an efficient regulatory body, and discredited at the same time.

Other conditions, outside the Commission, contribute to the Commission's inability to do its job effectively. Some licensees defy FCC rules and falsify records. KOMA, Oklahoma City, for example, received notice of liability for a $10,000 fine for willfully and repeatedly transmitting a signal far exceeding its authorization in direction and power. Seven violations were cited. KDWB, Minneapolis, was cited for operating at night with a daytime-only license.

Music Corporation of America witnesses in California hearings in 1960 defied the FCC examiner's requests for various materials. This case has now been taken to the Supreme Court. Forcing an overloaded FCC to go through all the delays of litigation discourages it from too much activity of this type. The

FCC staff comes to dread the prospect of encounters with the huge legal staffs of large firms. We have noted that most of the limitations of the FCC's powers and freedom can be traced to congressional action. The reason can be found in the fact that some thirty senators and congressmen are owners or part-owners of television or radio stations.[1] When to part-ownership in stations is added part-ownership in newspaper interests and in corporations owning and operating broadcast stations, and membership on the boards of various organizations with large stakes in large broadcasting interests, the propriety of such holdings by congressmen becomes questionable; this is especially true in the case of the members of Senate and House committees directly involved in FCC and regulatory matters. Should not legislators as well as members of the executive branch be forced to divest themselves of such interests? Or at least disqualify themselves from voting on such matters? If the Congress can override executive agencies, it does little good to make sure that regulators and cabinet members have no such conflicts of interests.

The FCC has admitted that it deliberately favors station-applicant companies in which congressmen have stock; in some cases it seems not only to favor congressional or other important political figures as applicants but also to help them preserve their monopoly. Moreover, congressmen and senators often act as errand boys on behalf of their constituents. When broadcaster friends who give them all the time they need on television stations are in trouble, they do not hesitate to go to their assistance. In this way the activities of the FCC are further impeded. Phone calls, petitions, new bills, investigations, and veiled threats are all successful tactics used by friendly congressmen or senators making sure that a friendly station's interests are well protected. In return, the networks do not forget favors done them. CBS reported that, from 1929 to 1940, senators addressed radio audiences more than 700 times and representatives more than 500 times over CBS stations. Friendly networks and stations can also expedite the airing of recorded and filmed programs from Washington in home-town areas where elections are decided.

Add to the harassments of congressmen and senators interference from the executive branch, as in the case of Sherman Adams, or through direct presidential action and pressure by one of the most powerful lobbies in Washington, and you can see why the FCC is effectively crippled. It goes through the motions or pretense of regulation, keeping a broadcast service going, but it is incapable of controlling what it does. Those of its statements and regulations which come closest to regulation fail because of the FCC's inability to enforce them. Those of the FCC's regulations which are effective are principally concerned with operational details. It has power to outlaw certain quiz and payola practices, but none to control the basic policy structure of the industry of which these are only symptoms. The Justice Department in several administrations has indicated that option-time provisions of network affiliation contracts, which are the very heart of the present network-based system, themselves violate the antitrust laws of the nation. The "weakest sister of the regulatory agencies," as the FCC has been called, hardly meets the needs of the nation today.

In 1961 General Electric, Westinghouse, and other large corporations were found guilty of antitrust law violations. What would the FCC do when these firms' broadcast licenses came up for renewal? In spite of the fact that the FCC noted that the "numerous violations" to which General Electric and Westinghouse officials pleaded guilty "were of recent vintage, flagrant and based on persistent unlawful acts over a period of time" the licenses of the stations these firms owned were renewed. This conflicts with the law that clearly states that conviction for federal offenses should disqualify an applicant for station operation. If these firms had been individuals, the flagrancy of such violations would be more obvious. But regulations written, and agencies created, with *individuals* in mind, as was the case of most licensees in 1934, are incapable of coping with the anonymity and power of the giant corporation, which now controls most of broadcasting.

The study made of the FCC by James Landis for John F. Kennedy before his inauguration stated that no other organization had been more subject to pressures, more subservient to industry, and more in need of freedom from these pressures than the FCC. FCC Commissioner Rosel Hyde in 1959 expressed his opinion that good programming ought to pay. If it does not, he surmised, perhaps we are making a mistake in keeping broadcasting a competitive rather than a regulated, public-utility type of industry. On the basis of the record and the declarations of industry leaders, good programming does *not* pay. Alternatives must therefore be considered.

In the consideration of these alternatives, the choice is not, as is so often alleged, between "freedom" and government censorship. The setting of standards by government is neither censorship nor a violation of democratic principles nor a threat to public freedom.

Wall Street objected to increased regulation. Yet there was no question, as there is none now about broadcasting, that such curbing was in the interest of the economy and the national welfare. Competition was alleged by plant owners in the United States for years as making it impossible to eliminate sweatshops, child labor, and conditions conducive to high accident rates. Government regulation in the form of the Wage and Hours Act and minimum safety provisions made a change possible by making it mandatory. This was not censorship or restriction; it was liberation through the setting of minimum standards. The public and the workers profited, yet profits were never higher than they were under the new laws.

The analogy with traffic is a valid one. As automobiles become more numerous, we begin to perceive "effects" from them which we did not earlier foresee. Little by little higher licensing requirements for drivers are necessary, just as closer scrutiny of the real qualifications of station licensees becomes necessary. More safety features are needed. Antipollution measures are required, as they are in France, where relationships have been established between the fumes from diesel fuel and leukemia and between automobile exhaust fumes and respiratory problems.

All institutions in industrial society seem to be subject to the same aging process that has occurred in broadcasting—from youth through maturity to old age. The richer and the older they grow, the more resistant to change they become. Their insistence on the *status quo* slows the nation's social progess, for in a democracy dynamic change is the only hope if the extremes of revolution and decadence are to be avoided. The passing of obsolete concepts concerning the role of networks or of corporations in broadcasting may be greeted with regret by those whose monopoly it reduces. Yet it should be welcomed by the public, for it clears the way for new institutions, better fitted to meet present needs.

It is an unfortunate fact that the problem of the regulation of broadcasting cannot be handled by further tinkering or patchwork efforts with a basically unsound structure. The problems to be considered are fundamental ones, such as the role of the corporation; the validity of present concepts of the regulatory agency;

the propriety of the ownership of stations by congressmen, senators, and other officials; the reliance of elected officials on the generosity and friendship of broadcasters for election under present laws and practices; and the overlapping and conflicting roles of other government agencies which also are charged with parts of the problem of broadcasting.

In the final chapter of this book a few approaches to these problems are suggested.

5

The Hidden Economics
of Broadcasting

In the United States "free" or advertiser-supported broadcasting
is supposed to cost its audience nothing. In testimony before the
Senate Committee on Interstate and Foreign Commerce on April
25, 1956, the spokesman of the National Association of Broadcasters stated that the United States broadcast system made available "at no charge the finest programming fare of its kind in the
world." He added: "Never, either in success or failure, has our
industry levied one cent of tribute from the American people to
see or hear our broadcast performances." [1] This idea has been
repeated hundreds of times by United States broadcast leaders in
speeches to the public, and in testimony and statements before
congressional committees and the Federal Communications Commission.

In 1932, however, W. W. Splawn, counsel for the House Committee on Interstate and Foreign Commerce, claimed that the
costs of telephone, telegraph, and broadcasting were fairly considerable. The American people, he said, are entitled to know
what they are paying for such services, and whether or not they
are being overcharged.

Americans traditionally believe that he who pays the piper
has the *right* to call the tune. By giving the public the impres-

89

sion that television's costs are paid by advertisers rather than by viewers, broadcasters hope to create a passive audience. At the time of the quiz scandals, for example, one viewer, in a letter to the editor of a national magazine, reminded his fellow citizens that *they* were not paying for these programs; they therefore had no right to complain. The belief that broadcasting is free to the public is now widespread—and it serves broadcasters well to perpetuate it.

There are, however, many channels through which funds are secured from the citizen to pay for broadcast service. They are indirect, and they may or may not be too high. They are, however, very real. They include what he pays for receiving equipment, installation, upkeep, and electricity or batteries; what part of the price of television-advertised products goes to pay for television time and talent costs; and various other expenses which will be discussed later in this chapter.

The figures quoted here are taken from regularly published reports: *Television Digest*'s annual *Television Factbook; Broadcasting Yearbook;* the Electronic Industries Association reports on set production; annual reports of the Federal Communications Commission and various other government agencies as well as the larger corporations, which are readily available; and figures on stock holdings of various individuals, which are a matter of public record, filed with the Securities and Exchange Commission. Even a reasonable reduction in any of the costs listed here, or correction of any of the figures about which there might be disagreement, still makes evident a very considerable investment on the part of the public.*

* A May, 1964, study of 26,000 sample households by the U.S. Bureau of the Census revealed the following:

TV SETS IN UNITED STATES HOUSEHOLDS, MAY, 1964

	Number in millions	Per cent
Households in U.S.	56.2	100.0
Households with TV	52.1	92.8
Households without TV	4.1	7.2
TV households with one set	42.6	81.8
TV households with more than one set	9.5	18.2
TV sets in one-set households	42.6	68.1
TV sets in multi-set households	20.0	31.9
Total household sets in service	62.6	. . . .
U.S. population (of 188 million) in TV households	178.0	95.0

Eugene Paul, in his book *The Hungry Eye*,[2] suggested that a family spending $5,000 a year on living expenses pays about $183 a year for its "free" television; this includes amortized set cost, electricity, and repair costs—as well as some $55.33 per year in television "advertising tax" (a term which will be discussed later). In its brief before the FCC on pay television, International Telemeter Corporation listed the public's investment in television equipment and upkeep between 1949 and 1954 at 16 billion dollars and the annual average individual family's cost at $86.01. The Kimble Glass Company, the picture-making subsidiary of Owens-Illinois, estimated such costs at $81.14 per year. These are among the lowest estimates found—but by now they have risen considerably.

Speaking before the Committee on Interstate and Foreign Commerce of the United States House of Representatives in 1958, Mr. Robert Sarnoff said that in television's first ten years, it had caused the American people to invest more than 15 billion dollars in forty-seven million sets—in other words, an average capital investment per family of $319. Mr. Gene Wilkey, of CBS station KMOX-TV, St. Louis, in an address at Southern Illinois University, May 15, 1962, spoke of the public's investment of 23 billion dollars in television sets during the previous twelve years. Hence, for the approximately fifty million families involved, the cost was $460 per family. Since installation, repair, parts, and electricity are approximately equal to the amortized cost of the set, each of the above figures could safely be doubled. Some of these sets and parts, of course, were exported. However, since many Japanese, German, and other sets are also *imported*, the cost to the public would probably not be greatly reduced.

A few other statistics deserve to be noted. TV set production in 1962 was reported at a little over six million sets, valued at something over 1 billion dollars. The estimated cumulative total of TV sets produced in the United States by the end of 1963 is ninety million. Mr. Frank Mansfield, director of marketing research for Sylvania Electric Products Association, has estimated that 26,123,000 sets were scrapped by the end of 1962.

Radio-set production has been running some seventeen million per year for the last several years, for an annual retail value of some 315 million dollars. Since 1922, according to annual industry totals, some 350 million radio sets have been produced; the public has paid something over 9 billion dollars for them.

The latest available production figures showed the following for 1962 and 1963 in retail prices reduced to the nearest round numbers.

Table 1

TV and radio receiver and tube production, in dollars,
1962 and 1963
Source: Electric Industries Association *EIA Yearbook, 1964*

	1962	1963
Television receivers	$953,000,000	$1,030,000,000
Home radios	205,000,000	177,000,000
Auto radios	181,000,000	206,000,000
Receiving tubes	301,535,000	273,670,000
TV picture tubes	173,661,700	167,269,400

Table 2

Number of TV and radio receivers in use, in millions,
1962 and 1963
Source: *TV Factbook, 1964,* quoting various sources

	1962	1963
Television receivers	60.8	65.0
Home radios	108.0	111.0
Auto radios	43.0	45.0
TV sets scrapped:	4.3*	

Using cumulative annual production figures, it is safe to estimate that since 1922 the average family has spent on radios, parts, and service $30 per year.   Over the thirty-five-year period that America has had radios, this total amounts to approximately $1,050 per family.

The two or more television sets which the average family has bought since the beginning of regular television broadcasting— including finance charges, installations, parts, repairs, and electricity—have cost about $1,000; in other words $2,000 per family for both radio and television.   In view of the many figures which are higher, this total of $2,000 per family appears very moderate. By the mid-sixties, the modest-income family which wishes to *budget* its radio and television capital and upkeep expenses would do well to set aside at least $110 per year.   As soon as the family buys a color set, it should budget at least $190.   If it has a second television set, it should budget a total of approximately $250.

It is unfortunate that there is as yet no single, central source

* For cumulative total, through 1962, of 26,123,000.   Author's estimate through 1964 (at 4.9 million per year): 35,000,000

of such statistics. However, pending the availability of such figures, it should be remembered that the purpose of this exposition is not to get at the exact costs but to indicate that these costs are substantial. This latter fact is important especially for two reasons. First, the money paid goes principally to many of the same firms which operate broadcast stations. A large percentage of its goes to RCA, which receives in addition patent and royalty income on many equipment brands other than its own. By 1923 Americans had already spent 175 million dollars for radio receivers. Much of this went to RCA, which was able to use these funds to finance NBC and its operations. Perusal of the names of some of the principal manufacturers besides RCA—General Electric, Westinghouse, Zenith, Philco-Ford, and Admiral; and in Canada Philco of Canada, Canadian Admiral, Canadian General Electric, Canadian Westinghouse, and RCA Victor, Limited—suggests how dollars paid by the public for equipment cross over into budgets available for broadcasting in the United States. It is especially ironic when such firms insist that the public pays nothing for broadcasting.

Second, broadcasting is unique in that the *capital* outlay necessary, as well as upkeep, repair, and power, is borne principally by the public rather than by the broadcasters. The only capital investment needed to receive magazines or newspapers is at most a mailbox. The publishers bear by far the larger share of the capital expense.

In order to understand more clearly the ratio of the public's expenses to those of the broadcasters, a few additional data deserve to be noted.

The *Report on Chain Broadcasting,* based on the Federal Communications Commission's study of network practices, in 1941, stated:

> The broadcasting industry does not require large capital investments. The NBC and CBS investment in tangible property devoted to broadcasting at the end of 1938 totaled $9,276,019. In that year their net operating income ($9,-277,352) was actually in excess of this investment in tangible property. . . . NBC's investment in tangible property at the end of 1938 totaled $4,284,032. Its earning for that year ($3,434,301) equaled 80 per cent of this investment. CBS had an investment in tangible property at the end of 1938 amounting to $4,991,988 and during that year its net earnings ($3,541,741) equaled 71 per cent of its investment

in tangible property. NBC and CBS profits have been large, and for the most part have been distributed to stockholders.[3]

In probably no other business in the United States has the profit return on capital investment been higher. FCC figures for 1960 showed a TV-industry profit of 244 million dollars, or nearly $5 per United States family. Since 1951, industry profits have amounted to nearly 2 billion dollars, or nearly $40 per United States family. Approximately half of these profits have been taken by the networks, and their 15 owned and operated stations, as those they own outright are called; the rest have been shared among the some 550 other stations, with the lion's share going to a very small number of large group-owned stations.

Representative Emanuel Celler noted in hearings before the House Antitrust Subcommittee of the Committee on the Judiciary, July 11, 1956, that CBS and NBC revenues for 1955 were 41.99 per cent of the total income of the TV industry, CBS alone accounting for 23.2 per cent. WCBS-TV, the network's key station in New York, in 1955, he noted, had a net income before Federal income taxes of $9,375,339 on a net investment in tangible properties of $409,484, thereby recovering "2,290 per cent on its total investment in broadcast property," as Mr. Celler phrased it.

More recent annual reports of the networks and large group-owned stations show no slackening of profits in the 1960s. However, the principal interest of these figures at this point lies in focusing on the capital investment of the public as compared with that of the industry.

Figures for 1961, as included in the FCC's 1962 Annual Report, indicated that the 540 television stations reporting, which included network-owned and -operated stations and 525 other stations, of which 81 were UHF stations, had a total investment in tangible broadcast property of $531,030,000 original or $317,-364,000 depreciated cost. Seven hundred television stations, costing as much as 1 million dollars each, would cost only 700 million dollars. By contrast sixty million television sets, costing an average of only $200 each, represent an investment of 12 billion dollars, or seventeen times as much as all broadcasters' capital investment. Also, the public cannot write off depreciation as a business or tax-deductible expense as industry does.

Since NBC as a broadcast organization buys its equipment from its parent RCA, actual costs to NBC are considerably less than RCA list prices. The same situation applies for numerous other electrical manufacturers which own stations. Whether their station-equipment purchases are really costs is a very important question. To what extent might they be considered legitimate testing or demonstration facilities and expenses? If carrying or financing charges are added to the retail prices for television receivers, total costs to the public would probably amount to an additional 8 to 15 per cent, making the ratio of public cost to that of industry at least twenty to one. Industry's payment for credit, even when it must go outside the corporate family, is generally fairly low in comparison.

In brief, we have noted that the investment of the American public in receivers and upkeep since the advent of broadcasting, if divided by an arbitrary figure of 50 million families, amounts to an average investment of some $2,000, with the annual total amounting to from $110 to $250, depending on whether the family has one set or more than one set, color television or black-and-white. The average will probably come very close to $200 per year up to 1965. The capital investment of the public is some twenty times that of the broadcast industry. Operational ratios will be found to be the same, although as stations become more stable and color and UHF expenses come to hit the average family, the public-to-industry ratio for upkeep and electricity will rise.

Television's advertising tax is also very substantial. The FCC in 1961 estimated that the average family was spending $33.48 for television advertising per year; this did not include the *radio* advertising tax which amounts to approximately another ten dollars, for a total of approximately $45. Breaking some of these figures down in another way: in 1962, radio time sales were listed at some 620 million dollars and television time sales at some 1,200 million dollars. When the 15 per cent commission of advertising agencies, which is deducted in advance, and spot and local sales are added, the annual cost of broadcast advertising comes to approximately 2.2 billion dollars of the approximately 12 to 13 billion dollars *total* annual advertising budget. Divided by America's slightly over 50 million families, this 12 billion dollars total advertising tax amounts to about $240 per family. Broadcasting's share, 2.2 billion dollars, amounts to some $45 per family as the cost of TV and radio advertising. However, averages for both set expenses and television advertising taxes have very little meaning. A typical upper-middle-class family will frequently spend in any given year two or three times the sums given here, particularly for the broadcast advertising tax. Since a higher proportion of the price of smaller items, particularly cosmetics, cigarettes, and dentifrices, goes for broadcast advertising than is true for larger items, families with certain types of purchasing habits may well pay several times as much advertising tax as others. Many cosmetics firms allocate 50 per cent or more of their sales income to advertising. Procter & Gamble spends well over 100 million dollars a year on television and radio. A fairly considerable portion of television tax is collected as part of the cosmetics, toothpaste, shortening, soap, and detergent prices paid to Procter & Gamble.

A typical family, with $5,000 in disposable income—using the national television advertising budgets of only the top fifty advertisers—might approximate its television advertising tax for an average year as follows:

Cosmetics and toiletries	$12.00
Patent medicines and drugs	10.00
Dentifrices	1.00
Soaps and detergents	3.00
Cigarettes	5.00
Wine and beer	1.00
Soft drinks	2.00
Food	6.00
Car	10.00
Gasoline, oil, tires, and other supplies	3.00
Total per year	$53.00

Adding the tax on products of firms other than the top fifty, including a radio tax of approximately $10 per year, would raise this family's broadcast advertising tax estimate to $75.

What kind of car such a family buys may make a very great difference in its tax, for example. In an article entitled "What the Public Pays for Advertising," Fred W. Hinickle asks: "Did you buy a new car last year? If you did, then between $18.97 and $161.70 of the price you paid went into advertising. The smaller figure was for a Ford, the taller one for a General Motors Tempest. The average for all cars was $31.70." [4] Ford's five-year Mercury advertising campaign, drawn up in 1956, budgeted 14 million television dollars a year to sell 400,000 cars; this averaged $35 per car, excluding local and spot campaigns.

Cigarettes offer another interesting example. Advertising ratios, ranging from 7 to 25 cents per carton, vary greatly from year to year and brand to brand. In some cases a good deal of this goes to television. In other cases only about half of this sum is allocated to television; the rest is divided among magazines, newspapers, radio, and outdoor advertising. The January, 1963, issue of *Advertising Age* showed the tobacco industry spending 5.47 per cent of its sales income on advertising. This would amount to a little less than 14 cents per $2.50 carton.

After the Surgeon General's Report on the relationship of cigarettes to lung cancer, the advertising budgets of several companies seem to have risen. *Printers' Ink*, in its "Special Report," in the August 7, 1964, issue, showed Liggett and Myers spending $866.53 for total advertising costs per 1,000 cartons of Lark cigarettes; American Tobacco Company spending $589.79 for Montclair; and Philip Morris spending $516.05 for Paxton. Of course all were new brands, requiring heavy initial promotion.

Advertising budgets for dentrifices reveal that for six brands only, the 1961 television advertising budget was approximately 36 million dollars, approximately 72 cents per family. Adding spot, local, drugstore, chain, and other campaigns, and the many brands other than the six mentioned above, something over one dollar per family per year would be a fair estimate. What percentage this is of the retail price may be computed by each individual. If a family uses ten tubes a year, the figure would be 10 cents per tube. Since the public has spent about 250 million dollars per year on dentifrices during recent average years, the 40 to 50 million dollars spent on television advertising by all companies would average from 16 to 20 per cent of total sales.

Procter & Gamble is well satisfied with the results of its use of radio and television—for which it spends well over 100 million TV dollars a year. Dividing this sum by the nation's approximately fifty million families yields an average of $2 per family. By the time the budgets of several other firms making similar products (Lever Brothers, Colgate-Palmolive, etc.) are added, the average family budget is considerably affected. From 1950 to 1963 Procter & Gamble alone had spent some 850 million dollars on broadcast advertising, or approximately $17 per family of the fifty million families involved. Adding the budgets of its principal competitors, the total would be over $50. Are the soap operas and other program formats created by them worth this sum?

It would seem to make little difference whether dollars are extracted from the United States consumer as visible taxes or as increased product prices, which include hidden television advertising taxes. The effects on family budgets are the same. The deductions made by business for wanted or unwanted advertising costs, unlike real taxes, have never been voted on by the consumer or by a legislative body. They are taxation without representation, since in none of the advertising media circles does the consumer have a vote or a representative. Having or not having a television set, buying or not buying a given advertised product, provide no alternative to paying this hidden tax.

The broadcasting tax collected through advertising since commercial broadcasting began in 1922 amounts to between 20 and 25 billion dollars, or from $400 to $500 per family for radio and television. The retailer collects this amount in somewhat the same manner that he collects cigarette, sales, excise, gasoline, and other such taxes. The similarity of private and public taxation in this respect becomes increasingly obvious under analysis.

In countries where the broadcast systems are supported by direct and visible taxes, the tax normally averages from $2 for radio to $12 for television. In England the television tax is $8.40 for television, although commercial television is raising the total expense per family very rapidly. In France the tax is about $12. In Canada, with vast unpopulated geographical areas and a French- as well as English-language service, it is approximately $16 per year. One important difference between the situation in the United States and that found in other countries deserves to be noted. In virtually every other democratic nation sets do *not* have to be purchased from firms which also operate a large part of the broadcast system itself and to a great extent dominate the economics and development of set production.

Many broadcasters claim that if the viewer does not like the programs, he should simply turn the set off. The absence of logic, if not the outright insolence, of this reply is apparent—not only has the owner paid for the set, but his dollars have probably gone to the same corporate families which suggest that he turn his set off. Since the set owner paid for the set, and is paying taxes, insurance, and other expenses for it (just as he does for his car), he has considerable rights as well as investments at stake. He may even have designed his home or purchased furniture to go with his set; this additional investment may amount to many thousands of dollars. To tell the set owner to turn it off is to imply that it is the broadcaster or advertiser who bears the expense.

In his statement of June 6, 1955, before the Federal Communications Commission, David Sarnoff attacked allegations that television is not in fact free. Mr. Sarnoff said: "This argument is as absurd as contending that purchases of automobiles and clothing subsidize the press and that, were there no press, automobiles and clothing would cost the consumer less. Of course, *it is elementary economics that advertising produces increased sales which in turn make possible increased production, lower costs, and lower prices to the consumer."* * NBC Board Chairman Robert W. Sarnoff addressed the Chicago World Trade Conference on March 5, 1963. He reiterated this economic fact: "The encouragement of mass demand sparks mass production, which, in turn, decreases the cost and increases the availability of these goods and services."

This philosophy is not limited to the United States. Roy Thomson, a Canadian who owns commercial stations in many nations, has also devoted considerable time and effort to explaining that none of the cost of television advertising falls on the consumer. The August 31, 1959, issue of *The Scotsman,* the Edinburgh newspaper he purchased largely with television profits, explains: "It is an economic fact that the more of a product a producer can sell, the less the consumer has to pay for it. . . . Thus, far from the public being out of pocket through commercial television, they receive not only a free television service, but pay less for those commodities which successfully advertise in that service." Such is the traditional view—some challenges seem in order.

How can advertising appear to serve both the public, which wants lower prices, and business, which wants higher prices? How has this conflict been reconciled? What role *is* advertising playing, at least in broadcasting? There are scores of case histories available to provide the answers. Strangely, none of the recent case histories available justifies advertising's self-congratulation; most, in fact, seem to prove the opposite of what Messrs. Sarnoff and Thomson say.

Some of the most interesting case histories (Johnson's Car Wax, Revlon, Hazel Bishop, and Alberto-Culver, for example) illustrate the ability of advertising *to enable the producer to charge higher prices.* In fact, prices have been doubled or tripled as a part of many successful television advertising campaigns. In

* Italics added.

one campaign, the price of a car wax was raised from approximately 69 cents to $1.69. The success story of television advertising provides scores of other examples. Costs *are* lower, but despite greatly increased sales and production, prices *rise*. Television usually has had the inflationary effect of creating enough increased demand so prices can be raised, even as costs are lowered.

How and why price raising, rather than price lowering, occurs needs to be noted. It is not as new a development as one might think. In farm areas of the United States during the 1920s and 1930s, there were numerous instances of advertising campaigns which enabled farmers to receive considerably more for their produce. Advertising in 1921 enabled one group to get $3 more per barrel for cranberries. In 1929 an intensive advertising effort enabled the Simcoe Poultry Farms in Ontario to sell their eggs for 20 cents a dozen above the regular price.[5] This is how farmers, who *sold,* were taught by advertising men that advertising pays. How the producer can be assured that advertising will enable him to *raise* prices and profits, while the consumer public can simultaneously be assured that advertising will *lower* prices, poses an interesting question. Is broadcast advertising really primarily a service to the producer, the buyer, or the general public? Enough questions have been raised to suggest the need for a careful reevaluation of the role of advertising in a television age.

Late in 1961 the National Labor Relations Board ruled that a broadcast station's services can be considered a product in the meaning of labor law. In this sense, the broadcaster is not in the public service; he is an indispensable part of the production process. As the Board reasoned, the station, "by adding its labor in the form of capital, enterprise and service to the automobiles which it advertises for the . . . distributor, becomes one of the producers of the automobiles."[6] By adding such labor in the form of advertising in order to make the automobile salable, the radio station "becomes a very important producer."

This decision raises a very interesting question: How, since the broadcaster so obviously is to all intents and purposes an employee or partner of the advertiser and a part of the sponsor's team, can he legitimately claim to be representing or primarily serving the public? Or is the station license, to operate in the *public* interest, now primarily anachronistic ritual? On the basis of the price record, where do television's heart and loyalty lie?

With *raising* prices, as industry wants, or *lowering* them, as the public wants?

In a very large number of the most dramatically successful television sales campaigns, one of the first recommendations of the advertising agencies has been to increase the product price. Particularly in the case of cosmetics, automobile supplies, jewelry, and other articles sold on the basis of irrational appeals, the recommendation to raise the price is often made for prestige reasons. The irrational power of television advertising is obvious here: People do not want to be found using *cheap* products.

A few more specific examples of the uses of television advertising to raise product prices might be noted. The success story of Hazel Bishop cosmetics is one such. Hazel Bishop sales rose rapidly after the company began to advertise by television. By 1954 it was taking in 12 million dollars in sales, and allocating 50 per cent of this to advertising. Television advertising made it possible to *increase* the prices of Hazel Bishop products considerably.

Another success story is that of Revlon, many of whose most conspicuous gains were traceable to the popularity of rigged quiz shows. The increased sales and profits of Revlon made *possible* reductions in prices by 50 per cent or more. Revlon, however, preferred to pass these sums on to *stockholders,* in the form of increased dividends and profits, rather than to distribute them to the consumer public in the form of reduced prices. The Revlon Company also, with its profits, purchased interests and firms in a number of other fields: a shoe-polish company, a drug firm, and Schick, Incorporated. In this case the advantages of advertising are used to *reduce* competition. Profits on one product thus enable a firm to raise its other product prices as well, by buying out competitors and in other ways. Apparently the time to reduce Revlon *prices,* however, has not come. In fact, some price increases can also be expected in connection with the products produced by the firms in which Revlon now has control.

Pharmaceuticals, Incorporated, sponsor of the rigged "Twenty-one" program, found television such a profitable medium for advertising that it was soon spending about 40 per cent of its sales income on advertising. It reported selling over 25 million dollars' worth of Geritol while this show was on the air. No price decrease was noted as the result of the increased sales volume.

Finally, another brief look at the experiences of Procter & Gamble, as an old, established, yet progressive company, provides additional insight into the role and function of television advertising. An additional but familiar characteristic of its advertising is the extent to which these funds are used to finance what might be called "internecine mock warfare." Programs to prove that Procter & Gamble's Dash is "better than any other detergent," including Procter & Gamble's own Tide, Cheer, Oxydol, or Dreft, and vice versa, cost some 25 million dollars a year, or approximately 50 cents per family. This must be collected in the form of price increases for some or all of these products.

In case after case—cosmetics, dentifrices, automobiles, cigarettes, soaps, and detergents—the more the products are advertised, the higher the prices have gone. Will price reduction *ever* result from broadcast advertising—do the facts not indicate rather, that this myth is due for the scrap heap? Advertising, at least on television, seems principally directed at serving the producer rather than the consumer, and at raising prices rather than lowering them.

Additional questions about the economic role of television advertising might well be asked. Since less efficient producers as well as more efficient ones may advertise, does not television advertising often contribute to the preservation of inefficient firms and processes? Does this not constitute a loss rather than a gain to the economy? To what extent do competitive commercials cancel one another? How useful to the public is the sum total of contradictory advertising of this type? Consider the cost of the counter-claims of the various cigarette companies: 200 million dollars a year or $4 per average family; the Lestoil versus Mr. Clean contest: 50 cents per United States family; Anacin versus Bufferin versus aspirin: 35 to 40 million dollars or 80 cents per family.

The pretence that television advertising is free or that it results in lower prices to the consumer shows a contempt for common sense and a contempt for the public. Perhaps *television's* unique advertising power has reversed what used to be considered the "natural laws" of commerce. If that is true, to continue to quote such "laws" is to be something less than honest with the public and something less than up to date on our economy.

There is neither time nor space in a brief study of this type to probe adequately the many symptoms of economic imbalance being developed by present uses of television advertising. About all that can be accomplished here is to raise a few basic questions. It has been recognized in our industrialized, capitalistic system that the costs of product distribution are substantial. A Twentieth Century Fund study in 1929 found that 59 cents out of the consumer's dollar often went to distribution, leaving only 41 cents for production costs. At the same time responsible economists have repeatedly expressed concern when the cost of any one part of the production-distribution process becomes disproportionately large. Some have expressed concern when advertising begins to exceed more than 5 to 10 per cent of the sales income. One of the conclusions of a special study by the President's Communications Policy Board was that "dollarwise, the economy has been able to take just so much communications service." [7] The same rule would appear to apply to advertising.

Never, however, until the advent of television, have such alarming imbalances in the costs of the various parts of our production-distribution system developed. If 50 or 60 per cent of the sales price of a given product goes for television advertising, how much is left for transportation, wholesale commissions, and retail costs? In such cases is television a service or a disservice? If all aspects of distribution take up all but 30, 20, 10, or 5 per cent of the retail price, leaving only small shares to be divided among materials, labor, plant costs, taxes, and other production expenses, has not advertising economically decreased in efficiency?

In many cases, indeed, the point of dangerous imbalance seems already to have been reached. General Foods some years ago reportedly reached a point where it was spending over $1.50 on advertising for every $1 increase in its net profits—because the $1.50 was deductible for tax purposes. This becomes a problem not only in television but in our economy as well.

If television and advertising pressures are so inflationary, and if large corporations can create demand, how and where can the problem be attacked?

The danger is *not* that television advertising is inefficient—it is *too efficient:* its effects are not held in check by the other parts of the economic system.

It is a widely held belief that one of the principal functions of advertising is to provide information to consumers about new and improved products. This is supposed to compensate for the objectionable characteristics of advertising. Television and radio advertising has, on the contrary, frequently been found to provide more misinformation than information. As Federal Trade Commission annual reports reveal, deceitful practices and misrepresentation have greatly increased since the advent of television. The evanescent visual medium of television is easier to "rig" than the print media, which the consumer can always re-check later.

Advertising has failed to be informative—too frequently only fake or selected data are promoted. If television is to serve the public interest, should it not provide the whole truth, rather than merely the advertiser's rigged version of it? Would this not be more in the public interest than the service now offered? If giving truthful information about products is really to be the goal of television, is the correct and honest way not the one pioneered by consumer organizations? Are not product demonstrations by such groups now indicated? Could they not be broadcast on the same type of equal-time basis that is now used in other countries for such consumer services?

At present, misrepresentations and counter-claims about products are broadcast "free" to everyone. Yet if the consumer wishes the truth, he must pay for that separately; he does so by subscribing to the bulletins and periodicals of a consumer service. Should television itself not provide this service? Is the public not already paying enough to deserve it? Is not the allegation that advertising is the best way to inform about products now false and outdated?

Two additional questions of economic policy in broadcasting need to be raised in this connection. One has to do with television's role in eliminating competition. The second concerns our obsession with money making.

Network leaders have denied that small businesses are being frozen out of television. At the network hearings conducted by the Federal Communications Committee in January and February of 1962, NBC Vice-president Walter D. Scott decared that small advertisers were not excluded—they could buy participations on NBC for as little as $200,000 per year, and the NBC sales staff would like to talk to such advertisers. He did not say how much an advertiser could buy for this sum. The answer is: very little; certainly not enough to achieve the repetitive, multiple impact which is television's forte. But a further question needs to be asked: is $200,000 really a small sum? Is it true, as one witness told the Federal Communications Commission a few years ago, that a budget of $3\frac{1}{2}$ million dollars is the minimum sum needed if a firm wishes to use national television effectively? Do such rates provide equal opportunity for new businesses, or free access for new ideas?

The significance of the economic emphasis of United States broadcasting is more apparent when we recall that both nineteenth-century industrialism and Marxism emphasized economics. Political developments were seen as subsidiary to economic events. This appears to have been the greatest mistake and tragedy of recent history. The center of concerns should be man, not money. Yet we are dragging past the middle of the twentieth century anachronisms based on the supremacy of production—as if production were still a problem. That problem, a real one during our nation's early days, has been solved. The really crucial problems of the world cannot be solved by dollars or even goods. As long as people keep busy earning money and buying things, they think they are doing something. Money-making comes to be considered a goal instead of a means. Money-making may really be one of the things our nation needs least. It defers, day by day, the need to ask: what for?

Dangerous political implications are to be noted in present electoral practices in which it appears that broadcasting and economics have both gained control over political channels. If present trends continue, will anyone other than millionaires, with very rare exceptions, be elected to public office? Certainly the 1960 Stevenson-Humphrey-Kennedy contest for the Democratic candidacy for President would suggest the advantage of large funds for winning elections in an age of expensive television.

A sampling of individuals recently elected in this way would include well-known names: the late John F. Kennedy, Edward Kennedy, the late Senator Robert Kerr of Oklahoma, President Lyndon Johnson, New York Governor Nelson Rockefeller, and various members of the Taft and other well-to-do families, some with broadcast interests. Many more could be added. Are the pressures of the present system, which favors a small number of economically elite beneficiaries, being transferred to politics?

The costs of the 1964 national election were estimated by *Broadcasting* magazine (November 2, 1964) at over 40 million dollars, nearly three times the 1960 total of 14.2 million dollars. And this figure did not include production costs or primaries. Nelson Rockefeller was reported to have spent over 3 million. dollars, and several of the others listed above, over 1 million. Individuals without funds in this dimension could not qualify. Is it proper to set up such a "prerequisite" for nomination? Will we soon be able to select only from a slate of millionaires—as we are now able to select only from a "slate" or choice of westerns, crime programs, or family comedies? Are such instances as the above really only coincidences? Are larger numbers of television-made millionaires scheduled soon to move into positions of political leadership? Is this in the public interest?

Such are some of the fundamental questions which need to be raised about the role of advertising economics in American broadcasting.

But this is only one aspect of the real and total costs of broadcasting in America. Some of the greatest costs of broadcasting are difficult to measure in dollars, and in fact might be better called consequences than costs.

If television or radio advertising media make possible the construction of a certain type of industry in a given city, and if this industry is later found responsible for air pollution, how are the costs evaluated—and who pays them? How is the role of television in such a case assessed? If the resulting sediment and smoke keep other *businesses* out, then the costs are recognized as adverse. But suppose such pollution keeps out not dollars, but health or cleanliness? Some costs can be evaluated in terms of dollars, others cannot. The Mellon Institute years ago found that the costs of air pollution in Pittsburgh were $9,944,740 per year to the community. Not counting crop damage, health costs, accidents, and illness, the annual cost of smoke pollution to the nation has been estimated at over half a billion dollars a year. Industries can now explain on television, more convincingly than was ever possible before, why such pollution is not their fault, and have thus made it possible to pass such costs on to the public by calling pollution a *public* problem.

Teenage smoking, and the national consumption of cigarettes, are apparently greatly increased by television advertising. Television leaders and advertisers themselves are the first to admit how much more effective television and radio are than the print media in promoting the use of soft drinks, cigarettes, and other such items. There is a distinct connection between cigarette smoking and cancer. How, then, are the costs of cancer to be allocated?

But there are many other more visible costs. They are paid, like the costs of smoke or water pollution, from general federal tax funds collected as income and property taxes. For instance, the annual budget of the Federal Communications Commission for 1963 was about 14½ million dollars. A large proportion of this was allocated to broadcasting surveillance and regulation. Since stations for over forty years have paid no license fee, and even the fees effective in 1964 are minuscule, all such expenses have had to come from general tax funds, averaging—since 1934, when the FCC was created—perhaps $12 per United States family, whether or not it owns a set. Portions of the budgets of the Federal Trade Commission, the Department of Justice, and a dozen other government agencies also go for expenses which would not be incurred except for our system of "free" broadcasting. Agency and congressional antitrust actions, investigations, hearings, and other actions against large broadcasters consume hundreds of millions of dollars. Each 100 million amounts to another $2 per family. The hundreds of millions of dollars spent by the corporations to fight such cases and to pay the fines levied also have no other source than the public. The public and federal efforts to make the whole structure work is certainly an expensive one.

In recent years, many of those firms which spend the most money on television advertising, and which thereby set the example for others to follow, have been cited for deceptive advertising. The costs of investigations and citations against Lever Brothers, Standard Brands, Colgate-Palmolive, American Home Products, and many others are significant public agency expenses. So are the prosecution costs of the twenty-three large electrical contractors, most of whom are engaged also in broadcasting and the manufacture of related equipment, who have been cited for price fixing, overcharging of public agencies for equipment, and violation of the Clayton and Sherman Acts. The costs of the nearly twenty cases successfully conducted by the Department of Justice in recent years against General Electric alone, and an equivalent number against RCA, amount to many millions of dollars. Policing the large broadcast corporations is expensive, and there is no one but the public to pay the bill.

One of the most significant effects of such constant litigation, of course, is to paralyze and hamper the regulatory processes. Because the entire staffs of such agencies as the FCC and FTC are tied up in litigation, these agencies have neither the time, personnel, nor energy to concentrate on those broader regulatory functions which they should be performing. Their only alternative, as noted in our discussion of regulation, is to request appropriations for larger staffs, which in turn are overmatched by corporation staffs in a continuous, expensive inflationary spiral—thus increasing government expense and bureaucracy, even while denouncing them.

What are the costs to churches, juvenile courts, prisons, or correctional institutions of erasing behavior patterns implanted by television advertisers? Many judges, prison wardens, psychiatrists, and mental-health clinic directors indicate that these costs are considerable. With half of the hospital beds of the nation occupied by mental-health patients, what is the relationship of television effects to hospital costs, or health insurance rates? What is the relationship between our average individual's physical fitness and the twenty or more sedentary hours a week which many of us spend with television? Can it be that our most powerful communications medium has no effect, or only good effects, on the economics of the nation's health and social services?

Although broadcasting is generally thought of as an industry which serves other businesses, it is also in competition with them. The time spent in front of a television set may be accompanied by the consumption of cigarettes, soft drinks, beer, food, and electricity. It thereby serves these industries. But while viewing television, people are likely to wear out fewer baseballs, golf clubs, walking shoes, hunting equipment, musical instruments, typewriters, artists' supplies, tires and gasoline, games, hobby materials, and books. Therefore, in a sense, television is in competition with these industries, even though it may carry commercials for them.

Time also represents a cost. All of the world's major institutions have tried through history to control man's time. The church, the school, industry, political parties, adult education, civic clubs, hospitals, and labor unions are some of the organizations which compete against each other for man's time today. Sports, politics, civic service, reading, music, hobbies, volunteer services, and recreation illustrate the uses to which this time may be devoted.

The broadcast industry has only time to sell. For the industry to maintain that *its* time is precious, whereas the public's or the individual's time is worth nothing, is an inconsistency, to say the least.

The average adolescent and adult spend from two to five hours a day watching television. Certainly 250 million man-hours a day or more are devoted to watching television. This would amount to something over ninety billion man-hours a year. Vance Packard has estimated that a high consumer of television and radio is exposed to some six hours of commercials per week. This comes to over 300 hours a year. Whether, in this role of consumer, he received 300 hours' worth of entertainment, education, and other values in exchange for this "homework" is a question which might well be raised.

Gunther Anders has pointed out how the average citizen "performs his work—which consists in transforming himself into a mass man—through his consumption of the mass product offered him, i.e., through leisure. . . . To complete the paradox, the homeworker, instead of receiving wages for his work, must pay for it by buying the means of production (the receiving sets and, in many countries, also the broadcasts) by the use of which he becomes transformed into mass man. In other words, he pays for selling himself; he must purchase the very unfreedom he himself helps to produce." [8]

One other aspect of the time-payment made by consumers of television and radio programs deserves attention. The time devoted by the individual to television viewing or radio listening is only part of it. A considerable number of individuals spend many additional hours writing jingles, working puzzles, and performing other services for sponsors or media-operators. And still other hours are spent accumulating box tops, pasting trading stamps, and engaging in other activities which, if paid for, would be considered very dull work indeed.

Much of this activity would look to a man from Mars like slave labor on behalf of advertisers. Many of these hours are spent in working on slogans which will later be used against the individual and his fellow-citizens. Such an expenditure of time by the public is even more out of proportion than is its expenditure of money. To the extent that many of these hours might be spent in self-improvement, or actually working for payment, the viewer's or listener's time *is* money.

It is time now to see what benefits the operators of the nation's commercial services receive for *their* efforts and investment. This requires patient study. For as scholars or federal agencies seek access to broadcasting's profit-figures, a maze of secrecy, rigging, and distortion is encountered which is difficult to penetrate.

The temptation to use different figures on different occasions is very great. When reporting to stockholders, declaring superiority over competitors, or seeking a large account, networks are likely to announce with pride the highest profits in history. In meetings with affiliated stations they are likely to point out the diminishing share of the network in the total income, and the need to increase the network's percentage of the whole if it is to survive at all. And when they are under investigation by regulatory agencies or congressional committees, network officials are likely to point out how precarious their financial position is.

On December 7, 1961, Robert Sarnoff, chairman of the board of NBC, told an affiliates' meeting in Beverly Hills, California, that something would have to be done to increase the network's share of the entire group's income. It was a dangerous situation, he said, when "the network's risks and costs keep growing while their return keeps shrinking."

In its coverage of the story, *Broadcasting* magazine of December 11 pointed out that "all three networks have called attention to the dwindling profits of network operations and the rising profits that stations have enjoyed." [9] Apparently the networks were in trouble.

Meanwhile, in the 1961 RCA Annual Report—where it was reported that 22 per cent of RCA's income came from the television and radio operations of NBC—David Sarnoff, RCA board chairman, proudly stated that NBC's broadcasting activity that year "achieved an all-time high in profitability." "Celebrating its thirty-fifth anniversary," his report said, "NBC achieved the highest profits in its history."

CBS affiliates, like NBC affiliates (and ABC affiliates), had also been told of the serious financial plight of their network. This imbalance would require correction at affiliate expense, in the form of revised affiliation contracts. The CBS Annual Report for 1961, however, reported that CBS net sales were the highest in the company's history. Cash dividends of $1.40 per share were paid that year, along with a stock dividend of 3 per cent. According to the report, CBS has paid its stockholders over 128 million dollars in cash dividends since the formation of the network in 1927.

From the reports of all three networks, it appeared that CBS grossed approximately 280 million dollars, NBC 276 million, and ABC 191 million in 1961. These sums amount to approximately $5.60, $5.52, and $3.82, respectively, for each of the nation's approximately fifty million television families. This represents a total television tax of $14.94 per family.

In 1962 and 1963 earnings were even higher. The November 22, 1963, issue of *Time* magazine reported CBS earnings for

1963 as nothing short of phenomenal. They were up 97 per cent over even 1962 earnings, to more than 28 million dollars on sales of 395 million dollars. People who had purchased CBS stock in January of 1963 had doubled their money by year's end. CBS Board Chairman William S. Paley's holdings, even after selling some $3,675,000 worth of stock in 1963, were still worth nearly 70 million dollars. Dividend returns on such investments are, of course, considerable.

Standard and Poor, Barron's, and other financial publications reported during 1963 an increasing trend on the part of large financial institutions and investment firms to add CBS and RCA stocks to their portfolios. Fifteen broadcasting companies were listed in the holdings of various mutual and other old-line firms, although CBS was the most popular. By late 1963, CBS stock was listed as the thirty-fifth most widely held common stock of institutional investors. Dependable firms like Massachusetts Investors Trust and the Fidelity, Dreyfus, and George Putnam Funds all increased their CBS holdings substantially during the year, thereby probably contributing further to the rising value of CBS stock, which by the end of the year was scheduled for a two-for-one stock split and an increase in the quarterly dividend from 35 to 45 cents per share. The RCA year-end statement also reported all-time highs in both sales and profits. Only ABC-Paramount showed inability to match this trend. Its value dropped a few percentage points during the year, from an average of about 34 to around 32.

While nearly three-fourths of CBS's and ABC-Paramount's income is from broadcasting as opposed to other activities, only 22 per cent of RCA's income for 1962 was listed as from broadcasting. The Mutual Broadcasting System represents so small a share of parent Minnesota Mining and Manufacturing Company's income that Mutual's contribution to the company's gross income of 687 million dollars was not listed in its annual report.

Lest these figures and those to follow be misunderstood, no claim is made here that the profits of all or most broadcast stations are excessive. It is not without some reason that many independent station owners, under the constant pressure of a few giant groups, particularly networks, protest that *their* profits are modest. The fact that the *average* station in the nation is earning a 15 per cent profit is less significant than that several hundred stations are earning only 5 per cent or less, while the top fifty network and group-owned stations are earning from 75 to

200 per cent. It cannot be said that all or most television stations are exploiting the public. Under the steady pressure of a relatively few large group-ownership corporations many independent stations are gradually forced to sell out in order to salvage their original investment. Such is the rapidly changing ownership base of United States broadcasting stations.

The late Senator Bricker, in a report to a Senate Committee several years ago, observed that one network radio station in New York City had an income in 1954 of 8 million dollars, eighteen times the total cost of the station. The exact profit came to 1,834 per cent.[10] Canadian Roy Thomson's statement that his franchise to operate commercial television in Scotland was the equivalent of a "license to print money" seems to be no exaggeration. Television critic John Crosby said in 1960 that owning a television network affiliate in New York "was like owning an oil well"; he added: "It takes about as much brains to run one. Push a button and the money rolls in." By way of illustration, he said that WCBS-TV would that year gross roughly 15 million dollars with a net profit of approximately 7 million dollars.

From annual Federal Communications Commission reports, it appears that the three national networks, with their fifteen owned and operated television stations, receive nearly 50 per cent of the total profits in the industry. According to the 1961 FCC Annual Report, total television revenues were $1,318,000,-000; the three networks' share was $675,300,000. Since the networks claim that profits from their network operation are extremely low and are subsidized heavily by their owned and operated stations, it appears that profits from the fifteen network-owned and -operated * stations roughly equal that of the other 550 or so stations in the nation.

* Each network is allowed to own and operate seven TV stations, of which no more than five may be VHF. The nineteen stations once owned and operated by the networks have recently been reduced to fifteen, since the networks gave up operation of UHF stations earlier owned when they were found unprofitable. Network-owned and -operated stations for the three networks, in television only, are:
For ABC:
WABC-TV, New York; WBKB, Chicago; KABC-TV, Los Angeles; KGO-TV, San Francisco; and WXYZ-TV, Detroit
For CBS:
WCBS-TV, New York; WBBM-TV, Chicago; KNXT, Los Angeles; KMOX-TV, St. Louis; and WCAU-TV, Philadelphia
For NBC:
WNBC-TV, New York; WMAQ-TV (formerly WNBQ), Chicago; KNBC, Los Angeles; WRCV-TV, Philadelphia; and WRC-TV, Washington, D.C.

The broadcasting subsidiaries of Westinghouse, Whitney, Storer, and a score of other large group owners are similarly profitable. Storer Broadcasting Company, most of whose common stock is held by the Storer family, earned a net income in 1960 of over 5 million dollars. Similar earnings characterize other owners: Balaban, Booth, Cox, Fetzer, Gallimore, Glassman, Hearst, Knight, Macfadden-Bartell, McLendon, Meredith, Metro-Media, Midwest Television, Mrs. Lyndon Johnson's Texas Broadcasting Corporation (formerly the LBJ Company), Newhouse, Rollins, Steinman, Taft, and Time-Life. Many of these, it will be noted, are newspaper or magazine ownerships.

All New York newspapers together report earnings of between 2 and 3 million dollars in a normal year. This is a very modest return of 5 to 10 per cent on their capital investment as compared, for example, with the nearly 250 per cent return of CBS-owned stations on their capital value, and the 100 or more per cent which newspaper firms often realize from their station properties. That such profits are denied by the networks and others goes without saying. In hearings of the Bricker Committee, the several hundred per cent profits of CBS, once "put into perspective" by Dr. Stanton, were reduced to what looked like less than 2 per cent.

High network profits are all the more surprising since they persist in the face of extremely wasteful practices. CBS Television City on the West Coast, with its huge facilities and enormous investment, has stood almost idle for several years, at a loss of several million dollars per year.

Public relations efforts of the networks also constitute significant expenses. Millions go for image-building. Network and trade association brochures (anticipating and replying to criticism) cost hundreds of thousands of dollars for the fine paper and expensive printing. Self-praise is both extensive and expensive.

During the height of the threat to free television, which the industry saw in applications to test pay TV, CBS held a party for legislators. Some 1,300 guests attended. This is still remembered by many who believe it was an excellent example of expensive and skillful public relations. Expensive talent (Patti Page, Phil Silvers, etc.) and lavish entertainment were available. A convincing CBS broadcaster, preferably from each legislator's home state, was assigned to each senator and congressman to be sure he received the full treatment about the advantages of the present free television system, and the threat to the American way of life posed by pay television.

Publications for distribution to schools; films for club and group showings; speaker services; lobbying, writing, and editing; and a score of other such services run the total of public relations costs to millions of dollars each year. One of the principal objectives of such materials is to prove that free television is a strong benefactor of the American economy, and that it must not be changed.

The profits of the networks and large stations have come largely from station operation. A significant proportion of the income of RCA, CBS, ABC-Paramount, Westinghouse, General Electric, and several others also comes from defense contracts of various types—but there is yet another source of income which needs to be mentioned.

Among the largest financial transactions which take place in broadcasting is the sale of stations, frequently referred to as "trafficking in licenses." Approximately one-half of the television stations now operating, including most of the largest ones, were purchased by their present owners. What is of interest here is the nature of the profits made on such transactions. Since the physical assets of a given station usually amount to a small percentage of the sale price, it is the frequencies that are really being sold. For example, CBS paid some 20 million dollars for Philadelphia station properties estimated (briefly, before the sale) as worth 5½ million dollars. For tax purposes these properties might well be listed as far less than that. An NBC station in Kansas City, which was purchased for about 2 million dollars, and originally cost only some $150,000 to build and put on the air, was sold for 7.6 million. Trade publications in early 1962 described the $10,950,000 sale of one New York AM radio station, from Loew's Theatres to the Storer Broadcasting Company. A second radio station in New York sold for 10 million dollars; a half interest in a Pittsburgh television station sold for 10.6 million dollars; and a radio-television combination in Buffalo sold for 14 million. Stations valued at $200,000 in 1950 were selling for up to 15 million dollars in 1963. The physical properties of a radio station selling for 10 million dollars or so are probably worth between 2 and 5 per cent of the sales price. The rest of such sale prices represents the sale of public property: the airwaves.

The sales prices of the radio and television stations sold during the last ten years probably total one billion dollars. Probably 70 per cent, or over 700 million dollars (some 14 dollars per United States family), represents the profits to the various interested parties. Since the frequencies belong to the public, sellers are serving more as brokers of public property than as broadcasters. Profits of from 100 to 1,000 per cent are not unusual. With the advent of color this is likely to become an even more lucrative business. *This* function of licensees is quite different from broadcasting, and since the public's air is being sold, the public's right to know of such transactions—or even to insist on public disclosure of them—should not be seriously questioned. Since these transfers must be reviewed and re-registered by the FCC, at the public's expense, the interests of the individual citizen seem to be taxed financially as well as ethically.

With profits being made on this scale, it should not be unexpected if fortunes should have been amassed out of "free" broadcasting. Figures on the size and nature of these fortunes are less available here than they are in England—where Clive Jenkins' study *The Power behind the Screen* [11] traces the overlapping monopolies of commercial broadcasting, including American interests, and computes the fortunes made in commercial TV in Britain so far. The growth of an investment of less than $5,000 by Norman Collins into several million within seven years is typical. Mr. Jenkins' study also reveals other economic effects of commercial television in Britain.

The scanty information available in the United States conceals the most significant facts. Salaries of $200,000 or so are listed but not the millions in dividends, stock sales, deferred payments, and other benefits.

Although David Sarnoff disclaims interest in money, Eugene Paul, in *The Hungry Eye* [12] notes that his personal fortune is probably well over 60 million dollars.

The company which became CBS was purchased by William S. Paley in 1927 for less than half a million dollars. Mr. Paley reported in 1961 that the earnings of CBS were "greater than those of the other two networks combined." Its net income was listed as $12,653,513, for $1.47 per share return. Mr. Paley's sale in early 1963 of 75,000 shares of CBS common stock for $3,675,000 has already been noted. He retained 866,000 shares, worth $44,382,500. Dividends of even $1.50 per share on these 866,000 shares would bring Mr. Paley some 1.3 million dollars a year. When dividends run to over $2 per share, as they have recently, this would total 1.7 million dollars.

Many broadcast-related agencies also prosper. Mr. Paul has described [13] how Jules Stein has built a modest agency business from virtually nothing in a few years. Dr. Stein is now the principal stockholder of his Music Corporation of America (MCA).

In 1961 he held 1,419,000 shares, each valued at that time at $78 a share. The total value held by him alone was $110,682,000. Following a consent decree against MCA, for antitrust law violation, Securities and Exchange Commission listings showed him holding only 1,380,030 shares on January 2, 1963. The SEC listing for December, 1962, also showed MCA Director and President Lew R. Wasserman holding 702,800 shares. In recent years, although the salaries of Dr. Stein and Mr. Wasserman may have amounted to a modest $175,000 to $200,000 per year, their stock earnings, at nearly $2 per share, have rarely amounted to less than $1,500,000 per year. When other income, from expense allowances, retirement, and profit sharing, is taken into account, it appears that the income and benefits from broadcasting for a number of individuals is fairly substantial.

In many cases salaries could be declined, refused, or turned back, much in the way President John F. Kennedy declined his, and many network and agency executives would still have adequate incomes of over a million dollars per year.

The salaries of the five top executives of RCA were listed in 1962 as varying from $137,000 to $215,000, for a total of a little less than $1,000,000. In similar manner the salaries of Messrs. Paley, Stanton, Aubrey, Jones, Hayes, and other principal executives of CBS total only a little over 1¼ million dollars. In all such cases, however, there are benefits (listed for tax purposes as stock benefits, etc.) other than salaries.

By the time earnings are distributed to the executives of the networks, large station groups, and a few related agencies, one to two hundred million dollars have been distributed to a fairly small dynastic group. These sums are listed as legitimate expenses of the United States broadcast system, which they undoubtedly are by business and tax definitions.

When the distribution of salaries is taken into account, other economic aspects of television begin to appear. As Father Keller, creator of "The Christophers," remarked at a 1955 Catholic Broadcasters Convention, only some 3 per cent of television workers are creators in the sense of being writers, performers, or producers. The other 97 per cent are sales, executive, technical, and management personnel. Thus, a large proportion of the funds collected are distributed before programs are even considered. It is doubtful whether many other industries have higher overhead expenses.

Even within the talent budgets of on-the-air and program

personnel, the same disparity is noted that exists between the high incomes of a few celebrities and the very modest incomes of the majority of workers. Rates for producers, directors, writers, and actors (except for "personalities") are very modest. The highest salaries and fees are paid to comics and actors or former actors turned salesmen.

Actresses and actors who specialize in commercials command large salaries. At the working level, they are the elite of television. People (like Yale drama graduate Julia Meade) who demonstrate shavers, appliances, and a score of other items, often draw salaries of from $100,000 to $200,000. Individuals like Nelson Case, Frank Lescoulie, Bill Cullen, Alex Dreier, Gene Rayburn, and Robert Wright draw $100,000 a year or more.

The highest talent salaries, however, go to celebrities whom television itself has helped create. Milton Berle will draw nearly 2 million dollars over a thirty-year period at $60,000 a year. A single Bob Hope Show, paying Mr. Hope $200,000, costs at least $400,000. Jackie Gleason will collect something over 1 million dollars on a contract already signed. A score of others like Phil Harris, Leo Durocher, Eddie Fisher, Barbra Streisand, and Carol Burnett account for some 3 million dollars a year.

Ironically, signing celebrities to exclusive long-term contracts keeps many television viewers from seeing them—viewers who live in areas not served by the particular network might as well be in quarantine.

The large number of television millionaires includes celebrities who in many cases have been able to set up their own corporations. The television and radio station interests owned by Gene Autry, Bing Crosby, Frank Sinatra, Bob Hope, Danny Kaye, and a dozen other movie and television stars, like the corporations of Lucille Ball, Loretta Young, and Dinah Shore, are both substantial and profitable. They, too, emphasize "pure" rather than intellectual or cultural entertainment.

Payments for the old films of Jerry Lewis, Lucille Ball and Desi Arnaz, Walter Brennan, Burns and Allen, Dinah Shore, Bob Cummings, Gale Storm, Danny Thomas, and other old standbys also represent investments of many millions of dollars. These guarantee the continued use of secondhand material produced in an earlier style for an earlier era.

Many producers have noted that commercials used on a half-hour program often cost much more than the program. One-minute "spots" often cost from $5,000 to $15,000. The cost of

filming or video-taping spots, according to the rate cards available
for analysis, has risen some 1,500 per cent in the last ten years.
Spots which cost $750 to $1,500 in the early 1950s now cost from
$4,000 to $25,000 to film. In the advertising aspects of television,
many such inflationary pressures are notable. Indeed, pressures
other than inflationary have not been discerned in the economics
of broadcasting.

According to FCC reports, the gross profits of the entire television industry rose from 41.6 million dollars in 1951 to 244 million in 1960. This represented a 600 per cent increase in nine
years. During this period, network profits rose something over
1,000 per cent from 9 million dollars in 1952 to 95.2 million in
1960. Broadcasting, in other words, has been a gold mine for
a small number of large firms during the past ten years.

What is to be done regarding these inequities and problems?
As suggested in the recommendations to be found later in this
book, a national study is needed to inquire into the economic
effects of broadcasting and its advertising.

However, certain preliminary steps might meanwhile be
taken: for example, an excess profits tax similar to that in Britain.
It does not appear to be in the public interest to have virtually
all policy decisions made on the basis of profit earning, nor to
have perhaps 80 per cent of those profits taken by the top hundred broadcast- and press-controlling families. Some steps to
ameliorate this situation could be taken now. The Supreme
Court of the United States has repeatedly ruled that price control
was one of the means available to both the states and the federal
government through Congress. It not only can but should be
used for the protection and welfare of the nation, especially when
small groups appear to be taking advantage of the public. In
every case where a state's or nation's right to regulate rates has
been challenged, it has been upheld by the highest courts in the
land.

A second step that could be taken without waiting for a
national study is to require open books. Services which call themselves public should be so in effect. If legitimate profits cannot
be made by open and aboveboard procedures in broadcasting,
the present system should be changed. A system which practices
secrecy in its own affairs cannot be expected to be able to put
such habits aside in other matters. A list of those individuals,
families, or corporations which receive one million or more dollars
a year from our free television service might be published by the

Federal Communications Commission, in cooperation with the Internal Revenue Service. These are steps which are immediately possible. Very little additional authorization would be required. Meanwhile, the principal corporations and networks—and their principal stockholders—should be invited to prove that profits are not as narrowly shared as this study implies.

In some respects, our broadcast system appears to be economic socialism in free-enterprise disguise. It is a system based on the premise that "free" programs are possible only so long as the audience continues to pay hidden taxes. Instead of profits from these taxes being distributed to the citizens of the entire nation as lowered prices, they are distributed to an oligarchical group. That such a system is neither wholly free nor democratic is obvious.

Although the intention in this chapter was principally to indicate that television is not free, and to suggest how and where the money goes, the size of the sums glimpsed suggests other questions: In view of the total cost of television, is the nation getting the best possible service for its expenditure? If the same sums were applied to alternative services, what new kinds of additional services could be provided? There is no question but that the public should be expected to bear the cost of a broadcast service. There is a question, however, of how much this sum should be, and what the public has a right to expect in return for it. Another question which needs attention is how large a proportion of the nation's income can go to advertising without straining and inflating the whole economy. How expensive does broadcasting have to become before the nation may decide that it is paying too much for communications as compared with education, health, or other services? How much time as well as money can television take away from other aspects of our economic, civic, and political life before it becomes a disservice rather than a service? These are only some of the questions which need to be explored by a national study into the economics of United States broadcasting.

6

Ratings and Mass Values

Probably no single factor is more responsible for the principal practices of commercial United States broadcasting than the use made of ratings. Ratings determine, in large part, what programs will be retained and which will be dropped. It will be noted that the programs offered in the first place, however, are determined by the broadcaster.

Ratings and the use made of them have been repeatedly condemned—and not only by the usual critics of television. LeRoy Collins, former president of the National Association of Broadcasters, has called them "a maze of statistics built from scanty facts" and has noted that investigations into how they operate "call into question the truth of any rating delivered today." David Sarnoff has said that the rating services do not mean what they say and do not say what they mean. Robert Hurleigh, president of the Mutual Broadcasting System, has called ratings based on 0.0003 per cent of the population meaningless. They have been criticized as "much ado about (practically) nothing," in view of the millions of dollars and the showy electronic computers used to extrapolate microbe-sized figures based on inade-

120

quate evidence into "public opinion." Probably never have so many people and dollars been engaged to prove so much from so little.

Ratings are based on the premise that stations should broadcast What the Public Wants. This premise should be examined. Journalists a few years ago were criticized for providing too little news about nuclear fallout. Editors explained that before press coverage of this problem could be increased, the public must demand it. The chicken-and-egg relationship in such a statement is obvious. From what, if not from news, is the public to know that such information is available? Or how is the public to know that fallout is or was reaching dangerous levels, and therefore should be considered news? The market for news items, like that for products, can be either created or not created.

Years ago speakers, artists, and writers had things to say; the media available—print, podium, and radio—dictated only its form. The commodity viewpoint reverses this. Now the communicator asks: What do you want said? The dangers of carrying the What-the-Public-Wants practice to an extreme are obvious. Only in so commercially controlled an environment as broadcasting is such a perversion of the very definition of news imaginable. Do you go to a lecture to hear what a man wants to say about a subject? Or do you go to have him tell you what you want to hear? Does an atomic scientist change his subject from fission to his latest trip through the Alps because it would be more entertaining and he has excellent slides available?

But this is only a small part of the problem. The slogan "Give the public what it wants" implies, first, that the public knows what it wants; second, it implies that the public is an *it* instead of a *they;* third, it implies that there is a clear and accurate way for wants to be transmitted to the decision makers.

The Canadian scholar Alan Thomas [1] has analyzed the roles people play in relation to television as Audience, Market, and Public. As Audience, people are a series of unconnected homes or individuals. Because they are so unconnected and isolated from each other, they cannot set standards, as Frank Stanton and others say they do. The Audience exists only from moment to moment. The Audience's vote is expressed by ratings. And ratings count sets rather than people or likes and dislikes in general.

As Market, the people become buying units, economic rather than human entities. Market success is measured by sales and profits; i.e., dollars. Market, too, is temporary. It is created by advertising.

As Public, people exist in their capacity as citizens. People who may vote *for* a program as audience, through ratings, may also vote as Public (citizens) *against* the program if they find the sponsor dishonest. As a part of the Public, a man may even support stricter government regulation to correct indecencies, dishonesty, rigging, deceit, excessive violence, or any objectionable content in the very programs he voted *for* as audience, and may even have voted for as market, by buying the product. The role of Public makes the citizen ask himself what is the *responsible* thing to do, rather than merely what he likes or wants. This role is the only continuing and rational one of the three.

Only in the role of Public do the people operate as a nation. Only in this role have they an objective and accurate mechanism for voting. That is the ballot box. The Public has voted for the creation of regulatory agencies by voting for congressmen who wrote legislation to create them. As Audience or Market, people may want lewd programs, or dope; as Public, or citizens, however, they will ask for limitations on both.

The Canadian public strongly supports the Canadian type of broadcasting, although as audience many of the same people may watch television programs from the United States stations along Canada's borders. The Canadian Public is very Canadian. The Canadian Audience and Market are essentially American—very much like the people of the United States in the same roles.

Even in this country the behavior of citizens as Audience is likely to be quite different from their behavior as citizens, when asked for a considered, deliberate, and responsible decision for the good of their country, their children, and the general welfare.

The Public regulates. The Audience watches programs and laughs at regulation violations. And the Market buys. Only in their role as the Public do the people recognize their duties and needs as well as their wants in the perspective which democracy requires. To quote ratings is not to quote the Public; it is only to quote Audience—to quote appetite instead of hunger, want instead of need, irresponsibility instead of responsibility, short-term instead of long-term, irrationality instead of rationality. Yet Audience is the constituency which the broadcast industry so often quotes (by ratings) in support of its programming.

The findings of firms like Schwerin, which do not hesitate to state with authority that they can measure what people think of commercials, suffer from numerous limitations. Schwerin invites women in and has them push various "like" or "dislike" buttons and answer questions about various commercials. There is no question that they can accurately report the opinions of women willing to serve as guinea pigs in exchange for free tickets and door prizes. It would be more interesting to know what different types of women who will not consent to such a waste of time, or women who are perhaps at work at the time, would think of these same commercials.

The give-the-public-what-it-wants philosophy fails to take into account that the satisfaction of needs is more likely to ensure survival of individuals as well as of democracy than the satisfaction of wants. People do not necessarily want what they need, but needs are objective, and they represent requirements; they are relatively lasting. Wants are subjective. They are irrational and can be created by all kinds of irresponsible temptations, lures, promises, cheap offers, and other bribes. Something a man *needs* is something it is harmful for him not to have. What he wants may actually be harmful.

Newton Minow in 1961 told the industry that his personal random survey of children showed that most of them preferred candy to spinach, movies to Sunday School, and soap operas and game shows to school. There is nothing wrong, he said, with giving children some of the things they want. But the fact that democracy is based on laws indicates that you simply cannot let children do whatever they want. We legislate school attendance in violation of children's freedom. Even for adults, want is not a sound standard for determining value. Hunger and appetite are not the same. Traffic laws and the controls placed on the sale and dosages of certain drugs are examples of the rules needed in all areas of life. Neither the courts nor medical diagnosis can or should be run by what people want. Those who declare that they are simply giving people what they want often do so to mask their own power and to protect their freedom of action. This is the case with the broadcast leaders who manipulate the taste of the people to their own greatest profit.

An example of this is the industry's attitude toward UHF as compared with its attitude toward color television. RCA particularly expressed great concern over the 20 or 30 dollars extra which UHF would cost the unfortunate public, but did not hesitate to push color sets, which still required expensive experimental maintenance and which would cost the same public several hundred dollars more per family. The public is made to want what is most profitable for the firm involved, and not to want what is less profitable.

In the case of programs, support can be found for almost any decision. When Laurence A. Johnson of Syracuse threatened boycotts of certain talent and programs in 1951 and 1952, when the industry was beginning to blacklist many writers and actors, industry was able to quote *him* as the public. Another example, more encouraging but certainly no less questionable in principle, was provided in 1956. During the Suez and Hungarian crises, the networks did not carry United Nations discussions. Jack Gould of *The New York Times* attacked the networks for failing to live up to their responsibility. He thought United Nations discussions should be carried. There is no evidence that what the people wanted had changed greatly. But what Jack Gould, as self-appointed spokesmen of the people, wanted did seem to carry some weight. United Nations sessions were promptly given some coverage. This was good. But it was hardly the *public,* or ratings, that the networks yielded to; it was one man. In all such cases, the views and pressures of individuals or pressure groups have seemed more effective than ratings (or what the public wants) in determining program policy.

"Studio One," "Camera Three," and many other programs have had enormous audiences. The decision to cancel them came from the network, based more on competitive factors than on what the public wanted. In Washington, D.C., when the McClellan hearings were being televised in the Kohler strike, the company side of the case was televised. Later when Walter Reuther presented the labor side the hearings were not televised. What the National Association of Manufacturers wanted shown, not what the public wanted, seemed to be the governing factor in this instance. The many millions of union members might well have liked to hear Mr. Reuther, and the union's case.

When Mutual outlets in the Buffalo area rejected "The American Forum of the Air," several years ago, a program which many people apparently very much liked and wanted, station WBNY requested the right to carry it. The request was denied. What the people of Buffalo or a Buffalo station wanted did not affect that decision. People in other large areas of the United States were denied this same program. It was finally canceled because, executives said (quoting ratings), "the people didn't want it."

When CBS and NBC put on "White Paper," "Meet the Press," or "The Nation's Future," hundreds of affiliated stations do not carry them. The people of those areas are not allowed to vote for these programs by the only ballot available: the ratings. In most cases they receive old movies instead. They receive the films because the local station makes more money on them. Ratings then prove that the people want old movies.

Sports on television illustrate another respect in which what the people wanted was ignored in favor of training the people to want what the broadcast industry could make the most profit on. When policy decisions regarding sports were being made, far more people were engaged in hunting, fishing, hiking, camping, golf, tennis, badminton, croquet, horseshoes, and a score of individual sports than in football, baseball, basketball, boxing, and wrestling. Two factors seem to have affected the decision finally made regarding what broadcasting would do about sports: First of all, industry wanted to promote those sports which would keep the television viewer in front of the television set for long periods of time; this required pushing spectator sports. Second, the profits in the *big* sports were more promising.

Television could have promoted individual sports instead of passive sports. It could have featured programs which teach youths how to pitch a curved ball, shoot a basket, handle tennis rackets and golf clubs, recognize different kinds of birds, and track game. The effects of a passive, spectator concept of sports which broadcasting has imposed on the nation are beginning to show up in physical-fitness statistics, and in other sports developments. The slow starvation of baseball farm clubs, the adverse effects on boxing throughout the nation, and other such recent sources of concern reveal the power of television to dictate what people shall be allowed to want. Ad agency president Fairfax Cone in 1961 referred to a typical Saturday in Chicago when the public's entire range of choices for three hours on four television stations was one baseball game and three football games.

Another indication of contempt for what the public wants is found in such advertising approaches as irritation commercials, allegedly first promoted by George Washington Hill, an early executive of the American Tobacco Company. Irritation commercials frequently achieve their success by their residual but subconscious reminder value, based on the intensity with which they annoy, irritate, or upset people at the time heard or seen.

When an individual finds a store out of his favorite product, and selects a substitute, he may suddenly realize, on the way home, that the one he chose is one whose commercials he found particularly obnoxious, though he did not consciously recall this at the time of his purchase. These have great attention-getting power. They are effective. But is irritation what people want?

Children are offered fantasy programs because, the networks say, most children want them. Between 20 and 25 per cent of the time, however, there seem to be no other programs from which to choose at those hours when most children are free to watch television. Those who formerly did not like fantasy programs or preferred reality programs are simply *trained* to like fantasy. The same situation exists for grandmother, who really wanted drama, or old-time music, but who soon learns to like professional football. She'd better; there is nothing else available on those lonely week ends when all the young people are away. The children and grandmother soon turn up as digits in the pro-fantasy and pro-football rating columns. The people have "spoken" via ratings.

The industry is well organized and well equipped. The other side, the people, are poorly organized or wholly unorganized, defenseless, untrained, and unaware of what is really possible.

We have described how industry can generate pressure campaigns—as the networks did when they got millions of people to write their congressmen, protesting against even authorizing a test of pay television. Representatives quoted these letters in Congress. The people had spoken.

In Britain, an even better example can be cited. No evidence of any substantial interest in commercial television could be found in Britain in the early 1950s. J. Walter Thompson and other agencies found this a real challenge. Billboards and other media were used to cause Britain to want commercial television. Britain was threatened with saturation by commercials from United States firms based on the Continent. The promotion group engaged to put commercial television over even offered to draft letters to the editor for people willing to write the press. A whole new nitwit industry, as it was called, was born; "indignant citizen" letters written for people to sign. In many cases the people did not even have to pay the postage. These letters were quoted on the floor of Parliament. One distinguished British official quoted the large number of such mass-produced "letters to the editors" in provincial papers as *his* reason for switching sides, and favoring commercial television. Commercial television was introduced in Britain. Again, the people had spoken.

There are over two hundred rating services, or audience research firms, as they generally refer to themselves. Telephone coincidental, telephone recall, diary, attachment on TV set, diary plus attachment, and personal interview are the principal kinds of data collection used. American Research Bureau, Bureau of Broadcast Measurement, Robert S. Conlan, S. D. Crossley, C. E. Hooper, A. C. Nielsen, Pulse, Elmo Roper, Schwerin, Sindlinger, Daniel Starch, Trendex, and Videodex are some of the principal firm names as listed in recent trade directories. Several of these firms do fairly specialized studies rather than general audience research or rating. Pulse operates only in communities of 100,000 or over. Pulse studies therefore present only or mostly the urban viewpoint, as Nielsen is also inclined to do.

One of the best-known rating firms is the A. C. Nielsen Company. This firm bought out a device developed at the Massachusetts Institute of Technology and now called an Audimeter. This is attached to the television set and shows when the set is turned on and the channel to which it is tuned. These data are recorded on a film. The cartridge is picked up at stated intervals by a Nielsen employee, who pays the set owner fifty cents each time for his trouble.

Nielsen extrapolates the nation's taste on the basis of some 1,100 Audimeters attached to home receivers. Whether anyone is watching, or who, or how many, or whether the viewer likes or dislikes the program or is even paying attention, is of course not known. The fact that sets are tuned to a given station, of course, does not necessarily mean that the message broadcast was received or even perceived; only that it might have been. The program the set is tuned to, however, is counted as the "best-liked" or "What the Public Wants." The scanty figures secured are then extrapolated, and the trade press reports that *x* million homes preferred that program. Under certain conditions, as few as thirty or forty sets tuned to a given program may give that program a high "Nielsen," depending on the competition. By the time the public relations departments of the sponsors and networks finish interpreting such reports, these thirty or forty lackadaisically tuned and frequently ignored television sets, sometimes playing to empty rooms and at other times looking out at bridge parties, or at children sleeping or fighting, have frequently been transposed into fifty million people, pictured as smiling happily or as wildly enthusiastic about the show.

How typical Nielsen homes are in any given area is open to question. Few intelligent people seem willing to have gadgets put on their sets, checking on their viewing habits. Few, too, care to allow other than bona fide service men access to their home and television sets. The few cents a week which Nielsen pays them for the trouble also seems like a sum only large enough to secure the cooperation of atypical families at the lower end of the economic and educational scale, and of very atypical indeed, if any, bona fide members of the educated artistic or professional classes. Some professional classes, in fact, are excluded by Nielsen itself, to help keep the findings from being too highbrow. The Madow Report [2] states that only about 67 per cent of the homes originally designated permit installation of the meters. A third or more refuse to cooperate.

The adequacy of the size of the Nielsen sample can also be challenged. To what extent this particular 0.00002 (two hundred-thousandths) of the television homes in the United States is either typical or adequate or behaves normally once the Audimeter is installed are questions which cast serious doubts on the validity of results.

At any given time probably not more than about nine hundred of the Nielsen Audimeters across the country are in working order. Of those turned on, depending on the competition, which in turn determines how many ways the audience is split, in a typical area, perhaps 32 sets may be tuned to one station, 24 to another, and so on. Since about 25 per cent of the films are not usable because of human or mechanical failure, these 32 or 24 are reduced to 24 and 18, respectively. These sets bear the burden of reflecting the nation's taste. The House Committee which investigated ratings in March, 1963, found that one of the sets had been on continuously for seven days. Several had been on over twenty-four hours. One Nielsen customer explained that she had turned the set on as a baby sitter. Another noted that the Nielsen-equipped set was in the children's bedroom, where no one else watched. In some cases, there may be only two or three Audimeters in a given city. Such is the so-called rating research carried out with Audimeters and similar attachments. By concealing the small numbers involved in the sample through the simple device of transforming them into percentages, the illusion of adequacy is created.

While there is a gadget in one's set recording everything it is tuned to, the chances are slim that one behaves normally any longer. It is by now an established principle of psychology, often referred to as the Hawthorne Effect, that while people are under observation, or having attention paid to them, they no longer can behave "normally," however hard they may try. Most Audimeter families probably do not want to look atypical or odd. Like people being photographed, these families are no longer "free." Audimeter families, whose television behavior is being recorded, want to do what is expected of them. Their *followership* is then projected as what the people want, and this becomes the *leadership* factor on the basis of which future program plans are made. Thus, people of America are given what a few people, of dubious typicality, under abnormal circumstances, are reported as having turned on, or failed to turn off, at some time in the past.

Transformed into percentages, the Audimeter's findings are magnified with millions of dollars' worth of computers, fanfare, and expensive printing, and then published. They then appear on virtually every broadcast executive's desk. Perhaps nothing in United States broadcasting provides a more discouraging commentary on the quality of its leadership than the fact that these men believe and quote these figures. As Representative John Moss said of ratings during the Nielsen testimony in March of 1963: "They are incredible. The fact that a major industry has placed any reliance in them amazes me. It is fantastic." [3]

Apparently the broadcast industry, including all the network presidents and vice-presidents, finds nothing wrong or out of proportion in the expenditure of 20 million dollars on Nielsen contracts alone. In a single city such samples might be statistically valid. But spread over wholly different areas of the United States, however large the staffs and hardware used to manipulate them, the imperfections in these samples can never be taken out. Once all the ingredients disappear into the broth, they cannot be seen or retrieved for checking or analysis.

There are, of course, other types of ratings than Nielsens.

Telephone coincidental surveys ask whether and what people are viewing. Here again, the tiny evidence in numbers is rigged to look like something dependable. In the forties the statistical validity of telephone coincidental surveys was tested at a university in the United States over a three-year period. The commercial firms operating in that area boasted that they were making 4,000 calls. In the university study, 6,000 calls were made. Of the approximately 5,500 calls completed, only two or three listeners were found for some half-hour periods. Percentages based on such figures appeared to have doubtful validity. There are over 200 half-hour periods in the 8 A.M. to 10 P.M. broadcast week. If forty persons are called during each of only 150 periods in a week for a total of 6,000 calls, ten callees (25 per cent) may have their sets on. Three of the individuals spoken to may not know what program or station they are either listening to or viewing, or may not be paying attention to the program. Percentage charts, however elegant, based on the remaining seven listeners for the given period have dubious validity in determining what a nation wants in program fare. In many cases it has been found that a rating of thirty to forty, which is high, and may affect broadcast trends for years, is based on as few as ten or fifteen sets tuned to the program in question.

Another kind of survey is the diary type. The Madow Report found that only 57 per cent of diaries recovered are usable. In diary studies there is even more opportunity for falsifying than in most types. A wife is unlikely to record in a diary, where her husband or the rating company can see, that she loafed and watched television all day instead of doing the laundry. Another may hesitate to indicate whether she preferred Nixon to Kennedy, or may not wish to admit seeing a program favorable to Castro. Another may not admit viewing a certain program because it turned out to be so bad. Moreover, about a third of the diaries are never recovered. Whether those recovered or those not recovered would be more accurate is not known. How typical those recovered are is also questionable.

Interview-type rating services also contain many flaws. The tendency of people to say they watch popular programs, or to say what will make them look better in the eyes of the interviewer, casts serious doubt on most types of interview surveys and ratings, whether by personal interview or telephone coincidental. Gallup, Roper, and other firms are frequently engaged to study the public. They generally seem to have proved whatever the firms paying them wanted proved; when they did not, their studies were not widely reported. This tendency simply to withhold adverse or negative data is one of the most regrettable practices found in the rating or poll business in broadcasting. He who pays determines how much of what is found out, if any, will be used and how.

Better methods for testing viewers' tastes and habits have existed for some time. Instantaneous feedback could have been built into the broadcast system of the United States if management had desired it. It still could be. The broadcast industry's failure to change to such improved methods suggests that the ratings give them the results they want. Innovations seem welcome in the rating area, as they are in the program or broadcast equipment fields.

Professor Charles Allen at Oklahoma State University has invented what he calls "the DynaScope." This device photographs the area in front of the receiver. It often reveals no viewers. At other times it reveals children who have gotten out of bed to watch television after the parents have retired. The number of people who fall asleep, or are fighting, or are doing homework while viewing is also revealed. So are expressions on viewers' faces. This device has been available for several years. But networks seem to prefer to have such devices kept off the market, in order not to disturb the picture now current of a loyal, satisfied, enthusiastic television audience. Hence, it would not be surprising if little further is heard of such devices for some time, even if their patent rights have to be purchased so they can be suppressed.

As if the flaws already described were not enough to cast doubt on ratings, they are extensively rigged. In a Midwestern city a rating firm was hired by one of the two radio stations in town. Ratings showed that station to be far ahead of its competitor in its number of listeners. The competitor hired the same firm some six months later. By some odd circumstance the situation was by then reversed. The station which *paid* each time won: Advertisers were confronted with proof that both stations were first, though the same firm did both studies.

In some cases this situation is created by the station itself. Running various types of special stunts the week the ratings are being conducted *does* often make that station first—for a while. Stations have been known to jump from last to first place within a period of weeks on the basis of special promotions and give-aways. Treasure hunts, special offers, guest stars—these are the bait. "Hypoing" the ratings of individual programs is also possible. This term refers to the practice (similar to the use of hypos and drugs on race horses or athletes) of creating an abnormal short burst of activity, or interest, by various stunts or personalities, at the time surveys are being conducted. The slow rise of the Dave Garroway Show, for years, was discouraging. J. Fred Muggs sent the ratings up rapidly. What the people of America wanted, obviously, was chimps.

An additional distortion of rating results consists in giving the impression that they show what the *majority* of the public is viewing. In a metropolitan center, assume there are approximately three million television homes. If one-third of the sets are on, this means one million homes. Two million sets, or the majority, are turned off. Of those sets turned on, an average rating would be 8 or 9 per cent. To be more than fair, assume a rating of ten for the average of the most popular program at any given time. This means that 100,000 sets are tuned to it. Far from being a majority, this is one out of twenty available sets, or only 5 per cent of the total. This is often concealed under the words "share of audience" (the percentage of those sets turned on, rather than the percentage of sets in homes). Even a rating of thirty, which is rare and high, often represents only 15 per cent of the sets in an area. Certainly no majorities are involved in such ratings.

The ratings of educational television programs have often been referred to as too small to justify the time and expense they require. Yet the average ratings of such programs have consistently been equal or virtually equal to that of soap operas. Of the sets tuned to soap operas, 1 to 5 per cent is described by industry as "everybody." The same number, tuned to educational fare, is referred to as "nobody" or "only the eggheads."

If all three or four stations in an area are carrying films, the fact that all the viewers are watching them does not prove they want films. They may very much want something else. But they have no mechanism through which to express their desires. The industry has devised equipment which works in only one direction. The program watched most may be only the least (but still considerably) disliked, or the one with the fewest commercials. It may even be simply the one coming in clearest.

Urged on by the inclusion of many stars, or by a great deal

of publicity, people may tune in on a special program only to be disgusted and disappointed. They are still listed as fans. They push the rating *up*, not down, as they might wish. The Audimeter or other rating shows they chose this program; interviewers have no spaces on most of their industry-financed blanks to show that, although the viewer tuned in the program, he disliked it and soon turned it off.

When asked what are their *favorite* programs, people in various studies have often not listed the top-rated ones. In fact, many of the highest-rated programs appear, year after year, on "dislike most" lists.

Several companies have given up using telephone surveys because people lie so frequently over the telephone about their television-watching habits, or even about what the set is tuned to. Other firms have abandoned plans to use Nielsen-type gadgets; it was found that some families turned sets on before going out at night, so the house would not look empty. Others turned on the President so the Audimeter tape would show they had been loyal and patriotic.

In March of 1963 Representative Oren Harris began hearings on ratings, before the House Special Subcommittee on the Investigations. Frank Stisser, president of Hooper, whose Hooper Ratings dominated the industry for years, declared: "It's purely a calculated guess," when the validity of figures regarding listenership and viewers were found to be ambiguous. The president of Sindlinger and Company remarked, "I don't think the industry wants true figures anyway." Certainly, according to evidence revealed at the hearings, it was not getting them.

As *Newsweek* noted in a short piece entitled "Bugged," [4] American Research Bureau reports for Birmingham, Alabama, showed 57 per cent of the 11 A.M. "Bugs Bunny" viewers on Saturday mornings were adults, although retail studies and other accurate data proved that few adults were even at home during those hours. Each such oversight or slipup, once discovered, is profusely apologized for by the rating firm and explained away as an "error" in a manner reminiscent of the way in which quiz-rigging accusations and disclosures were handled. Videodex, Inc., of New York, when called on in these hearings, was unable to produce for the subcommittee even a single copy of its vaunted diaries. The Kansas City firm of Robert S. Conlan Associates turned out in hearings to have a somewhat smaller staff than its publicity indicated. The experts, verifiers, editors, tabulators, calculators, supervisors, researchers, and checkers it boasts of all turned out to be one fairly tired Mrs. Jones. William Hurwitz, chief of the statistical division of the United States Bureau of the Census, stated that the nonresponses of 35 to 45 per cent accepted by rating services did not meet Census Bureau standards and that he would not consider using such "samples." [5]

Rating studies, even those that are honestly done, pose many problems. For interview studies, the selection and training of interviewers is very important. Statistics show that most interviewers are middle-class individuals likely to be dominated by middle-class values. Interviewees will try to please them. When interviewers nudge or explain questions, the nudges are likely to be good middle-class ones instead of neutral ones. Well-trained, qualified, and carefully selected interviewers could balance or correct for such biases. But that type of interviewer will not work for the kind of fees paid by most rating services, either for personal or telephone interview work. Unemployment offices are usually among the first contacted when a firm comes to a city to do a study.

Mary Field, distinguished British researcher, gave up the use of questionnaires for film research. Interviewees, she said, too often reply whatever comes readily to mind. Some interviewees are eager to please while others are impatient or cynical. The answers are replies often obviously intended to please, shock, or mystify.

It has often been asked why presidential preference polls can be so wrong. The answer is either that the sample was not an accurate cross section of the eligible voters, or that the interview techniques contained significant flaws. It appears that both conditions prevail. But so does the fact that some interviewees have not made up their minds and others change theirs. People are neither as rational nor as stable in their tastes as is generally believed. More recently, Gallup Poll results from a study of television as a news medium have differed from Roper studies about similar problems, significantly enough to raise further questions. Yet both these firms are far superior to the average rating firms in their integrity, direction, and personnel.

Another research firm conducted a quantitative study in 1956 of how many readers of a certain national magazine attended the opera. It found that over ten million did. This was several times as many as could possibly have crowded into all the opera seats for all the opera performances in the United States during the entire opera season.   Similarly, several million people have been reported viewing given television programs on nights when these programs were not broadcast.

Fairfax Cone, distinguished advertising agency executive, spoke in 1961 of the battle for "the gum chewers, the lip movers, and the bulk of the no-opinion holders" who were glued to television sets for the quiz-type program.   He warned that the rating and audience fight was probably for less than one-third of the sensible Americans of whom industry should be thinking.

At the time of the quiz and payola scandals, ratings were blamed, but, as we have discussed earlier, the networks must take the ultimate blame, since they assure government that they *are* responsible for all their programs.   The use, or misuse, of rating results by the networks is at least as questionable as the ratings themselves.   They become a rationalization for decisions even more than a basis for them.   The rating companies have pointed out that *they* cannot be blamed.   They would be willing to devise and carry out quality as well as quantity rating studies, if the networks would buy them.

When Steve Allen beat Ed Sullivan's ratings, as he recalls, "You would have thought I was a great hero."   Phil Silvers tells how, after receiving a higher rating than Milton Berle, the CBS secretaries stood in a body and applauded as he stepped off the elevator—perhaps the only "ovation" ever recorded in that lobby. More than ovations result from ratings: Millions in bonuses and renewed contracts follow from high ones; low ones often result in actors' and producers' thoughtfully rubbing their necks at the point where a guillotine blade would have fallen in an earlier day.   To many former actors, actresses, and writers, ratings are equivalent to fate.

William S. Paley in 1934 is said to have decided to offer New York Philharmonic programs on Sunday afternoons.   When told there was no audience for classical music, he replied that CBS would create one; and it did.   Later CBS and NBC created audiences for soap operas, professional football, and quizzes in essentially the same way.   Yet while it is claimed by the networks that Mr. Paley wanted to give the country classical music, soap operas, it is claimed, are what the *people* wanted.   Ratings do *not* dictate decisions.   They only rationalize decisions made by the networks.   But "the people," whose decisions these are then said to be, have no effective way of making or influencing *those* decisions.

Yet there is some evidence that rating personnel are not the wholly, objective, scientific, poker-faced, data providers that they appear. A Trendex spokesman protested being blamed for many practices, saying he was only a nose-counter. But a Nielsen pamphlet notes the adverse effect on listenership, in a given case, "caused by a long-hair presentation." The terms used by the raters and the prejudices they share seem to be the same as those of the networks.

The most famous defense of ratings is that given by Dr. Stanton, who sees ratings as a basic element in implementing cultural democracy. Giving the people what they want, Dr. Stanton believes, is the very essence of democracy. He has repeatedly stated that he knows of no satisfactory alternative to letting the people set the standards of programming by the simple act of accepting or rejecting what is offered. But (besides being unrealistic) how democratic are ratings?

When speaking of majorities, minorities, and people's rights, it is easy to forget several things. For example, historically majorities have often been proved wrong. True democracies keep the channels open to minorities to make sure that majority rule does not become the tyranny of the majority. But in radio and television where no single majority exists, the tyranny being developed is really a tyranny of a small, middle or lower plurality, a minority as compared with the entire public. This consists of perhaps 20 per cent or less of the total population. Bad as a tyranny of the majority is, a tyranny of a minority —however it is concealed under ratings, or even if it is called a majority or the will of the people—is worse. This seems to be neither a real democracy nor even a cultural democracy. It resembles totalitarianism in its disregard of both the desires and aspirations of the rest of the people.

When Richard Nixon was Vice-president, he took exception to publication of the fact that 80 per cent of the mail received by the State Department at one time opposed the United States policy on Quemoy. Mr. Nixon pointed out that policy decisions cannot be made on the basis of opinion polls. What the public says it is for or against is often based on too little information or misleading information. Only leadership, he said, could know all the factors involved. Ratings as a device for indicating what broadcasting should be doing are equally inadequate. The people are kept too much in ignorance about ratings even to raise the proper questions. Station managers quote ratings to church and school groups to prove that people do not want either religion or education. Yet many millions of people spend millions of dollars and hours on religion, education, and adult-education courses. The lowest possible ratings can always be guaranteed by placing programs properly in the schedule, as well as by moving them around.

Years ago the British Beveridge Commission pointed out that the use of ratings would result in a constant lowering of the forms of entertainment. The late Carl Jung expressed in interviews grave concern for the creation of faceless, totalitarian averages. As he once pointed out, if each stone in a yard is weighed and the average is found to be two pounds, the person we tell this to still knows very little about what the individual stones are like. All may be gravel-sized except for one or two rocks each weighing several tons. There may be no single stone which weighs two pounds. The statistical method, and the use of averages, falsifies rather than reveals the true nature of the stones. What is distinctive about men is their individuality, their uniqueness, and their irregularity. Ignoring, concealing, or distorting man's individuality as ratings do is precisely the opposite of democracy. The *typical* or *normal* pattern of viewing may be far different from the *average*. Yet ratings average everything: likers, dislikers, ignorers, rapt viewers, sleepers, and talkers are all "fans."

The networks prefer a program watched indifferently by two million people to one watched, and desperately needed and utilized, by only two hundred. They are free to do so as long as there is no system for ascertaining the good done by a program, the quality and attention it commands, or the understanding or incentive to useful action which it communicates. If ratings are to be useful, they must be both improved and supplemented by far more accurate and qualitative systems of measuring public opinion.

At present the use of ratings tends to equate wholly different forms: slapstick and religion, sacred music and singing commercials, madonnas and bathing beauties. All are lumped together. Instead of lifting people to the level of art, art is lowered and vulgarized to the supposed level of the mob: the digits revealed by ratings. Yet this process does not reflect what people want. No one person has such homogenized tastes.

Dr. Stanton's cultural democracy levels everything and everyone. It is neither culture nor democracy.

Once this leveling has taken place, popularity—or what the ratings register as popularity—becomes the only criterion of value. If a program or a star attracts millions, those numbers in themselves prove that he is good. Exposure constitutes celebrity. The effects of this criterion of quality are especially dubious for young people just forming a sense of values.

It is natural for broadcast leaders to rely on ratings, since they conceive of television as a mass medium. Yet what is a mass? And can television viewers be considered a mass? Television viewers, as we have seen, behave at different times in different roles. At one moment they are a part of one group; the next moment they are part of another of the several minorities. But no one of these units is stable from moment to moment. Nor is any one a majority except, possibly, fleetingly. That is why the term *mass*, which implies such stability, does not describe a dynamic and open society.

The job of such a democratic society is the formation of individuals. Totalitarianism, under whatever name it may operate, reduces man to a unit or cog. Whether he be thus dehumanized for political, economic, racial, religious, or broadcasting reasons is of less significance than that he *is* dehumanized, less than free and less than fulfilled.

Management of television and radio in the United States decided to apply mass-production techniques to broadcasting, not because they were inevitable or better but because they were more profitable. As the reasons are examined for considering television and radio as mass rather than minority or pluralistic media, it appears that they are mass media principally because they were *made into* mass media by their uses and their users. United States broadcasting aims at the largest possible audience available at any given time. Yet one of the dangers of thinking of the media in terms of the mass is that as the size of a group grows, so does the number of compromises which need to be made to avoid talking over the heads of lowbrow members or antagonizing certain minority members.

In a mass-dominated society individual features become blurred. We see only faceless crowds. The symbol of the society becomes the blank look, the look of people whose irrational appetites are manipulated by an elite who control mass media.

Nothing could be more of a contradiction or parody of true democracy than this mass or "cultural" democracy.

While Frank Stanton and his compatriots have said for the United States commercial system that a mass medium must concern itself with the common denominator of mass interest, the BBC's first director general, Lord Reith, has never considered television and radio to be mass media. He sees not a mass but a series of different publics, each of which must be treated with respect; not as targets for advertisers, but as human beings capable of cultural and intellectual *growth*.

Robert Sarnoff has said that television is "the broadest of mass media." Yet in education, which has always avoided mass tactics by making age, grade-level, subject-matter, and other non-mass divisions, television has been marvelously successful. Doctors learning from specialized television uses how to save patients' lives by new surgical and radiation techniques illustrate non-mass uses. Talk-back and question techniques by radio, providing instantaneous feedback, daily illustrate non-mass techniques in the use of radio and television. Radio stations KPFA in Berkeley and WFMT in Chicago, "class" stations with small but loyal audiences composed largely of culturally oriented individuals and community leaders, illustrate non-mass uses. All serve their areas. All reach large groups, but preserve them integrally as desirable and separate minorities. All are in a fair way to disproving the mass concept of Frank Stanton, who claims that every mass medium must "cater to the middle" or cease to exist.

Mass culture is fabricated by technicians and profit-seeking administrators who find that the mass status of the people requires less trouble and less imagination, and yields higher return on investment. The analogy to industrial production is obvious: The bigger the volume and the fewer the styles or models, the bigger the profits.

But to those who have seen other masses created and manipulated, the way in which our media create and wield masses is strangely disquieting and ominous. Only thirty years ago masses assembled in the sports arenas in Nuremberg or Berlin, shouting *Sieg heil* with spine-chilling monotony. And other millions in Rome cried *Duce! Duce!*

Philosophers and historians have warned of the dangers to be faced unless the American can shake himself loose from the hypnotic influence of totalitarian mass behavior and psychology.

The American seems to be becoming more unable to demonstrate the individuality which democracy requires. Continuing hypnotism, emulsification, and homogenization of men by the media is the opposite of what our nation needs. The United States was not, in its beginnings, a homogenized nation. Perhaps no nation was composed of more varied racial and national stock. Old-world traditions provided a diversity that most nations could not match. Yet today, so far as the media are concerned, we are treated as a nation of standardized, interchangeable parts. The indoctrination has not been forced, nor has it been official, yet it is debilitating and dangerous to democracy.

Since present network leadership was being determined and radio was shaking down into its permanent mold in the 1930s, the totalitarian characteristics of media orientation should not surprise us. This was the time when totalitarianism was in the air. Hitler and Mussolini were on the rise. And the Japanese empire was seeking a place under the world's sun. In the United States, Father Coughlin, Huey Long, and others were given or sold radio time to declare similar philosophies. .

World War II swept the mass concept out of the politics of many nations, and even out of the radio systems of Germany, Italy, and Japan. United States advisers there realized that powerful corporate monopoly leads to totalitarian practices and the corporate state as surely as does government monopoly or control. Only in the United States did the original occupants and controllers of broadcasting remain. The cartel in this country was preserved.

However painful to present broadcast leadership, and even if it reduces profits, the dehumanization of democratic man by television and radio must be halted if democracy is to survive. At least two steps are needed if the present dangerous mass concept dominating the use of television and radio is to be stopped. The first is to introduce into the one-way system we now have the much more rapid feedback that leaders in a democracy require. This involves recognition of the fact that television and radio are first of all instruments of democracy rather than of commerce. The leaders of the broadcast system also require more dependable feedback than ratings provide. Channels must be found through which the members of the public can express themselves to leaders of all kinds. This will mean setting aside air time for serious, unrigged discussions. It will require the introduction of the kind of *talkback* that has been developed by education. The use of telephone lines has been described whereby listeners and viewers may participate while educational television programs are on the air. By the reservation of a few frequencies for the viewer and for feedback, the great dialogue which democracy requires is still possible. Old ballot approaches devised two hundred years ago are too slow today. Electronic guidance in the form of reaction to dialogue, and the feeding in of ideas on an instantaneous basis from the people to government, are now possible. If commercial media do not provide this service, government itself must have its own broadcast and feedback system to make it possible. It is electronically feasible now to have instantaneous feedback from every television viewer in the United States. A few rating services already are using, or misusing, such devices. Broadcasters can know instead of guessing about qualitative reactions of viewers. Many practices which are denounced today as economically unfeasible can become realities tomorrow—but only if the present monopoly is broken and the present mass concept of the media abandoned.

Second, programming for the cultural subgroups of the nation must replace mass-audience programming. This is not to say that fewer people should be served. It is to say only that fewer people will be served at a time. Selective viewing and selective programming must be promoted. Instead of reaching a majority by homogenizing most programs, a majority would be accumulated by adding together the many individual minorities who want something more specific than the present fare.

It is ridiculous to believe that television and radio are not innately as capable of non-mass uses as the book, the magazine, or the film. The principal obstacle to such development is the mass-media concept now prevalent.

Ratings *could* be useful. But they are now being used to defeat rather than to serve the public interest. Good editors have reported that when readership surveys have revealed low interest in foreign news, they have used these surveys as guides for *improving* or *increasing* their foreign news, not for replacing it with comics. Ratings should challenge rather than defeat.

The people of the United States need to be lifted to the level of today's problems. The media, more than the schools or any other institutions, can do this. So far, the problems have been lowered or watered down. We have heard that education, culture, or many other things cannot be forced down people's throats.

Yet soap operas have been.   And so have westerns, quizzes, wrestling, game shows, thirty-year-old movies, and professional sports.
Judge Learned Hand challenged the allegation that the people have consented to what exists.   They have not.   They are
only too unorganized, too inert, or too uninformed to do anything about it.   The only true rating of what the people want
must take into account what they would choose if it were offered, if they clearly saw its importance, and if they were left alone
and allowed to act rationally.

Lord Reith of the BBC gave his view of the responsibility of
leadership as early as 1924.   He said: "As we conceive it, our
responsibility is to carry into the greatest possible numbers of
homes everything that is best in every department of human
knowledge, endeavour, and achievement, and to avoid the things
which are, or may be, hurtful.   It is occasionally indicated to us
that we are apparently setting out to give the public what we
think they need—and not what they want, but few know what
they want, and very few what they need.   There is often no difference. . . .   In any case it is better to over-estimate the mentality
of the public than to under-estimate it." [6]

7

The Effects of Television and Radio:
Some Burning Questions

Broadcast-industry spokesmen generally maintain that little is definitely known or can be proved concerning the harmful effects of television. They declare that there has been little research on this subject. This position is unacceptable to educators, mental-health clinic directors, and officials of correctional and law-enforcement agencies who test, question, and treat children every day and know that television is one of the most powerful parts of their environment. Radio and television not only can and do teach, but cannot help teaching. There is no longer any question of *whether* they teach. It is only a question of *what* they teach, whether intentionally or unintentionally.

The first careful and complete studies which dealt with such effects were the Payne Fund Studies on films and their effects on children. These investigations extended over a four-year period, from 1929 to 1932. The results were published by Macmillan in some twelve volumes between 1933 and 1935. These studies are relevant here since these films, and others like them, make up a large part of the fare offered over most United States television stations.

In 1961, UNESCO published an annotated International

Bibliography, *The Influence of the Cinema on Children and Adolescents.*[1] The data, research, and studies it cites come from several hundred correctional institutions, hospitals, schools, juvenile courts, psychiatric clinics, and mental hospitals around the world. The 491 books, articles, and journals it abstracts contain several hundred additional references in their own bibliographies. Hundreds of doctors, educators, researchers, and organized child-welfare and religious groups in many nations have spent long hours collecting and analyzing the most authoritative evidence they could find.

Research activities abroad—the studies of Mary Field and J. P. Mayer in England, of Erich Wasem and a dozen other researchers in Germany, of Enrico Fulchignoni and colleagues in Italy, and of Henri Storck in Belgium; studies at the Children's Neuro-Psychiatric Center in Paris; studies by the Czechoslovak State Cinema; and extensive studies in Japan, Russia, Australia, New Zealand, Portugal, Spain, Italy, Austria, India, Denmark, and Switzerland—refute any belief that there is a shortage of data available on this problem.

Files kept for years by German juvenile courts have been studied for clues as to causes of delinquency. The files of the Spanish Guardianship Courts have been found to yield helpful information. The reasons behind the decision of NHK (the Japanese national television system) to forbid the showing of violence, or any weapons that could be used for violence, on any of their television programs have been clearly spelled out for the sake of their fellow broadcasters around the world.

The quality as well as the quantity of recent research in the United States has often left much to be desired. Studies in the United States often quote what viewers or children say, or allegedly think. But the distinguished New Zealand scholar, Gordon Mirams, in commenting on a Danish study, noted in the March, 1961, UNESCO *Courier:* "Contrary to common belief, many cartoons and Tarzanlike films frighten very young children; some cried and tried to leave the cinema, others had nausea, and parents later reported cases of bedwetting and nightmares. Yet the same children *said* they thought the films were funny. They at first refused to admit they were scared."[2]

The inclination of United States researchers in all too many such instances has been to quote children as saying they liked very much whatever they saw and were not frightened. Such quotations, obviously, have little or no validity.

The problem attacked here is a serious and complicated one. Every new technology catches its age unprepared. Television audiences are the largest ever known in the history of communications. We have been told by the nation's greatest teachers that television teaches more powerfully than any previous instruments available to society. Senator Thomas J. Dodd, chairman of the Senate Subcommittee to Investigate Juvenile Delinquency, pointed out in the June, 1961, hearings that the excerpts of scenes of violence and sex which he and his fellow committee members viewed were from programs which had had, in effect, a cumulative audience of 66,318,000 children. In an average week, when 50 per cent of prime time is devoted to such programs, there will be over 200 million exposures of children to such scenes and programs. Of these 200 million, 130 million will be twelve years old and under. Many children are saturated by such programs before they can read.

Mass media used this way cease to be instruments of communication and become instruments of social control. These are totalitarian rather than democratic uses. Farfetched as it may now seem, historians of the future may conclude that never before was there a period during which control of the thinking of a nation was exercised in a more totalitarian manner, or by a smaller group, than it is now by television and radio.

There is evidence that a given program will do one person harm, and yet cause no apparent harm to another. Industry spokesmen exploit these contradictions. Since the operators of the mass media find it most profitable to define and operate these media as *mass* media, the average becomes the normal. Cases which do not conform are simply dismissed as deviant or atypical. But it is this dismissal that most educators cannot accept. A disease may leave one child unharmed and kill another. To say that the average child is left only half-dead, or still alive, is to conceal what is really happening.

Human beings cannot be averaged as if they were numbers. A small group of children, done harm, may well be more important than a thousand times as many who are done no harm. The quantity criterion cited by industry does not hold up when human beings are at stake. It takes only one child to kill or maim another, derail a train, or burn a building.

Instances of people harmed by television will not be found in averages or statistics, but in hospitals and prisons. They are specific tragedies. Factory owners used to deny that there were significant adverse effects on children from working in mines or mills. Coroners' records and hospital visits finally lifted the veil.

To say that television is *the* cause of delinquency and mental and physical unfitness would be unfair; to say that television is not *a* cause, and an important one, in view of the evidence now available, is no longer acceptable.

The late W. W. Charters, Director of the Payne Fund Studies, was a serious scholar who weighed his words carefully. Soberly he wrote in 1934: "Sexual passions are aroused and amateur prostitution is aggravated. The fast life depicted by the movie characters on the screen induces desires . . . for such a life. . . . *From all these data collected about the content of pictures the conclusion is inevitable that from the point of view of children's welfare the commercial movies are an unsavory mess.*" * 3

Dr. Charters continued: "The Big Three among the themes in 1930 were: love 29.6 per cent, crime 27.4 per cent, and sex 15.0 per cent. . . . Under the 27.4 per cent of crime pictures were included those dealing in a major way with: Blackmailing; extortion; injury, hate and revenge. . . . It is inevitable . . . that producers of motion pictures who have a love for children and an interest in their development must address themselves to the problems of children's movies as the publishers of books have attacked the problems of providing a children's literature. . . ." 4

Dr. Charters was not talking about films now buried. Most of the same films evaluated in the Payne Fund Studies, many of which were banned in certain areas or not shown to children, have now been repeatedly shown throughout the entire nation by television.

In 1955, when pay-television exponents were seeking approval to test a system whereby viewers who wanted films could pay for them, while "free television" might concentrate on non-film fare, sales reports indicated that over 3,000 old feature films had been sold for television showing for 200 million dollars, final payments not being due until 1968. The revenue-producing potentials of even the worst films, if reshown fifteen to thirty times, are immense.

By 1959, WPIX, New York, was running over forty hours of film a week, of which one-third was first-run and two-thirds were second-run. Some of the heaviest users of old films are the most prosperous stations in the nation. Many are the network stations themselves. New York's WCBS-TV showed 1,600 dif-

* Italics added.

ferent first-run films between February, 1951, and 1959. By 1959, is was using approximately 1,200 film bookings a year. A typical week on that station would include twenty-four feature films. Program listings for November, 1961, for the seven New York television stations showed 104 different movies, programmed 130 times. Over half were pre-1948 films. WCBS-TV led the group with thirty-four hours. CBS-TV Vice-president Aubrey, in the January, 1962, Federal Communications Commission network hearings, estimated that about 50 per cent of CBS's television programming in prime time was on film. The remainder was either live or on tape. By 1963, over half of NBC's prime-time offerings, like ABC's, was made up of film. In an address in Columbus, Ohio, April 26, 1961, Washington television critic Lawrence Laurent noted that "Susie," a series about a private secretary, was then being telecast in Washington for the thirteenth time. The January 29, 1962, issue of *Newsweek* magazine reported that 80 per cent of the programs on the air each week "came out of a can from the West Coast."

Films, far from being less dangerous when shown on television than when shown in theaters, seem merely to present several *different* hazards and problems. First of all, films that have been denounced as unfit for children or found objectionable or banned by local, state, or city censoring groups, or films that are usually shown only in small art theaters, with unusually sophisticated audiences, may all be shown on television. Television, in other words, is a channel which bypasses censorship or adults-only limitations. The implications of this are obvious.

The use of old or used merchandise has helped broadcast leaders expand television to eighteen hours a day rather than limit its hours to what it could do live and do well, as some countries decided to do. It is paradoxical that a medium whose advertising is so completely devoted to urging viewers to replace old items by new should itself depend on discount, used, rejected, damaged, and secondhand materials, many dating from the early thirties.

Even movies which failed by box-office standards are being reshown and reamortized on equal bases. Moreover, once the practice is started, it affects even the pattern of new, original films. Supply rather than demand seems to be a dominant factor in determining what films will be shown to the United States public. Investment, in itself, becomes the reason for showing. One of the most regrettable results of television's use of film has been to mix two art forms which in many respects are different. Ralph Vaughan Williams saw in the film an art form for combining all the arts to achieve a beauty which the individual arts could never achieve. Television as an art form offers even greater possibilities. It offers the unique qualities of intimacy and immediacy which the film cannot equal. The use of so much film by television has probably been a factor in making television something much less than its promised potential. Instead of becoming an art form in its own right, television became merely a conveyor belt, a "common carrier" for imperfectly delivering the products of other art forms, with those interruptions, dilutions, transformations, and limitations which television imposes whenever it is used at less than its full capacity.

It is significant that network executives urge critics to ignore films in evaluating television and to concentrate on live television. Psychiatrists have repeatedly warned that nothing affects people as much as that which they do not take seriously. And courts have repeatedly declared that the powers of motion pictures as organs of public opinion are not lessened by the fact that they are designed primarily to entertain.

Radio and television are in certain respects unique instruments, different from anything humanity has ever encountered. Like water or fire, television has a powerful innate attraction because it moves. Substantial evidence indicates that people often hypnotically watch whatever is offered. To maintain that this *watching* is an endorsement of what is on the screen is to confuse the form of the medium with its content.

Learning and enjoyment derived from the printed word, as compared with those derived from the modern time-oriented media, are slow and incomplete. Print is lineal—it is read word by word. Ideas and impressions come gradually, at a relatively slow rate, largely through the eyes and intellect alone. Ideas emerge at a controlled rate from a succession of relatively frozen images. The reader determines the pace; he has time to stop, analyze, reread, or challenge. He remains in charge.

Radio and television, on the other hand, are all-engulfing; they involve the whole person—kinesthetically, subliminally, and emotionally, as well as intellectually. The medium, not the viewer, determines the pace.

Like certain types of modern art, television criticism requires a new concept of what is form and what is content. It has been difficult for many students of art to grasp the peculiarities of modern art, in which the subject of the painting is the painting itself. Similarly, the electronic media are not merely the envelope or carrier of a message—they are important influences in themselves.

Research carried out at the Psychological Institute of the University of Rome years ago revealed how the rhythm alone of film images influences the spectator's respiration and other metabolic behavior. The spectator of a film or television program becomes much more emotionally involved than he does in print media. Before a child learns to read he is learning what life is about. Long before he goes to school, the child is learning what values are important, what is truth, what is honesty, how adults behave, how people succeed. Martin Keilhäcker, in his 1958 studies in Germany,[5] has pointed out that at this age, children are not so much spectators of a film as they are co-actors. They live it. And nothing conditions a child more than experience. Elisabeth Würth, the Austrian scholar, concluded from her studies [6] that a child of five or six is not yet sufficiently grown to be exposed to films without detriment to his personality development. The studies of many European groups, such as the Catholic Association for Radio-TV and the West German Television Committee, strongly warn against *any* television viewing by children under age six. The business-oriented custodians of television in the United States have so far refused to recognize adequately the effects of television on small children. But if the television industry is as concerned as it says it is about the nation's and the world's children, present practices are due for more profound examination.

The answer to the problem of children's programs is not to do less for children, but much more. Disease, scientific discovery, social and international problems, the opening up of new nations and cultures, the stimulation of artistic achievement, heroes who are winning battles over all kinds of natural forces, pressures and ignorance (not merely over gangsters and villains) all suggest new kinds of adventure programs which television might promote.

Of course, most broadcasters insist that they count on the family to balance and control television uses. The effects of television on the family itself, however, make this a less reliable control than it used to be. The role of the family, and the proportion of the total environmental influence it now exerts on the child, has greatly changed from pre-television days.

Miss K. Taggart, Regional Administrator of the Department

of Social Welfare at Regina, Saskatchewan, Canada, has explained this situation thoughtfully. Speaking of the family problems raised by television, she told a conference in Regina, April 27, 1956:

> To bring the family together physically is really begging the question. It is just these hours which were formerly the most important time for the family which are the principal time for television now. These were the critical three hours for the family, at the end of the day, when they had an opportunity to share their experiences. They are now the most popular time for television. We should look at this thing which we are taking away from the family. The mere physical presence of the family in the room is not enough.[7]

Television leadership must recognize that unwittingly it may have taken away as much as it has given. By its attractive nuisance value it may have deprived parents of the time and opportunity necessary to do what television leaders tell them they must do to balance television impressions. In many cases also, family members, saturated with television values, are merely propagators of other television-transmitted values. Some parents are as subject as their children to overconsumption of television program types, and are as much in need of nontelevision counterbalances as any of the children. This circle of effects is rarely perceived. Besides the time people spend viewing television, additional hours are spent talking about what they have seen and heard on television. This discussion displaces that which used to occur before television came to occupy so much of the environment. The family and other groups come to reflect and reinforce the attitudes communicated by the media. There is thus no escaping the influences of broadcasting, for what does not reach the individual directly from it, reaches him indirectly through his peers and reference groups.

The effects and influences of television, then, are far more pervasive and are exerted in many more ways than most people suspect. It is now time to look at some of these effects more closely.

Values Promoted by Television

On television the mediocre and the great appear side by side. Singing commercials are heard more than great music. Pressed by television, the other media adopt this same approach. Starving children and cigarette models face each other in color. The coexistence of the cheap, the vulgar, the violent, and the sacred, give the impression of almost complete valuelessness. The danger in this is that the listener or viewer himself grows indifferent. As broadcasting does not discriminate between opinions, the listener-viewer also becomes undiscriminating.

If television can be said to have any values at all, it is those of the salesmen, big businessmen, manufacturers, and showmen who control it—essentially materialistic values. And, like those who control it, television shuns everything which does not fit with these values.

Randall Jarrell has noted how the media ignore those things which would be disruptive of the value-systems and "happy" picture promoted by their managers:

> I come to a long row of one-room shacks about the size of kitchens, made out of used boards, metal signs, old tin roofs. To the people who live in them an electric dishwasher of one's own is as much a fantasy as an ocean liner of one's own. But since the Medium (and those whose thought is molded by it) does not perceive them, these people are themselves a fantasy; no matter how many millions of such exceptions to the general rule there are, they do not really exist, but have a kind of anomalous, statistical subsistence; our moral and imaginative view of the world is no more affected by them than by the occupants of some home for the mentally deficient a little farther along the road.[8]

Television extols the spender. He is portrayed by the stars. He buys everything. He knows that it is a duty to free enterprise to spend, rather than to save. Unlike the networks, which use the same films year after year, he is told to throw away the old and buy new. Whether he needs a product or not, if he is not to be a saboteur of our economic system, he must buy. This value is used as a lever in various ways, affecting even the respect of son for mother and vice versa. If children do not spend on mother, on Mother's Day, they obviously do not love her. Affection or loyalty, like success, is measured in dollars.

The saboteur of our economy is the tightwad father who wants to use the old car another year, or who objects to the rapidity with which items are made obsolete. Since it is believed that fathers most often exercise a restraining hand on spending, television programs ridicule such fathers as much as possible and hero-worship the woman, who spends more readily. Another of the conspicuous values taught by television is conformity or adjustment. Viewers and listeners are urged to do as the person on the screen does. "Buy item X. Use like this." Television market research proves that this motivation is very effective—and that people *do* do as they are shown. Television defines the good citizen. He is happy and carefree. He spoils himself. He does not walk when he can ride. The well-adjusted, happy individual goes along with the gang. He does not raise unpopular questions. If the craving an individual has is not satisfied by things, he is obviously a deviate. He who is not satisfied with what the media offer is obviously out of step. He is an enemy.

Television exalts celebrities, treating them as society's most valued members. It is taken for granted that on the basis of both salary and prestige, except for corporation executives, show people are the most important people in the United States. They are paid more and imitated more than scientists, artists, journalists, composers, teachers, doctors, or government employees. The best programs on television are tributes to them. The public knows what products are good by noting what products the stars use.

What kind of values do the stars demonstrate in the roles of hero and heroine which they portray? The Payne Fund film studies indicated that the hero had little reluctance to use violence, or to kill if necessary. The hero was responsible for fifteen of the seventy-one deaths by violence found in one group of films. Even the heroine committed some of the murders shown. The violent and illegal use of weapons and other instruments (such as cars) is promoted by television and films. Lessons in how to use such tools for crime (rather than for hunting or safe driving) are, of course, included. So far as respect for education or serious careers is concerned, in 115 films reviewed, scientific or educational achievement is shown as a desirable goal in only four.

Lest the problem of violence or weapons be oversimplified, however, it should be made clear that the position taken here is not simply that violence is always bad. Nor is the showing of the use of weapons necessarily bad. The situation is not that black and white. Cars may be used as weapons, to kill. Guns, used legitimately for sports, recreation, or law enforcement and crime prevention, are surely not bad in themselves.

David Martin, an Australian scholar, after studying the content of violence in Australian television programs (principally of United States origin), finds most of them dangerous and objectionable. The sadism, irrational crime, brutality, sexual promiscuity, and mental-health habits they *promote*—rather than merely reveal—is of concern to him. But his reasons are rational instead of emotional: "Such films should have a level of aspiration higher than in crime (and most Western) films; in other words, films in which decency, after a struggle, has a chance to triumph over something apart from murder. *It would seem that this is more to the point than the debate whether violence is acceptable, what kind of violence is and is not, and how much of it can be assimilated.*"

But a number of the other points Mr. Martin makes are also relevant. Slightly abridged and paraphrased, four of the most important are:

1. Some psychologists overlook the fact that *much television crime drama is written by people who appear to be neurotics* and who, all too often, succeed in projecting their own guilt.

2. The fast car is to the crime film what the horse is to the Western—a primary gratification on several levels. It is far too late in the day to do anything about this, but it is well to acknowledge that *careful driving is not one of the messages of the police crime film.*

3. At the time of his survey (December 1960-January 1961) the Australian content of non-institutional and institutional crime films was zero. He states: *"It is much to be desired that a film, or series of films, based on crime detection or prevention in Australia be initiated which, from the very start, would take into account a correct psychological approach full of action and dangers and triangles, but with mature solutions of latent conflicts."*

4. Mr. Martin recommended establishing some liaison with Mental Health Authorities to bring them into the discussion. "It is hardly to be expected that television plays a part that can be grasped directly. In many breakdowns the problem is a good deal more complex and pervasive than that. *However, it might be found, for instance, that a high frequency of viewing television crime films is an additional, and perhaps critical, factor in the building up of unresolved anxieties."* [9]

This excellent study, like many other foreign ones, deserves the attention of American broadcasters.

As Edgar Dale noted (thirty years ago) in his analysis *The Content of Motion Pictures* in the Payne Fund Studies, revenge (which the NAB Code outlaws as a motive) ranks fourth as a motivation and was found in 25 per cent of the films. In the group of films studied, five heroes, eight heroines, and ten villains were moved by revenge. Revenge motivated more heroes and heroines than villains.

One recent shift in the qualities of heroines and heroes, as compared with those found in most of the films reviewed in the Payne Fund Studies, is to be noted. Heroes, especially athletes, used to be associated and identified with wholesome food, regular hours, exercise, and self-discipline. Recently, heroes are shown associated with soft drinks, shaving materials, beer, tobacco, automobiles, and luxuries.

The kind of woman who gets ahead is well illustrated in westerns. Young ladies who wish to succeed may study them each evening on television. The pure and virtuous woman is dull. She is spurned by the marshal, the hero, and other males who are worth having. If a woman wishes to be interesting she must have a past. To have fallen at least once usually qualifies her. In his factual study of the Westerner, Robert Warshow writes: "Those women in the Western movies who share the hero's understanding of life are prostitutes (or, as they are usually presented, bar-room entertainers) . . . 'fallen' women." [10] Such a fallen woman can, of course, understand the marshal, or other interesting men, in ways which the wife cannot. The old Anglo-Saxon belief that chastity is important, or a virtue, seems to have been largely modified to meet modern television needs. So is the idea that women should not drink too much. In popular television programs the woman most admired enjoys drinking and knows how. The social graces which television shows as desirable seem related to the various liquor and tobacco interests, which are important sponsors. Skeptics see the suspicion of a payola type of relationship. Just as Hollywood films were a powerful force in securing the repeal of Prohibition, television and Hollywood films now seem to be proving their effectiveness in establishing drinking, smoking, and several types of cosmetic, hair, and clothing practices as uniformly desirable social graces.

How heavily tobacco is promoted on television may come as some surprise to people who think it is promoted only, or principally, in paid commercial time. Before smoking by women was widely accepted, Edgar Dale wrote, in *The Content of Motion*

Pictures: "We note that in 26 of 40 pictures the hero used tobacco in some form; the heroines in about one-third of the pictures. . . . The hero did the major part of the smoking. The heroine smoked more than either the villain or villainess and the villainess tied with children for last rank. . . ." [11] As this is written, TV is on the verge of beginning to show cigars being smoked by women—there is, or so the "message" goes, less risk of cancer and none at all of appearing unladylike.

What constitutes acceptable romance is also an interesting indication of television values. Smartly dressed girls are, of course, most popular, and most likely to find romance. The need for spending on clothes, make-up, perfumes and lotions, and hair preparations is demonstrated frequently and in many ways. This, too, is related to the large expenditures of sponsors (the cosmetic interests) in television advertising. Dressing scenes showing various degrees of nudity appeared in 23 per cent and undressing scenes in 30 per cent of the films analyzed in the Payne Fund Studies, and still seen on television. Romance appears to be principally a premarital phenomenon, or one experienced with someone else's husband or wife. The pleasures and joys of married life itself are rarely shown. In fact, marriage appears to dampen romantic and love interests considerably. It is a social convention still endured, but with little glamor or enthusiasm.

Enough of the technique of love-making is shown in sufficiently alluring fashion to provide incentives for imitation. Of 252 delinquent girls studied by Professor Herbert Blumer and reported in *Movies, Delinquency and Crime* (one of the Payne Fund Studies), one-quarter of them admitted engaging in sexual relations after being aroused by movies. The boys who were studied reported how "when you see these hot love pictures it makes you feel like going out and having sexual relations." The number of both boys and girls who successfully tried out the techniques shown was substantial. One girl, seventeen, reported how such films taught her how to "kiss, love, drink, smoke, and lead up to intercourse. It makes me all stirred up in a passionate way." Several of the girls found these films useful guidance in party behavior, petting leading up to intercourse, and teaching them how to "lead men on," as one of the girls described it. Of the 252 delinquent girls studied by Blumer, 41 per cent traced some or all of their difficulties to such movies. How many others unconsciously were also taught or triggered by such movies is not known. Some, no doubt, would have fallen without such

exposure.   But delinquent males frequently mentioned the usefulness of films in getting the girls worked up to the point of
willing intercourse.

Fredric Wertham who, as Consultant Psychiatrist of Queens
Hospital Center in New York, has devoted many years to this
problem, pointed out in the February, 1960, *Ladies' Home Journal:* "The connection between violence and sex, as presented on
the screen, is particularly apt to arouse fantasies and/or facilitate
the transition from fantasy to action. . . . I have known of cases
in which boys as young as eleven have been sexually excited by
them.   Sadistic daydreams, whether or not accompanied by mas-
turbation, are certainly not good for children and may instill a
liking for sadism that will cause serious trouble in later life." [12]

Such are some of the values reflected in current television
offerings.

Educational and Anti-educational Effects

The effects of commercial broadcasting on education in the
United States have been analyzed in many sometimes contradictory ways.

Stephen White, in an article in *Horizon* magazine in September, 1961,[13] points out to people who are dissatisfied with
the level of television programs that raising tastes is a job for the
schools—not for the advertising media.   He urges people who
wish to help raise the educational levels of broadcasting to write
the United States Office of Education instead of the Federal Communications Commission.

The distinguished semanticist, S. I. Hayakawa, takes a contrary view.   As he sees it:

> Our job as teachers is to inculcate habits of rational choice
> and decision.   The advertising profession, however, with
> all the technical resources of art, expert copy, color print-
> ing, radio, and television at its command, spends most of
> its efforts in the encouragement of irrational and impulsive
> choice. . . .   When home economists urge government
> grade-labeling to encourage rational choice, industry and
> the advertising profession cry, "Socialism!" . . .   The teach-
> er's job is to encourage intellectual and moral self-disci-
> pline; the job of the advertiser of consumer goods is to
> encourage self-indulgence, even at the cost of life-long
> bondage to finance companies. . . .   So basically the adver-

tising profession and we in the teaching profession are at odds with each other. . . .[14]

Many educators and psychologists hold that in determining how well educated an individual is, the total environment is as significant as his time in the classroom. Each year less of the learning which shapes children takes place in the school. A child normally begins to watch television long before he can either read or attend school. Through his school years, the average student spends far more time per year (about 1,200 hours) with television than in classes. This situation is even more pronounced in pre-school and post-school years. So it would be strange if television's influence were not one of the most powerful forces, educational or anti-educational, which shapes young lives.

Respect is one of the greatest tributes that can be shown education, and one of the principal ways in which it, as well as its products, which are educated individuals, can be promoted. Whether education is respected, or whether it is placed high or low in a nation's priorities, depends on the environment created for it. Radio and television have made professional football, cigarettes, rock and roll, and many other products and activities popular. In its ridiculing of the teacher, the serious student, and the professor; in its aversion to intellectuals, whom broadcast leaders frequently attack; and in its historic opposition to educational broadcasting, it has done far less to create respect or support for education than it could have done. Yet neither universities nor schools, particularly with their present budgets, can do much, if anything, beyond making education available. It depends upon other agencies, like broadcasting, to stimulate demand for it.

Many of the obstacles thrown in the way of education by broadcasting are perhaps unintentional. They are none the less real. The late Richard Neuberger, on the floor of the Senate, March 21, 1958, protested against the falsification and perversion of history by television westerns. He noted with regret the effect of such mass media falsehoods in counteracting the teaching of the schools. Senator Neuberger, who was then chairman of the Subcommittee on Indian Affairs, protested against the distorted picture of the Indian, for example, in "programs which portray the American Indian as a hideous, barbaric savage, who would lie in wait to torture the kindly innocent white people who came across the country, and had only benevolent thoughts for the poor Indian."

Related complaints have been expressed by many educators and writers who ask how we can condemn children for lying when they see such activity practiced daily by grown men on television, who are paid hundreds of thousands of dollars a year to do this. In fact, perhaps one of the most powerful effects of television has been to teach a national tolerance of falsehood, exaggeration, and distortion. Parents who ask their children to tell the truth must explain that of course a certain cereal will not transform them into great athletes, as the highly paid announcer says, nor will the drug mentioned really cure hemorrhoids, or cancer, or arthritis. The announcer is really lying. Nor will certain cosmetics or cars guarantee success in romance, as is implied. Somehow the parent must explain that truth is to be expected of the child individually, but that a huge industry can be based on falsity, exaggeration, and distortion. These are the lessons of the unofficial, commercial mass-media education, which is gradually and relentlessly squeezing official education into a more difficult position.

The good teacher and the good school teach thrift, self-denial, self-control, activity, and emphasis on long-term goals. The commercial media teach self-indulgence, immediate gratification, and shortcuts to success via product magic. To berate and denounce children for practicing the values taught by the unofficial rather than the official educational system of the nation is to condemn only the victims, as was done in the quiz scandals. They are only practicing what they are taught, regardless of the source.

The slogans, catchwords, values, mottoes, and other lessons tattooed on young minds even before young people learn to read are not educational but commercial. They displace, contradict, and cancel, in many cases in advance, those lessons and values which education seeks and will seek at public expense to teach and inculcate.

Effective education requires wide-awake children, eager to learn. Dr. Charters reported in the Payne Fund Studies, even before the days of television, that heavy consumers of films "average lower deportment records, do on the average poorer work in their school subjects, are rated lower in reputation by teachers on two rating forms, are rated lower by their class-mates on the 'Guess Who' test, are less co-operative and less controlled as measured both by ratings and conduct tests, are slightly more deceptive in school situations, are slightly less skillful in judging what is the most useful and helpful and sensible thing to do, and are slightly less emotionally stable." [15]

Schramm, Lyle, and Parker, in their studies of the effects of television viewing on schoolwork, tell of "cases of drowsy children the morning after late and popular programs, of day-dreaming that might well be connected to the fantasy of television programs . . . a tendency on the part of some pupils to expect to be entertained passively in class, as they are before the television set. Some of the teachers said laughingly that they had a pretty stiff standard of entertainment and production to compete with. . . . After watching television, is school dull? A very large number of students say that it is." [16]

Students who are high viewers of television know more about cowboys, chorus girls, actors, and dancers than low television consumers. They are also more inclined to accept as natural such habits as drinking, smoking, and various acts of violence. Low television viewers know more about places, people, and events of a nonentertainment type, and have more respect for and interest in intellectual activity. Such are Schramm's findings.

Perhaps one of the most serious obstacles which educators have to overcome in students is the inattention which the young people must develop as protection against the TV practice of repeating, over and over again, the same commercials. This deadly practice, forcing individuals, if they are to preserve their sanity, to "tune out" these commercials after they have seen the same ones perhaps a dozen times, *ad nauseam,* is not merely a broadcasting, advertising, or even educational problem. In the glazed eyes and dazed state of many individuals—including adults —who are excessive consumers of TV, is one of the most common problems which mental-health clinics and school psychologists encounter today. This practice seems to be one of the principal reasons why so many people fail to hear what they should hear, if they are to live normal lives and fulfill their roles as parents and citizens. The tendency of many citizens to leave their attention "turned off" too long, while appearing to be viewing or listening, could well be a serious civil-defense and national-emergency problem as well. Many people have protested that they "did not hear" warnings which were plainly and clearly broadcast. The viewers thought that they were only commercials. Certainly, the extent to which this deadening practice may be a disservice to the public interest should be studied. Does making TV a narcotizing instrument not merit study? Other intoxicants and narcotics are subject to strict controls—why not the TV commercial? Over two hundred years ago, in *The Rambler* of March 31, 1750, Samuel Johnson observed how young people learn. When they note an obviously successful individual, he said, "they fix their eyes upon him with closer attention, and hope, by observing his behavior and success, to regulate their own practices."

Day after day, year after year, commercial broadcast media provide models and teach lessons which directly challenge or contradict the lessons taught by school and church. However unintentional such practices may be, they are dangerous. And how much more of this type of discrediting can American education take from commercial broadcasting before there is a complete breakdown?

Language

Television influences education through its uses and misuses of language. Television allows wordsmiths and advertising copy writers to invent much of our language and terminology; consequently, many of what were thought to be natural language laws are violated each day. Language, which used to be made in novels, schools, and science, is fabricated, like public opinion, on Madison Avenue and in Hollywood. It is created by announcers, salesmen, and commercial-slogan inventors instead of poets, lecturers, or journalists.

If a reliable and accurate means of communication is to be maintained, it is essential that the "value" of words, to use a metaphor of currency, be kept dependable and standard. Progressive use of superlatives and exaggeration requires the consumer of the language to "discount" what is said. Television and radio today use large words and florid language for clothing small values and thoughts.

Paul Merrill, in the *Scientific Monthly* of January, 1947, though describing poor writing generally, ironically described broadcasting's techniques with language: "Avoid being specific; it ties you down. Use plenty of deadwood: include many superfluous words and phrases. . . . A cloud of words may conceal defects. . . . Poor writing, like good football, is strong on razzle-dazzle, weak on information. Adjectives are frequently used to bewilder the reader. It isn't much trouble to make them gaudy or hyperbolic; at least they can be flowery and inexact." [17]

Commercials mangle language with incomplete comparisons like "better" and "finer," and with salesman grammar: "Winston tastes good like a cigarette should." Many of these techniques are evasions encouraged by the NAB Code and FTC regulations.

The criterion of successful language in television advertising is the extent to which it moves goods, whether it has meaning or not, the degree to which one can imply, suggest, hint, and *almost* say things which codes, rules, regulations, or good taste forbid. If it is too definite, the commercial may be accused of lying. The use of language in broadcasting for purposes of *evasion* rather than specific declaration is one of the most powerful of the lessons taught by broadcasting. The way it affects children and the schools is observable daily in the problems faced by teachers seeking to teach communications, oral or written.

The effect of telegraphy on the language of fifty years ago has been noted by many scholars. The effects of commercials alone, to mention only one aspect of broadcast effects, is much more significant. Consider the effects of 25-, 50-, and 100-word "spot" commercials in radio days, and of commercials of prescribed length on television. In some cases the same kind of pruning which one learns for telegrams is applied. In other cases five-word ideas have to be expanded to fifty words, because the sponsor bought fifty. The inverse ratio between value and volume, noted above, begins to be evident. One effect is the creation of children who follow similar practices and are, therefore, unable to express themselves succinctly. The younger generation is found unable to read or write decent English, in spite of the desperate efforts of the schools to counteract such trends. Day after day teachers hear, "I heard it on television" as an excuse for every error. Yet the fact that television is teaching the nation more English than the schools are is not widely realized. This power—the ability of the most illiterate television celebrity or wordsmith to override the influence of the most fully certificated teacher, or the most excellent school system, or the hundreds of years of slow but controlled linguistic evolution—seems to have been ignored in most analyses of the so-called crisis in education. To blame the fact that Johnny can neither read nor write on the schools, which do not have access to the children until they have been taught for several years by television, seems to be blaming the wrong villain. At least the responsibility must be shared.

Music and the Arts

Broadcasting, especially television, affects the fine arts—including music—at least as powerfully as it does both education and language.

Anthropologists have found that the lyrics of popular songs are one of the most dependable indices of the cultures of nations studied. If such criteria were used to measure the United States, the most adequately financed type of music would be found to be the singing commercial. Orchestra leaders in the United States note the growing number of requests at dances and parties for such ballads as those extolling certain cigarettes, beers, detergents, or clothes. Albums were already on the market by 1962 which contained the most popular singing commercials of the day. It should not be long before many of them are among the top ten, or top forty, tunes of the day.

Singing commercials become popular music simply because the public hears them so frequently. The difference between music and nonmusic disappears. As in the case of words, the most insignificant is often played louder and repeated more often because of its very insignificance. This repetition and volume, in turn, *give* it significance and prove its popularity. This was and is the basis of plugola practices. How often a tune is played, rather than how well it is liked, determines its popularity. This repetition moves it up the scale to the position where it becomes a model for imitation. What is imitated, played, and called music, *becomes* music, by broadcasting's definition.

Whether *some* of the arts, like music, should be reserved for the praise of the higher values in life is a question not often raised. Perhaps it should be. Radical as the suggestion may sound, it is possible that it might be in the public interest to outlaw singing commercials. Certain nations and cultures have found it desirable to make it unlawful to use certain precious materials except for specific purposes. Certain poor nations with no such metallic resources as aluminum, for example, find it unforgivable to use this precious mineral to wrap baked potatoes. The same criteria might be used in deciding to what uses such intangible resources as music and the arts might be put.

Since broadcasting has erased to a considerable degree the difference between music and nonmusic, it is not too surprising to find that the subject matter and lessons of what is called music are essentially the same as that contained in westerns, detective programs, and commercials. Many of the disturbing or distorting elements responsible for creating mental and emotional problems are traced by mental-health specialists to the life values propagated by popular music as much as to westerns, detective stories, or old films.

Probably the greatest danger of today's practices with reference to art, however, lies in the low status granted the artist. The business structure of broadcasting is unquestionably such that the sales executive can and does dictate to the artist. He can hire and fire artists by the score. He can decide whether artists shall have access to channels to the people, or whether the public shall have access to the greatest artists via the new media. If the artist wants to earn a living he must do not what he wants, but what salesmen want.

The point that may be missed is that artists and poets are not useless, or impractical parasites on society, or nuisances. A nation needs them. They are the antennas of the nation, as essential to a nation for direction planning as radar is for navigation. Their sensitivity is needed. They detect in advance dangers and threats and tendencies which a nation should know about, and which other people often miss.

Is it good that artists are so often pictured in the mass media as effeminate and nonessential? Is it good that art, other than "commercial" art, is belittled rather than made attractive? Is it good that the arts are usually shown as if they were merely play or hobbies, or therapy to which people escape from careers that are *important*, like advertising or selling or being a soldier? The status accorded to artists, educators, and the intellectuals in a society or in a communications medium is likely to prove to be very important indeed.

Physical Fitness

Numerous statistics and studies—the Kraus-Weber tests and the studies of Cureton, Pohndorf, and others—warn us of the deterioration of the physical fitness of United States citizens. While it would be unfair to say that television is the cause or creator of the flabby American, it is clearly one important contributor to the softness and physical unfitness of Americans. Perhaps television, the automobile, cigarettes, and alcohol are almost equal causes of the physical decay sometimes noted in America's younger generation. The effects of television on physical fitness are of several kinds. The Payne Fund Studies of the sleep patterns of 163 children indicated that seeing certain types of films was more disruptive of peaceful sleep than staying up until midnight. Some films affected children as adversely as drinking two cups of coffee in the evening. These disruptive effects often extended far beyond twenty-four hours, depending on the age, sex, and mental level of the child. The conclusion drawn was that unwisely chosen films had definite and measurable deleterious effects on the health, happiness, well-being, and growth of children, partly because of the loss of sleep they caused.

Television, moreover, keeps young people from engaging in the physical activities and outdoor exercise which doctors and physical educators agree are desirable. President John F. Kennedy, in his analysis of the causes for the softness of American youth, did not hesitate to mention television first: "The television set, the movies and the myriad conveniences and distractions of modern life" are among those he mentioned. He blamed the poor condition of youths and adults alike on the fact that our principal sport seems to be sitting. As columnist and editor Ralph McGill has said, any time this nation wants to experience profound humility it has only to look at its selective-service rejections. These still run approximately 50 per cent.

Broadcasting has contributed significantly to killing off minor sports, and to replacing many individual sports with spectator sports. Television has aided in the demise of small-club boxing. It has helped kill minor-league baseball. Small neighborhood clubs, like union meetings and city council sessions, go largely unattended. Too many boys are sitting beside Dad, with a beer, watching instead of doing.

The rigging in wrestling is obvious. Boxing, like wrestling, is no longer a sport. Once the time is set, if two *good* boxers cannot be found, two poor ones are matched—the show must go on. Television seems to be having essentially the same quality-lowering effect on sports that it has on the arts. This is perhaps not surprising, since in TV's first days programs were received by most people in noisy, smoke-filled taverns, where the crudest story and the loudest sound track were the most effective. The tradition, once set, is difficult to change. Sports used to be something wholesome that people did. Now it is something they watch. It now means passivity. Television *could,* of course, have promoted hunting (as opposed to manhunting, and the use of firearms for violence), fishing, tennis, hiking, camping, and so on. Present practices keep the viewer quiet and passive before the television set, where he is available for sales messages. He must not be allowed to get away. If television were to teach how to play various sports, or how to engage in scores of physical activities outdoors in person, from hiking to gardening, or even in simple home gym arrangements, the nation's public health interest would be better served. But these individuals would be lost to sponsors during the hours they were thus active. This tendency to keep viewers immobilized, as receptors of commercials, is particularly unfavorable for young children, who need activity for growing and learning. Simply sitting, for hours on end, is likely to have many adverse effects on young people aside from what they view during those hours. Other countries have limited the hours of television to permit more physical activity, yet United States broadcast leadership shows no evidence of changing its practices.

Mental Health

Symptoms of mental health are less easily recognized or measurable than those of physical health. Yet there are many specialists who assure us that these symptoms are very real and recognizable.

The conflict between the value systems taught by Christian doctrine, the school, parents, and the laws of the land, on one hand, and those taught by the mass media on the other, creates a strain under which many people break each day. The need to reconcile such conflicting views and value systems has many effects—one, noted by several doctors in many subjects, is an increased national incidence of schizophrenia.

The demands made on children to reconcile conflicting values, to adjust back and forth many times a day between the values taught by television fantasy and the values that the reality of his personal life requires of him, constitute strains that not all are capable of meeting. Mental hospitals and prisons are full of people who could not make such adjustments. Prison records reveal criminals who feel that prison is more endurable than conformism and imprisonment in a society which is seemingly full of contradictions.

What is the effect on many people of being perpetually shown, and urged to buy, items which they cannot afford? How do such appeals affect poorer individuals who cannot buy the things they are made to want? Or on people so insecure that they will steal what they see proffered so irresistibly in order to enjoy briefly the sense of satisfaction which the commercials promise in such glowing form?

Norbert Wiener has compared computing machines to the brain and the central nervous system. He has explained how nervous breakdowns are similar to the breakdown of a machine which receives an excess of input instructions or is fed contradictory material. There is a question of how much noise and contradictory urging even the strongest human system can endure before breaking down. Far be it from the broadcast industry, however, to worry about how much of this the nation can endure. What is the breaking point of people subjected in commercials to parades of physical ills; bombardment by slogans; rumors and tales of violence; sales messages in musical, visual, and spoken form; and the volume of claims, counterclaims, accusations, and counteraccusations which make up much of television and radio offerings? How many irritation commercials can people stand? How many suggestions of infirmities does it take to create hypochondriacs?

By the time individuals are urged to do several hundred things a day, there is little time to do any of them. They begin not to do what they feel they should—and to worry about not doing it.

Enrico Altavilla's studies of the effects of gangster films on young adolescents in Rome illustrate the danger. To quote the UNESCO summary: "Gangster films are the cause of dangerous psychological complexes, not so much because they encourage the crimes they portray, as because they give rise to moral disturbances which may lie at the heart of numerous offenses. Mythomania, in particular, may induce in the child a conflict between two sets of ethical values, those of the gangster hero and those of the family. The former, through its intensity, may prevail over the latter." [18]

Jean Giraud, in his 1956 studies [19] of the causes of maladjustment in Paris reformatory inmates, found a large number of emotional disorders traceable to films showing violent emotional experiences of various kinds. In Bombay, Oluf Bruel found numerous phobias of young people traceable to film experiences.[20]

We have discussed the problems raised by current "mass" concepts of the audience, and of the medium of television itself. This problem is particularly acute when the viewer is, through no fault of his own, not a part of the mass but one of the "bad guy" groups shown, or a member of a ridiculed or reviled minority. *Most* people will identify with the good guys. What about the rest? Negro writer James Baldwin describes the problem in these words: "You go to white movies, and like everybody else, you fall in love with Joan Crawford, and you root for the Good Guys who are killing off the Indians. It comes as a great psychological collision when you realize all of these things are really metaphors for your oppression, and will lead into a kind of psychological warfare in which you may perish." [21]

Hans Luxenburger, in *Psychiatric and Mental Hygiene Problems of Films,* reports: "The influence of films on the mentally-retarded child, who cannot understand them either emotionally or intellectually, is unpredictable and quite likely to be harmful. . . . The film tends to reinforce emotional immaturity. Antisocial behavior may be provoked by films in children who are emotionally immature. A film of artistic quality can have a therapeutic effect if it gives a true picture of life." [22] The dangers noted come from films based largely on violence or conflict. Factual or problem-solving films have positive and healthful effects. *Good* films can help prevent mental illness or help cure it.

Gerhard Clostermann in *Artistic Education through Films* [23] shows how building-in constructive follow-up activities—to enable children to express the feelings stimulated or aroused in them by the programs, through drawings, painting, or other creative outlets—can have therapeutic instead of harmful effects. The activity suggested by the film, to be done after viewing it, may be more important than the viewing itself. In all too many cases in United States films based on violence or conflict, the only built-in therapy cues are stimulation and demonstration of actions of violence which can be particularly dangerous for a child who is not artistic, but strong, brutal, aggressive, or frustrated.

Qualified authorities have pointed out the dangers of introducing frustration, whether by overstimulation or by causing the viewer to want something he cannot afford, or will not ever be able to have for physical, racial, or other reasons. Seeing certain programs may cause certain children to *want* to commit certain violent acts. If they cannot, and no crime results, the need to suppress the urge may place a burden on the child's mind and set up a conflict which will later manifest itself as either mental illness, delinquency, or other antisocial behavior or attitudes.

Ralph Steven Banay, a research psychiatrist from Columbia University and consulting psychiatrist for the United States Bureau of Prisons, testified before a congressional committee April 6, 1955, that "juvenile delinquency is primarily a problem of emotional health or emotional disturbance. . . ." Dr. Banay flatly stated that: "If the proverb is true that prison is a college for crime, I believe for young disturbed adolescents, television is a preparatory school for delinquency." [24] The committee concluded by observing that the additional testimony generally supported Dr. Banay—enough to arouse deep concern; it called for "the immediate establishment, by legislation, of a Presidential commission" which would "study and investigate all media of mass communication as they do or may affect youth and children . . . , report periodically to the President, the Congress and the public . . . , and encourage and stimulate the undertaking of basic scientific research" in this problem area.[25] It is regrettable that this recommendation, like scores of similar ones, has never been carried out.

Since most advertising is directed toward arousing in people discontent with what they have, or are, it creates frustration on a national scale through television and the other mass media. The creation of dissatisfaction, even though it is obviously to the advantage of both sponsor and broadcaster, may well be contrary to the broad public interest. By denying the relation of television to such problems as mental health, the managers of the mass media may be making it impossible for the nation to come to terms with the problems of delinquency, physical unfitness, and mental illness.

Violence and Juvenile Delinquency

The December 13, 1963, issue of *Time* magazine told of the concern of the New York Transit Authority when it learned that NBC was to present as the televised Du Pont Show of the Week, "Ride with Terror," a TV play in which hoodlums terrorize subway riders and kill one of them. Nothing like this had ever occurred on the New York subways. The morning after the play was presented, in spite of the Transit Authority's protest, an off-duty detective was killed by teen-age thugs on an IRT train in Brooklyn.

This episode illustrates the sometimes unexpected and tragic effects that television drama or news may have, however innocent their motives may be.

The study of Herbert Blumer and Philip M. Hauser, *Movies, Delinquency and Crime,* one of the Payne Fund Studies, was based on the careful study of ninety boys from a high-delinquency area, forty boys in a house of correction, twenty backward and delinquent girls, and fifty ex-convicts. These records were supplemented by shorthand records of interviews with 258 convicted boys and 118 convicted girls. These case studies reveal the active role that films played in awakening sexual passions, stimulating desire for the gay life they saw portrayed, arousing hunger for luxury and smart clothes, which the individual often could not afford, and showing undesirable and criminal ways of satisfying the desires and hungers which were aroused. They reveal the dangers of *demonstrating* socially undesirable behavior and criminal techniques. They indicate that both are as effectively taught as are those lessons which are *deliberately* taught by educational films in and out of the school.

The Spanish Guardianship Tribunals records of 1944–1953 [26] indicated that 37 per cent of the delinquent boys arrested had been influenced by films which "showed them how," justified or rationalized the kind of behavior involved, disoriented the boys' consciences, and introduced immoral or criminal interests or desires into their plan of life.

Extensive hearings on television and juvenile delinquency were held in 1956, before the House Committee on the Judiciary. The report of these hearings contains the testimony of several hundred authorities. Among them is this statement by psychologist Lucille Emerick: "New York City today is clamoring for more policemen, more narcotics men, more social workers and psychiatrists, more jail space, and more hospital facilities for young drug addicts. Meanwhile . . . we countenance the spending of millions of dollars annually to instruct our youth in the arts of crime, to instill in their minds the fallacy that all law-enforcement officers are stupid or corrupt, and to keep them in daily contact with gunplay, murder, kidnapping, torture, and brutality in all its forms. I am referring, of course, to the vast amounts of money spent annually by the foremost advertisers on radio and television in the children's market." [27]

Reporter Sherwood Ross has told of a flood of letters following a crime wave in a previously quiet small Ohio community. Two stabbings by thirteen-year-old boys resulted in 330 letters from citizens to the Federal Communications Commission. Mr. Ross says: "Like many other Fulton County residents, its prosecuting attorney, John H. Barber, has nailed his indictment to the door of the television industry. . . . Across the nation today, millions of Americans are haunted by the growing suspicion that television violence has a corrosive effect on the public conscience in general, and on juveniles in particular. Even the most cursory observer will note that the indexes of juvenile crime—which President Kennedy has stated is costing the nation 5 billion dollars annually—have taken their most pronounced and alarming up-turn since the advent of television." [28]

Justice Curtis Bok of the Supreme Court of Pennsylvania, on the basis of his study of crime records, has listed crime and violence shows on television as one of five primary causes of delinquency. James V. Bennett of the United States Bureau of Prisons has spoken of the imitation of television techniques by young offenders, which makes television a school for crime. He is joined in his belief by J. Edgar Hoover. Mr. Hoover's May 1, 1958, letter, "To All Law Enforcement Officials," warning against "a dangerous trend which is manifesting itself in the field of film and television entertainment" is included as Appendix C of this book. Judge Frank J. Kronenberg of New York has expressed concern at the way in which television teaches that violence is an accepted way of life.

Records of all children's courts in Germany in towns of 10,000 or more population were studied by Hans Wilhelm Lavies and published in Weisbaden in 1954. The report of these records is summarized in the UNESCO bibliography mentioned earlier.[29] The judges were asked to comment on the part played by films in each case of delinquency. While the magistrates were careful not to indict films for all or even the majority of cases, their replies did indicate that *many* of the juvenile delinquents were influenced, and several "activated," by the viewing of crime films. Several thousand judges, prison directors, medical and mental-health authorities, psychologists, ministers, and educators are on the record with case-by-case citations to prove a connection between television programming and both juvenile and adult delinquency. What further evidence the broadcast industry needs is not known.

W. W. Charters admitted thirty years ago that we had delinquency before commercial motion pictures were invented. But never so much. For crime movies, he noted, were handy, and it was easy to learn from them if one was interested in delinquent behavior. Audio-visual instruction is very effective demonstration. As Dr. Charters put it, "One's education in crime advances more rapidly by means of crime pictures." [30] With television the young student of crime does not even need to go to the theater. And to the thousands of these Hollywood-produced films of years ago, television has added its own versions in enormous volume.

Many television programs, including old films, appear to promote disrespect for law and law-enforcement officers. Mickey Spillane teaches that it is quite proper to ridicule police officers, or take the law into one's own hands, thus replacing legally constituted authority. Private eyes save America nightly, often by unlawful means and in violation of human and constitutional rights, from whatever they (not the law) define as bad.

James V. Bennett, Director of the Federal Bureau of Prisons, several years ago protested that ABC's "Untouchables" defamed and undermined the integrity of the federal prison service and law enforcement. In 1956 [31] Mr. Bennett protested that most frequently justice on television takes the form of brute force, or of tactics on the part of representatives of the law which are little better than those of the criminal. If the criminal meets destruction, it is not as a result of the evil he has done, but because he is careless and incompetent as a criminal.

Arthur W. Wallander, former police commissioner of New York City, told the House Committee, mentioned earlier, that crime programs on television and radio characteristically glorify the criminal and the private-eye detective and "glory in making the policeman look dumb." He went on: "Not only the child, but the parents themselves, tend to lose all respect for the very man they are supporting as their front-line defender against crime. This breeds not only disrespect in the child, even to the point of making him a cop-fighter in aggravated cases, but it makes the parents cop-fighters in the mental sense, too." [32]

Another respect in which such programs seem contrary to the public interest is the way in which they teach that violence is an acceptable solution for life's difficulties. The implication is that the solution of basic problems is to be found in the use of brute strength. Courage is equated with the willingness to use violence. Courage which stands *against* violence is rarely shown and virtually never extolled. In all but the most exceptional cases, in order to survive, the heroes of American television finally have recourse to arms and violence.

Several years ago Siegfried Kracauer studied the extent to which German films between 1922 and the advent of Hitler prepared the way for totalitarianism. He found that most German films produced during that period revealed certain attitudes toward violence and human dignity which foreshadowed later Nazi practices. In 1946 Kracauer examined Hollywood films from the same point of view. He was especially concerned with the sadistic violence they contained and their emphasis on psychological destruction. Mr. Kracauer noted the resemblance between this type of violence and horror and that found in the films of the pre-Hitler period in Germany. [33] For what are such films and TV programs training United States citizens? Television and radio programs in America frequently teach lessons not only of violence but also of totalitarianism and militarism, courage in opposing soldierly or militaristic methods being branded as cowardice.

Callousness, also typical of totalitarianism, results from constant exposure to violence, according to many mental-health and child-welfare authorities. Frequently, police records report individuals or crowds who watch impassively while policemen, bus drivers, or other innocent victims are beaten, robbed, or killed. Fatalistic acceptance of violence, characteristic of systems other than democracy, begins to be widespread. Trained to watch violence about which they can do nothing, many people still sit helplessly by when this violence is seen in real life. Is there no connection? Reluctance to become "involved" becomes widespread.

Fredric Wertham, previously quoted, warns:

> What children see on the screen is violence as an almost casual commonplace of daily living. Violence becomes the fundamental principle of society, the natural law of humanity. Killing is as common as taking a walk, a gun is more natural than an umbrella. . . . It would seem that these violent shows lead children to expect, and in some cases to crave, a kind of violence that they will not encounter in real life unless they stir it up themselves. . . .

With the progress of civilization we have learned, slowly and painfully, that violence is not the best way to settle human differences. But we seem to be using the marvelous technical media of movies and television to teach children that it is the only way.[34]

In a study of the young United States ruffians who smeared Nazi-style swastikas on synagogues, movies and television were cited as sources of their ideas. That some of the televised movies they used as models were even anti-Nazi did not reduce their influence. What the boys saw in them was a glorification of militaristic, militant, and violent behavior, regardless of the cause involved. What they saw illustrated were techniques of violence which they wanted to try. This particular cause simply proved to be a convenient pretext. Several of the boys denied being anti-Semitic and insisted that they were merely applying the kind of behavior they had seen demonstrated on television.

Yet despite the evidence, broadcast spokesmen still insist that television does not teach techniques of crime. Every day they give killing, robbery, brutality, beatings, and other antisocial behavior many hundreds of times the wattage available to educational stations demonstrating socially useful skills. To deny that these programs *teach* seems unrealistic if not outright dishonest. Studies of the attraction of daytime serials by the industry itself have repeatedly shown that one of the principal so-called values of these programs was in teaching women how to meet daily problems. Broadcasters themselves stress that these programs help orient viewers to their environment. Yet they refuse to admit that old movies and the more popular programs in the evening are similarly teaching all kinds of lessons in living and behavior to wider, more varied audiences.

In a November, 1961, holdup of a bank in New York, the young robbers reported the usefulness of television programs for learning techniques useful in bank robbery. They had studied carefully and long by television. They mentioned especially a program entitled "The Perfect Crime."

In the Payne Fund Studies, Herbert Blumer lists techniques which young criminals said they learned from films, including how to open a safe by the feel of the dial, how to force house windows and car doors, how to neutralize burglar alarms, how to pick pockets; how to make and use blackjacks, how and when to slug people, where to strike in order to maim or disable, and dozens of others.

When young people daily see attractive characters solving life's problems through violence, with specific illustrations, there should be no great surprise when these patterns show up in real life. It should be noted, in passing, that such violence is not found merely in dramatic or film materials. In *news* as well as in popular music, entertainment, and children's programs, there is emphasis on violence. Many a newscast is little more than a list of accidents, deaths, conflicts, or crimes.

One of the statements often made in defense of television violence is that it does not cause normal children to commit violence; only children who are already unbalanced or predisposed commit such crimes or acts. Yet anyone who has seriously studied the statistics of the more brutal crimes during the last few years well knows how large a number of them have been committed by a very small number of psychopaths. Many psychopaths and future psychopaths live among us, unrecognized. In many cases they consume large numbers of television programs. It is the Oswalds, Rubys, and Gambrills, * not *normal* individuals, who endanger us daily as a result of broadcasters' irresponsibilty.

Moreover, the argument that television "only triggers" those individuals who are already predisposed is hardly a reassuring defense for industry leadership to use. "Triggering" is precisely what determines whether individuals, or nations, will live or be destroyed.

Catharsis

One of the defenses cited for programs of violence is that they provide catharsis for young viewers. The idea that violence is worked out by watching violence is based on misrepresentations. Sociologist Leonard Berkowitz has written:

> The evidence is not overwhelming in every study of this problem, but it is consistent. The research will suggest media violence is more likely to incite children to acts of overt aggression than to "drain" them of their hostile energy. . . . There is no need for theoretical twisting or

* In March, 1964, Michael Lee Gambrill, a nineteen-year-old Marine on leave, reported that after watching a horror movie on TV, "something came over him," which caused him to kill his father, mother, and sister with a hatchet.

turning on this point; there simply is no adequate evidence that hostility catharsis occurs through vicarious aggression. . . .[35]

Summarizing many experiments and findings, Professor Berkowitz concludes:

> On the basis of these findings we can hypothesize that people with strong aggressive predispositions will display a relatively strong liking for aggression in television, movies, and comics. There is no evidence, however, that their hostile predispositions are weakened by viewing fantasy aggression. If anything, experimental results suggest that scenes of violence depicted on the screen will have a much greater tendency to incite children to later aggressive acts than to "drain" them of their aggressive "energy." [36]

Isidore Ziferstein, a psychiatrist with years of experience in child problems, has stated flatly that rather than producing a release of emotions, the constant dosage of violence provided by television results in an *increase* of tension, anxiety, and violence-seeking outlets.

Yosal Rogat, in analyzing the effects of sadism in connection with the Eichmann trial, raises a basic question of logic regarding the catharsis theory. He asks: "Is it certain that people simply become shocked, disapprove, and do good when they see terrible acts of sadism? On this simple psychological assumption, we could eliminate criminals by showing movies about violent crimes. Unfortunately, it is necessary to consider the possibility of reactions considerably more complex and less benign; those, for example, which psychoanalysis explains by concepts like identifying with an aggressor." [37]

Aristotle wrote of purification through pity and fear in Greek plays. But violence was not shown on the Greek stage. Freud wrote of relieving repressed emotions. But this was to be achieved through analysis and understanding, not by exposure to scenes of violence or, indeed, any mass or impersonal therapy. Most authorities do not believe that showing sex scenes purifies young viewers. Incitement is recognized as a triggering factor in various kinds of antisocial behavior; yet the nation has for years accepted the allegation of television leaders that scenes of violence on television do *not* incite to imitation, but, if anything, provide catharsis. A perverted concept of catharsis has joined that of the inevitability of the mass nature of television and radio in order to establish a profitable rather than a careful and responsible program tradition. The time has come to challenge this position.

Passivity

One of the most disturbing effects of television appears to be the creation, in some people, of passivity. If this seems contrary to findings just reported, indicating that television is responsible for much delinquency, violence, and the teaching of specific techniques of crime, it is well to recall that this is not a simple problem. Just as children will be differently affected by the same schools, lessons, and teachers, so are children differently affected by television.

The recent passivity of Americans surprises and alarms many of our foreign friends, as well as physical- and mental-fitness authorities in the United States. Social scientists point to endless hours, night after night, year after year, spent before television sets, consuming, drinking in, and vegetating. By taking the citizen away from public affairs—town meetings, citizen councils, neighborhood groups, church and discussion goups—how many vital functions of our nation have been dried up by television? How does television's "freedom" to compete in this way square with its responsibility to contribute to, and not counteract, democratic processes and strengths? Does television not have a responsibility itself to supply the functions of those meetings and activities it starves out by keeping people at home or inactivated?

Political scientists and great psychologists like Carl Jung have warned us that it is the dictator state which keeps citizens passive, reassured, and politically inactivated. How long can democracy survive similar treatment, even if it is imposed by economic rather than political controllers?

Martin Grotjahn, a psychiatrist, has said:

> We can observe the development of a new style of living which I call, for want of a better term, "television living." This is characterized by the assumption that we do not do our living ourselves any more but that, so to speak, "we are lived" by the television screen. All that we have to do is sit passively in front of the screen which lives, thinks, sees and hears for us and gives us the proper conclusion. This leads to such increase of all dependent tendencies that it hampers the free development of people into independent individuals capable and willing to form their own opinions,

to develop their own personality, and to live actively. Frequently television children are at a complete loss for any spontaneous imaginative activity. . . .[38]

Television has brought a great change in the status of the "idler" in society. Many years ago the nobility was considered to be the idle class. With the coming of industrialization came pool halls and taverns. Those who frequented them were generally treated with contempt by society; loafers were not popular. Today the person who loafs in front of his television set is likely to be admired for he knows more about celebrities and products than most other people. He is the model viewer. Is television creating a huge class of idlers whose productive efforts could more usefully be channeled? Certainly there are dangers which grow out of habits of idleness which need to be taken into account: the effect on relief rolls and taxes, and the extent to which missing exercise and activity affects performance on the job (to mention two obvious ones).

Many researchers, like Schramm, Lyle, and Parker, have noted how television leads many children into a withdrawal and private communion with the picture tube. It is something to which a child surrenders himself, something that is done to him, something that he does not have to work for; he merely soaks it up or absorbs it. Is this effortless satiation related to the increasing effeteness we observe? Certainly such problems deserve study.

Broadcast leaders speak much of the broadcast freedoms. So far as viewers and broadcasters alike are concerned, how permissible is it for a democratic people to have the freedom not to worry, the freedom to abstain from politics, the freedom to be irresponsible, or the freedom to be passive and let others do what needs to be done? Democracy will not survive if those freedoms instead of more responsible and positive ones are promoted. Psychiatrist Eugene David Glynn believes television *can* activate. And he suggests how:

> It must find ways to encourage active audience participation; programs which will not satiate but stimulate its viewers . . . showing not a baseball game, but how to pitch a curved ball; . . . sending its audience on nature hunts, into club activity, to the library for books. . . . With this orientation, television can overcome the dangers pointed out and find its way to being highly growth-promoting. Otherwise it will find itself degraded into an instrument for the

shaping of a group man: . . . the natural foil of any authoritarianism, be it left or right.[39]

The shrillness of the competitive appeals for attention in the mass media has become increasingly intense. Such stridencies have forced us, in self-defense, to develop an ability to "tune out," which no previous generations had. Americans have been conditioned to not hear, even while listening, and not see, even while looking.

Some Implications for Politics and Public Opinion

Imperceptibly, the irrational vote of the individual as consumer has come to replace the deliberate, considered ballot of the individual as citizen in much of today's decision-making. Some advertising and broadcast executives have even gone so far as to say the votes cast by citizens in the role of consumers are more democratic than the ballots they cast in the voting booth.

The old concept of the people instructing their executive agents and representatives through their votes seems to have lost ground in the age of television. For the people we have substituted the public. Decisions are no longer made through channels involving the people's ballot. For the will of the people we have substituted public opinion. And public opinion, under present conditions, can be fabricated almost at will by those who control the media. Instead of serving as communications media or vehicles for political discussion involving individual opinions and ideas, television and radio have increasingly become tools of political management and manipulation.

The control of the broadcast media by public-relations experts has reached a point where, if they are provided with enough money, they can virtually give a money-back guarantee to get a potential candidate elected to office. The efficiency of such public-relations teams as Baxter and Whitaker in California, in handling election campaigns, proves that this procedure is effective to a frightening degree. When a candidate is *not* elected, it is likely to be because of his appearance or personality rather than because he lacks the qualifications which used to be thought important for leadership.

Candidates are no longer elected; they are merchandised—in a manner which is reminiscent of the way Nazism was merchandised in Germany. The crises and reforms and daily steps so occupied the German people that the gradual breakdown of the democratic process was not noticed. A hard look at what is happening to democracy in America, under the pressure of the mass media, is in order. Certainly, instead of the consent of the governed, it appears that the governing of consent, the manufacturing of public opinion, prevails more and more. Since access to the media is determined by whether or not individuals or parties have the large sums necessary to finance their campaign, the whole concept of paid political time may well be fatal to true democracy.

José Ortega y Gasset years ago predicted that industrialization would change democracy (in which qualified, elected leaders bear the responsibilities for policy-making decisions, advised by specialists and experts) into what he calls "hyper-democracy," in which the nation's decisions are "born in the café." His vision has come true; everyone, however uninformed or ill qualified, can "vote" in one way or another, on everything from fluoridation or pay television to which types of airplanes the United States Air Force should use. But the café he feared is replaced in America by the television screen. Less-informed people are asked to decide between increasingly complicated and confusing alternatives; television is used to trigger these decisions, often by precipitating floods of telegrams or letters, or by other forms of pressure.

"Get out the vote" campaigns of this sort are a disservice rather than a service to responsible government. Evidence indicates that many of the people who go to the polls do not really know the issues involved or the real qualifications of the candidates. They have only superficial impressions based on sincerity, personality, or family.

Television should urge the citizen *not* to vote until he is sure of the issues. But it is unlikely that the nation's broadcasters will promote the examination of evidence and the interests of the voter when in the rest of their operations they are not above assisting advertisers to *conceal* facts from the public, or urging views to make purchasing decisions on the basis of the flimsiest kind of evidence and irrational considerations.

In fact, the present system of broadcasting can scarcely be expected to promote democracy in view of the way it is organized internally and in view of the "outsider" status it gives to labor, education, religion, agriculture, the unemployed, the poor, and other groups which, both in what they need and in what they have to contribute, are important elements of the nation.

Management aims to keep people viewing as much as possible; as we have pointed out, this in itself hinders democracy, since it keeps people from fulfilling their duties as citizens. As Barbara Ward has put it: "Again and again in Britain, in Australia, in America—extremists or dishonest leaders have been able to manipulate a trade union election because they did not go home to look at television and the majority of their fellow workers did." [40]

In the past, elected executive officials were expected to be generally wiser and better informed than the "little people." Today specialized knowledge and training are little respected. Floods of telegrams tell representatives what to do, and threaten them with defeat unless they do it. Walter Lippmann long ago warned of the need to protect the executive and the judiciary from mass opinion. The same need is beginning to be apparent in other aspects of responsible political decision making.

The story of the effects of broadcasting in the United States is largely the story of the warnings of professionals denied and contradicted by the sales-trained corporate men of the media. The fact that the unintended "fallout" from present television and radio programs, at home and abroad, may be having almost as powerful effects as atomic radiation should do more than cause concern. It should and must precipitate specific action. As more color television appears, with its enormously increased impact, and as the United States becomes involved with other countries in cooperative satellite broadcast projects, it becomes more important for American television to put its house in order.

8

The United States and Its Image Abroad: Broadcasting and International Relations

At a time when new nations are seeking models on which to shape their political, economic, and broadcast systems, the United States enjoys a unique situation. No other country is in a better position to guide new nations from colonialism into dynamic democracy. And in no field other than mass media is there more opportunity for reaching and helping new nations.

In no enterprise in the United States are there more dedicated disciples and apostles of the free-enterprise system than in the broadcast industry. Perhaps one of the principal characteristics of broadcast leadership is dedication to our commercial system. An editorial in *Broadcasting* magazine in March, 1955, told of the alleged victory of the American broadcasting plan, which has "prevailed in all democratic nations," over the so-called British Plan. The editorial concluded: "Henceforth the lexicon will change. It will be the 'American Plan' versus the 'Totalitarian Plan' until the latter collapses." [1] Similarly, *Advertising Age* in November of 1959 observed that "Nations that have resisted commercial tv have made little progress." "Nations that have adopted commercial tv have made rapid strides." [2] The implication in such statements is that the United States commercial broadcast system is finding a ready acceptance. Such is not always the case.

Few publications have noted or reported the sometimes ruthless tactics used by United States firms to *force* the United States commercial broadcast system on nations less than eager to adopt it. These pressures are expressed in many ways. One of the most conspicuously successful is that described by W. W. Wilson in his book, *Pressure Group: The Campaign for Commercial Television.* As Professor Wilson says:

> Britain was given commercial television against the advice of almost all the nominal leaders of society in education, religion and culture, as well as significant sections of the business community. At no time was the British electorate, or even the rank-and-file Conservative voter, given an opportunity of passing on the merits of the case. Lord Hailsham may have been extreme in characterizing the submission of the television bill to Parliament as a "shoddy and squalid constitutional error," but many believed there was justification for his criticism of the Government for its "deliberate concealment," in not presenting the issue for debate in the General Election.[3]

Professor Wilson traces "the defeat of the Conservative Party leadership by a very small group of nominally politically insignificant Conservative backbenchers," but observes: "Actually, of course, they were not insignificant, because they were, in effect, spokesmen for powerful economic groups—e.g., the radio-television manufacturing industry, major American and British advertising agencies, and financial institutions."[4] As Professor Wilson points out "the evidence would seem to support the contention of Mr. John Rodgers, M.P., that major credit is due to the 'five or six Conservative backbenchers who worked day and night on the project,' "[5] namely, securing parliamentary approval of commercial television.

Why did those who opposed commercial television, calling it a "national disaster," capitulate? Because of the threat that if Britain did not *itself* develop a commercial system, it would be flooded by commercial television programs from United States firms on nearby bases in Europe and on ships off the British coast. Why these could not be considered mere empty threats will be noted later. Norman Collins, who left the BBC, embittered, to lead the campaign to give it a commercial competitor, gave many speeches during the period described in Professor Wilson's book. As Professor Wilson states, "In one widely reported speech he warned that Britain might be deluged with propaganda by American-owned stations on the Continent. 'I know all the technical objections, but I also know how far American plans have advanced,' " he declared.[6]

Opposition to commercial television collapsed only when the Conservative Party leadership became convinced of the danger of broadcasts from "uncontrolled commercial" stations on the Continent, in Eire, and on ships. There were rumors that Radio Andorra, Radio Luxembourg, and other facilities would be purchased and taken over by United States broadcast firms. Magazine articles, possibly planted, quoted plans to use Ireland and other areas as bases. A threatened "commercial invasion" from United States firms appeared to be a real danger.

Lord Hailsham on November 25, 1953, observed in Parliament that "the introduction of commercial television is to the advantage of the very large agents, particularly those which are branches of big American agencies." [7] Particularly active among the agencies which put over the campaign were the J. Walter Thompson and Erwin Wasey agencies.

However, it would be a mistake to believe that only United States advertising agencies were involved. Equally involved were United States equipment manufacturers, film companies, networks and the trade press. In its November 30, 1953, issue *Broadcasting* magazine carried an editorial, expressing confidence that the tentative first steps of commercial television in Britain would soon be more confident and steady. It concluded with the jingle:

> Dear little John Bulls,
> Don't you cry;
> You'll be full commercial
> Bye and bye.[8]

Commercial television in both Britain and the United States seems to have been adopted in the same way: pressure groups and pressure tactics were largely responsible. So were irrational appeals of all kinds, so characteristic of broadcasting and advertising techniques.

But why would anyone believe that Britain could be flooded by United States commercial television programs? Was this not unrealistic? The answer to this question is found in a second case history of United States pressures on other countries: the operation of so-called "pirate" ships off the coasts of Britain, Scotland, Sweden, Norway, Finland, Holland, Denmark, Belgium, and several other countries. The story of such pirate-ship operations is a long one, replete with concealed ownerships and disregard of international accords. They are referred to as "pirate" ships because of the frequent absence of national registration, as will be noted below. Although there were several modest efforts to establish pirate ship operations in the mid-fifties, the first significantly troublesome pirate station was the 50-kilowatt FM Radio Mercur (or Merkur), which, anchored in international waters off Copenhagen, began operations in July, 1958. By 1959, Radio Mercur was grossing $150,000 a year from the commercials it sandwiched between popular American music records. Principal sponsors were such United States firms as Ford, Lever Brothers, and the American Tobacco Company. By 1960, its income had risen to $450,000 a year.

Radio Mercur was followed by a number of other pirate operations: Radio Nord (North), Radio Syd (South), Radio Veronica, Radio Eulenspiegel, Radio Atlanta, Radio Caroline, and finally, by late 1963 and early 1964, various television transmitters on ships and artificial islands outside the territorial waters of Holland, the British Isles, Denmark, Belgium, Norway, and Sweden. These were outlawed in 1965.

Perhaps one of the most interesting of these ships was Radio Nord, broadcasting from the ship *Bonjour,* a former German coastal freighter. This ship did not begin operations until pirate ships had been discussed and denounced at the highest levels by various national and international bodies. A *New York Times* dispatch from Stockholm (correspondent Werner Wiskari) on April 2, 1961, told of Radio Nord's initial broadcasts on March 8. American-owned, the ship flew the Nicaraguan flag, was registered in Liechtenstein, and had a Swedish crew. Jack S. Kotschack, a Finnish-born Swede of Polish ancestry, produced in Stockholm the programs and tapes used by Radio Nord. He told correspondent Wiskari that the *Bonjour* was "the property of Nord Establishments, a Liechtenstein company with American owners. The owners plan to install another radio ship off Goteborg and a third in the Mediterranean, near France." Radio Nord operated outside the four-mile Swedish territorial limits, off the Stockholm Archipelago. It broadcast on 606 kilocycles, which provided considerable interference to a legally licensed, land-based station in Lyons, France.

Since the owner of Radio Nord was reported to be an American by the name of Thompson, the *Times* checked with him directly. As the April 2 story concluded, "Robert F. Thompson, reached at his home in Dallas, Texas, said he was the owner of Nord Establishments. Asked if he was aware the *Bonjour* was broadcasting commercial radio into Sweden [which forbade it] he replied: 'I ought to know. I own her.' "

The next day the *Times* carried a follow-up story on the American firm which had provided the equipment for the ship. The equipment, costing $350,000, had been sent to Hamburg and then to a Finnish port for installation. Bert Kupperman, export manager of Visual Electronics Corporation, was reported to have told the *Times* that Radio Nord was making "substantial profits." The April 3 *Times* story noted: "In Dallas, Mr. Thompson said the enterprise had about seventy advertisers, half of them American."

On April 11, 1963, the Board of Swedish Telecommunications, in a letter to the author, told of legislation passed after considerable Parliamentary debate "to prevent the commercial radio transmission to Sweden from outside territorial waters." The Board also reported the results of a police court interrogation (of Mr. Kotschack) which confirmed the ownership and other details given above. In the correspondence on this matter another American from Texas, Gordon McLendon, was frequently mentioned. When asked later about his role in pirate-ship plans and operations, Mr. McLendon told the writer that, although he had served as a consultant in such operations, his firm had not been directly involved.

By May 6, 1962, Sweden had passed legislation aimed at controlling pirate broadcasting. The Swedish steps were followed in quick succession by similar controls decided on by Denmark, Norway, and Finland. Radio Nord ceased its broadcast at the end of June, 1962. A few months later, however, reports received by the United States Information Agency indicated that Radio Nord had been sold, and converted into another pirate operation, Radio Atlanta, destined for Mediterranean operation. By 1963, Radio Atlanta had shown up off the coast of England. In 1964 it teamed up with Radio Caroline, which began commercial broadcasts to England from outside British territorial waters.

Pirate ships, and their involvement with American broadcasters, advertisers, film and record producers, and agency representatives, did the American image no good. The participation of Americans in this operation is all the more regrettable since it followed a most bitter denunciation of such practices by legitimate European broadcasters.

In 1960 the European Broadcasting Union devoted considerable time and attention to such "pirate" stations. Attorney Jens Evensen of the Norwegian Supreme Court, on behalf of the Norwegian Broadcasting Corporation, prepared a study [9] on the questions of international law which were raised by "the operation of pirate stations from ships and airplanes." In general it noted that such operation was in flagrant and cynical violation of international practices of many years' standing. Mr. Evensen's report said that " the attempts made lately to operate radio stations on board ships or airplanes outside the territorial waters of a country, in contravention of the valid telecommunication conventions and regulations of the world, are illegal and cynical attempts to evade the law."

Since international law and telecommunications agreements signed by virtually all countries made clear that this was a violation of the rights of such countries, Mr. Evensen concluded that the operators took advantage of the fact that "in this field the rules of international law and of domestic law are so weak and so confusing, and the enforcement thereof consequently so ineffective or haphazard, that their illegal activities will be tolerated."

This entire case illustrates an interesting role of the United States corporation in international relations—it is this role which results in anti-American steps, whether it be legislation of the type listed above, or the establishment of quotas for films and television programs. It is important at this point to note American broadcast holdings abroad and their effect on broadcasting in other countries.

United States law forbids granting a license for a television or radio station to a corporation in which there is foreign ownership. The opposite is not true. American ownership in foreign broadcast systems is considered legitimate. Considerable United States influence has been noted for many years in certain foreign systems. The British Broadcasting Company, for example, was first housed in Magnet House, the General Electric Building in Kingsway, London, and H. M. Pease, an American representing the Western Electric Company (owned by AT&T), was one of its first directors. Associated Television, one of the largest producers and contractors of programs for British commercial television, is the United Kingdom contractor for Muzak, which is owned by the (American) Jack Wrather Organization. Wrather and its alter ego, Associated Television (ATV), own one-half interest each in Independent Television Corporation, a joint United States–British enterprise, although Mr. Wrather, as chairman of the board, retains control. ATV also controls the Macquarie firm in Australia, which has stations in Sydney, Adelaide, and Brisbane. Warner Brothers also has large investments in British commercial television.

CBS helped devise commercial television in Western Germany; it also operates, in various partnership arrangements, television centers in Argentina. NBC also has an interest in Argentine and other Latin American stations, networks, and sales organizations. Moreover, NBC is the United States partner with the Nigerian government in Nigeria's NBC. Many of these foreign holdings have grown slowly. Already in 1941, before the days of television, NBC announced the formation of an affiliated twenty-one-station Mexican radio network.

ABC-Paramount is one of the better examples of American broadcasting in foreign systems. Formation of a Central American television network was reported in February of 1960. The ABC Division of ABC-Paramount was reported to own 51 per cent of the new network, the balance of the ownership being distributed among the participating stations. At the time of its organization, Donald Coyle, ABC vice-president in charge of the ABC International Division, announced that the El Salvador, Guatemala, Honduras, Nicaragua, and Costa Rica stations would carry film shows from United States firms; this included ABC-TV, which itself owned and exported such programs as "The Untouchables."

ABC International also in 1961 announced that Television Manila had affiliated itself with ABC, thereby helping to develop ABC's worldwide television network. Besides "The Untouchables," the Filipinos began receiving and broadcasting such United States programs as "Maverick," "Rifleman," "Surfside 6," "Gunsmoke," "Restless Gun," "The New Breed," "The Rebel," "Mr. Lucky," and "The Hathaways." In 1961 Oliver Treyz, then vice-president of ABC-TV, in reporting on ABC's acquisition of a minority interest in twenty-two stations abroad, noted with satisfaction that "The Untouchables," "77 Sunset Strip," and "Maverick" were top programs in Australia. Similarly, "Wyatt Earp" was an easy winner in Bangkok. Time-Life Broadcast, Inc., also has holdings in Europe, Latin America, Asia, and Africa.

Perhaps the most effective broadcasting bridgeheads for the United States are being established in the form of foreign branches of advertising agencies. J. Walter Thompson several years ago had wholly owned subsidiaries in eighteen countries. McCann-Erickson and Grant had similar foreign installations. Ted Bates and Company followed a more usual pattern by buying a London agency, John Jobson and Partners; this practice makes American ownership less noticeable to the British public. Benton and Bowles bought the British agency, Lambe and Robinson. McCann-Erickson's acquisition of the Australian agency Hansen-Rubensohn was also recently announced.

More surprising are the broadcast efforts or pressures of non-broadcast organizations. It might be thought that the Arab-American Oil Company (ARAMCO) is only an oil company. The efforts of this firm illustrate the extent to which American industrial activities frequently include the founding of cities, of entire educational systems, and of radio and television stations.

In Iran one of the most successful commercial stations is run by Habib Sabit, the nation's distributor for Pepsi-Cola and RCA. Obviously, this is useful for advertising Pepsi-Cola and other products. Here, too, the American system came as a part of a package. The foreign factories owned by RCA, General Electric, or other such firms would at first sight seen unrelated to the kind of broadcast system which these host nations have, but such is hardly the case. The availability of RCA advisers and equipment probably influenced the broadcast directions of many new nations far more than the Department of State or the United States Information Agency.

The corporate pressures determining broadcasting in new nations are of various kinds. This is quite different from the kind of aid and advice given new nations by official United States government agencies. For example, the consensus of United States advisers called upon to design broadcast systems for Germany, Austria, and Japan recognized that the imposition of the American form might have adverse consequences. The system recommended, therefore, was one based on a careful analysis of the economic, geographical, and other characteristics of the nations concerned and was designed to meet their democratic needs in the most satisfactory form. The corporate view, by contrast, is that no such analysis is necessary; the American system is best and will work everywhere.

Providing such pressure seems to be one of the principal

activities of the representatives of the United States networks and their parent corporations, film companies, advertising agencies, equipment representatives, and related firms. Probably no official or governmental pressure brought to bear on such countries, with the possible exception of that of the Soviet government itself, can match this pressure. The fact that it sometimes gives rise to resentment on the part of the younger generation, liberal political parties, intellectuals, educators, or other groups in these nations should be understood. They are not seeking to be anti-American; they usually only seek the right to decide what systems, or combinations of systems, will best serve their needs. In some cases these needs are very desperate ones in which public health, education, literacy, irrigation, agriculture, and other such problems are seen as a higher priority than entertainment or advertising. But regardless of the kind of broadcasting adopted, the foreign systems present a profitable market to American programs. Already in 1959 the income from abroad was estimated at 25 million dollars; with the mushrooming of new systems it probably totals well over 100 million dollars by now. In an article entitled "U.S. Television Abroad: Big New Business," John Tebbel reported export figures for 1962 showing NBC in first place, followed by CBS, ABC, MCA (Revue), Screen Gems (Columbia), and ZIV (United Artists) in that order.[10] The nature of the programs sent, how well received they are, and the image they convey deserve to be noted.

Since public affairs and documentary programs are more expensive and tend to become dated, most of the programs sent abroad are old movie films or kinescopes (films made directly off the TV tube). In 1962 "Bonanza" was listed as the world's most broadcast television program.

By 1959 NBC had sold the "Perry Como Show" in seventeen countries. CBS Films, Inc., had about forty programs which it was promoting abroad, including "Gunsmoke," "Whirlybirds," "Have Gun Will Travel," and "Perry Mason." ABC's top sellers late in 1959 included "Three Musketeers," "Sheena, Queen of the Jungle," "Twenty-six Men," and "Douglas Fairbanks, Jr., Presents."

Jack Wrather's "Four Just Men," distributed in fifteen countries by International Television Corporation, by 1959 had grossed 878 million dollars. ITC's top shows were "Lassie," "The Lone Ranger," and "Fury." ZIV's big successes were "High way Patrol," "Sea Hunt," "Bat Masterson," and "Cisco Kid." The rest of the most popular exports follows similar patterns. Programs like "The Gale Storm Show," "Tugboat Annie," "Abbott and Costello," "Ramar of the Jungle," "Sergeant Preston," and "My Little Margie" were also proving to be popular and profitable.

However, the figures on the volume of United States programs being broadcast abroad, like ratings, tell little of what people *think* of these programs or the extent to which they meet their needs rather than their appetites. A couple of months after ABC President Leonard Goldenson's visit to Australia, George Patterson, executive of one of Australia's still Australian advertising agencies, warned that perhaps a quota would have to be applied to prevent the broadcasting of too many American programs. Otherwise, he feared that the "creeping mediocrity," as he termed it, of Australian programming could not be halted.

Such quotas have been applied against American programs by many countries, including England, France, Canada, and Japan, and, since so much of television's gross income has come from foreign sales, their imposition has caused concern in broadcast and film circles in recent months. Why numerous countries are beginning to resist our television exports deserves to be noted. Perhaps one of the best explanations is that of the previously quoted Hugh Carleton Greene, director general of the British Broadcasting Corporation.[11] In scores of new countries millions of illiterates asking for education, help in health and agriculture, and orientation in democracy are huddled night after night around television sets watching western, crime, and adventure series. Many of these are the cheapest rather than the best of their kind. Profit rather than quality determines too much of what they get to see from and about America. Sir Hugh feels this is a great tragedy because the world needs the example set by American economic and democratic leadership, and also American materials—but not the present kind.

Some critics are less tactful and friendly. One of Britain's angry young men, John Osborne, has protested against the flooding of Britain with the "neuroses, sex, violence" and materialism that so many United States materials feature.[12] Such an image and such materials are not merely regrettable in themselves; they are tragic because they seem to indicate a moral failure on the part of our democratic and free-enterprise system. This is of far greater significance than we realize, for many new nations are at this moment trying to decide what kinds of governments they should have. They will decide on the basis of what they see and what kinds of life those systems reward, foster, and feature. Some critics of our present policy have sarcastically suggested that since the effects of some of our programs in some countries are so great and so negative (training in crime and violence), we should export such programs only to *enemy* countries. The adverse effects on certain groups of Russian youths who emulate some of the practices of our beatniks, and of our movie and recording idols, would suggest that their sarcasm is not unjustified.

One of the most regrettable aspects of this problem is that the very things our most enthusiastic exponents boast about are those most likely to do our image the most harm. Broadcasting and advertising agencies have, over and over again, emphasized our high standard of living. In an address July 17, 1961, C. James Proud, president of the Advertising Federation of America, said: "Flip a switch and we have music, opera, the best entertainment in the world, light, heat, air conditioning, news from all over the world, almost as it happens. Solomon in all his glory never had it so good." [13] From representatives of nations which know starvation, however, comes the reminder that "we could live in luxury on the garbage dumps of North America . . . real luxury from our point of view." [14] Foreigners tell us how they feel upon hearing about and seeing pictures of our luxury and waste, as they starve. How many friends, in this situation, do our present programs win? Or are they, perhaps, contributing to a tornado of fury which may break someday over our heads?

In Hong Kong, where "The Untouchables" and "Mike Hammer" are being urged on the population, 5,000 people each day are starving in the streets. Isn't the world we live in today so literally *one world* that we can no longer be indifferent to poverty, hunger, and misery anywhere on the globe? And what effect on starving people do our programs have—featuring waste, dissipation, violence, and luxury?

It is no doubt difficult for United States network and agency executives, whose diet is adequate, to realize that many Asians cannot work hard all day because both climate and malnutrition make it impossible. Many of the Asian's waking hours may be spent looking for food. If he spent much time before a television set, he and his family would starve.

Remembering how many thefts and break-ins and other crimes have been committed even in the United States by citizens with starving families, but with no money to buy the food and other items attractively shown on television, one can conjecture about the effect of such programs on the Africans and Asians who know that we annually waste and destroy enormous quantities of surplus food while they starve.

Anthropologist Ashley Montagu has reminded us that "at the present time human beings, in millions, are still living in caves. Not just in Mongolia or Arabia, but in Europe. At the present time there are over a million people in Spain alone who make their permanent home in caves." [15] Many friends of America, warning us, have been misunderstood and denounced as unfriendly.

Many of the practices seen on television raise many questions in the minds of foreign visitors who have noted that contrary to the U.N. Declaration of the Rights of the Child, children are open to exploitation. Are not children urged to insist that their parents buy certain brands of products and not to take No for an answer? Are not teen-agers lured into joining so-called credit clubs, buying all sorts of useless items, and wasting much time which could be better used if more wisely apportioned? Were not millions of children urged to ask their parents to oppose pay-TV, under the threat that they would lose their favorite free television programs?

Is America really a peaceful nation, dedicated to peaceful goals? Our belief used to be that a militarized nation is a totalitarian nation, that militarism is inconsistent with liberty and world friendship. How does this square with our present image and the treatment given military personnel and military leadership in United States broadcasting? When sponsors begin to specify that programs shall not discredit or criticize war or the military, are there not far broader implications at stake? Are friends who tell us that our image is all too often militaristic and totalitarian going too far? Is this not a matter of national concern, rather than merely a broadcasting and business problem?

Some critics are surprised at the apparent suppression of many items of news, consistent with our military orientation. How did it happen that no United States network carried Albert Schweitzer's appeal of April 24, 1957, for the cessation of atomic testing? Or Albert Einstein's similar appeals?

When the United States government blocked the efforts of the Food and Agriculture Organization of the United Nations to set up a World Food Council, why were United States broadcast listeners and viewers not told? When Russia suggested black-box inspection devices for atomic inspection, why was it not reported that this constituted acceptance of a proposal made by an International Pugwash Conference, rather than being an unreasonable *Russian* proposal? When United States television and radio reported imminent communist invasion in Laos in 1959, was a retraction issued when it was found that this entire crisis was a fabrication? Or were Americans told of the wholesale executions carried out by Batista, before the Castro victory? Was concealment of such reports related to the friendliness of Batista to a few large corporations in Cuba? And was the anti-Castro line not in some way related to the effects of agrarian reform on a very few United States corporations in Cuba, whose large holdings were broken up to create small farms for Cuban agriculture?

Yuji Isobe, editor of one of the largest Tokyo newspapers, *Tokyo Shimbun,* is a good friend of the United States. He is a good enough friend and a courageous enough man to have warned of the tendency of United States news services, and television and radio, to fail to report accurately news of Communist China. He felt this is dangerous and unforgivable, as he told a United Nations seminar in 1962. Other nations are likely to wonder whether a system which conceals so much from its own citizens—while repeating that the United States citizen is the best informed in the world—may not have fatal flaws.

Much of the world to which we now send television programs and films is populated by black, brown, and yellow individuals. What do our programs tell them? Foreign Minister Jaja Wachuku of Nigeria warned a conference of the United States National Commission for UNESCO in October, 1961, that the time was overdue for the United States to make some mental adjustments about Africa and the black race. He was especially clear in his explanation of the consequences for America of the second-class citizenship status of the Negro in American mass media.

As the black men around the world seek their picture in our television and films, they see only an occasional Negro— usually a waiter, janitor, or a comedy character. Such is the value set on them, the natives of Africa, by United States media. Certainly no race is more consistently debased and slandered in United States mass media than the Negro. This is costing us dearly abroad. Mexicans see themselves portrayed as lazy, shiftless characters, mispronouncing English and speaking through bad teeth with a foolish smile. The Italian, seeking his image, all too often finds it in the stereotyped criminal and gangster. Or what do the red and brown races see in our so-called historical westerns? ". . . great Indian killers, whose only virtue was that they killed large numbers of Indians, Indians who were most wickedly trying to defend their homes and their wives and their children, and their right to their own country." [16]

Politically, America proclaims, American labor is free. It is a bulwark against communism. The right to organize is a symbol of the freedom of the worker in a democracy. Yet in broadcast programs, labor unions are generally shown as corrupt and few union leaders are mentioned, other than those who are ruthless, dishonest, or criminal. Labor union strikes, violence, and disorder are emphasized by our broadcast media. Is this image of labor likely to enhance the world image of the United States?

New nations need educated individuals, yet in the United States mass media the teacher, the intellectual, and the serious student are shown more ridicule than respect. In many new nations the artist is considered as a leader, a welcome resource, a credit to the culture. What do such people and nations think of a broadcast system which so often shows artists as aesthetes, effeminate, weak, often homosexual, and generally worthless? Visitors to this country, and students from new nations, note in letters and reports that in the United States comedians are paid more than scientists, professors, or teachers; that teachers and intellectuals are among the favorite butts of television, film, and radio jokes; and that network executives blame intellectuals more than any other groups for being unreasonable in their criticism of the American system. The United States officially is spending millions to create respect for American art and culture; is the mass-media picture of the artist and the intellectual consistent with that effort?

Is a system which creates such contempt for intellectuals and which denigrates education, religion, and nonconformism alike, a good system for new nations to adopt? All too often they decide it is not; their greatest need is for education and educators rather than for commodities or salesmen.

There is a need for us to recognize that there is much more to life than air conditioners, Cadillacs, IBM machines, and luxuries and that there should be fewer broadcast hours devoted to promoting purchase, waste, popularity, "sincerity," sexual attraction, or movie or television careers. Our preoccupations with such qualities are seen by many new countries as irresponsible distractions from the *main* goals they need to achieve. They can not yet afford such decadent practices.

The materials distributed abroad by the Voice of America are scrutinized and criticized by many congressional committees. Yet they are heard and seen by only a fraction of the people who daily view and hear programs from United States commercial broadcasters whose materials are not subject to review. The effect of the Voice of America and the rest of the official United States Information Agency effort seems to be vitiated by such materials. The Voice shows aspects of United States life which are intended to generate respect, admiration, and emulation of our democratic political system in other nations. For United States television networks and film companies to inundate these same nations with programs which do the opposite appears inimical to our total national objectives.

In his address to the National Association of Broadcasters at their April, 1962, Convention, Edward R. Murrow said, "I suggest you would do well to acknowledge that in the volatile world in which we live celluloid and magnetic tape are a strategic commodity. Those who do export of it must show concern and consideration for its use. I have doubt that what is being said abroad about the people of this land is in accord with what the people of this land would have spoken in their name. . . . Not everything done abroad is perpetrated in the national interest." [17]

When it has been suggested that the image of America being exported by television programs and films is a tarnished one, industry spokesmen have denied it. NBC's Robert Sarnoff has said that our television programs reflect credit rather than discredit on the United States image. Many spokesmen have implied that criticism of American export programs is disloyalty and that critics who make such charges are trying to "sabotage the American economy," or to "cripple the United States trade balance." There is, in fact, one interesting trade-balance and foreign-aid question raised by present practices: How large a part of our foreign aid grants to the various nations concerned are, in effect, siphoned back into the treasuries of American broadcasting corporations? To what extent is it to the advantage of these nations, or consistent with our foreign-aid program, to follow this practice rather than helping them to set up their own broadcast production facilities, staffs, and traditions?

The realization that one of our largest and most important exports today is packaged information (about the United States and the world as we see it) is a new one. And it poses a problem that present rules and regulatory agencies are incapable of coping with. The fact that such materials may be labeled entertainment does not affect or reduce their informational and image-creating impact. The quality of such goods would therefore seem to be no less important than the quality of foods, drugs, currency, or other materials we export from the United States. In numerous other nations, national committees have been appointed to supervise the composition of such exports. Unless such care is shown, the funds spent on the Voice of America will be canceled daily in the battle for men's minds. The effects of American radio, television, and film programs abroad may well be more powerful, and sometimes more adverse, than those at home.

It is especially regrettable that controls are having to be exerted in the forms of quotas established by friendly nations to keep down the number of American programs broadcast, and sometimes to prevent the broadcast of certain acts which characterize so many United States programs, instead of voluntary United States industry measures. For such rejections reflect discredit on the whole American nation and are often interpreted as unfriendly acts.

The reluctance with which the national Japanese television system (NHK) has banned all programs showing deadly weapons or violence, hoping that this will not be construed as an unfriendly act, is revealing. Yet those responsible for NHK policy felt they could do no less. It reveals one of the greatest single reasons for objection to United States television programs, namely, violence. Whether United States broadcasters admit that violence has any adverse effects makes little difference. The representatives of other broadcast systems—the counterparts or equivalents of United States network officials—are convinced that showing violence as a solution to problems, or techniques of violence, or instruments and weapons of crime and violence, is not in their national interest.

Indebted as England was to America after World War II, British scholars and members of Parliament, studying the United

States commercial system with a view to possible adoption, soberly declared that the use made of television and radio by United States broadcasters should "serve as a warning rather than an example," as Asa Briggs points out in his book *The Birth of Broadcasting*.[18]

A bill, since passed, was introduced into the Mexican Chamber of Deputies in 1959, approving the recommendations of a special study committee. One of its provisions was to prohibit broadcasts "contrary to social customs or showing violence or crime in a favorable light." (The French have had a similar precautionary ruling since 1949.) Under other provisions of the bill, announcers would be required to exercise some responsibility: to state for each program whether it was suitable for minors; to alternate all alcoholic beverage commercials with educational messages on hygiene and nutrition, and to air them only after 9 P.M.; and to give sources for all news items.

The fact that nation after nation, knowing full well what United States practices are, should specifically write into their own laws and codes provisions to prevent such things in their own countries, speaks more loudly than anything they may say directly about United States programs themselves. If real exchanges of programs with such nations are to occur, in the kind of worldwide dialogue which television makes possible, some revision of our current TV value systems is in order.

Many countries feel that TV should be a limited-time service, rather than, like ours, a continuous service watered down to fill the day and night. This concept is based on a belief that television should be a special experience, of high quality. Several speakers in the British Parliament have expressed the opinion of leaders in many countries when they declared that television already takes up, even in England, all the time it should. Most nations would not deny to the United States the right to have television as few or as many hours per day as it wishes. But for the United States to cause virtually all countries to broadcast more and more television each day, by exerting various types of commercial pressures, package deals, and other incentives, is resented by many. Habits are more easily formed than broken. And this refers very much indeed to habits of watching television for long periods. Some nations, after observing our practices, have proceeded to enact legislation limiting the number of hours of television broadcasting, just as they (like us) limit the dosages and availability of certain drugs. These limitations, however, are very difficult to introduce once the American pattern or habit is formed.

Although they do not directly take issue with the ideas of United States television management on how much television children may watch, the Western German Television Committee and the code of the European Catholic Association for Radio and Television both urge limiting the number of broadcast hours, so those which *are* offered may be of excellent quality, realizing the unique qualities of television rather than using it as a delivery facility for the products of other media.

The Canadian Royal Commission observed in 1957 that there was no question but that Canada could have cheaper television and radio if she became an extension of United States practices, networks, and firms. However, it also asked, if the cheapest and easiest way were always chosen, "is it possible to have a Canadian nation at all?" Without denying the United States the right to run its own business, the report politely observed there was no valid basis for thinking the United States broadcast fare was desirable for Canada: "In a troubled and difficult world, Canada has a role to play that will be more valuable and useful if we are something more than a carbon copy of American views and opinions and aspirations . . . Assuming that their broadcasting system is satisfactory and suitable for Americans, this is no basis for thinking it is desirable for Canadians." [19] Such is just some of the evidence that all is not well in the effects of United States broadcasting abroad.

As ordinary Americans travel abroad, they learn that one of the clues by which they may judge other nations is how the people of that nation treat each other. Visitors to this country and consumers of American broadcast programs and commercials do likewise. And they remark on the way in which salesmen and advertisers on our television and radio commercials appear frequently to deceive fellow Americans, or try to lure them into doing irresponsible things. They note that most of our broadcast music consists of ditties in praise of products—especially cigarettes, beers, and cosmetics. They note how the United States allocates its resources and how education and intellectuals are valued. Still other lessons about us are revealed by the respect or condescension with which other nations are treated and viewed, especially those of other races. Our actions speak louder than our words.

Americans are likely to forget that a nation may be judged

more by what it seems to find enjoyable than by what its leaders say or what its ancestors fought for. We are also likely to fail to realize how the image of American women, husbands, children, family life, and social values may be understood or misunderstood by the simple people of other nations, eager to learn about us, but lacking in the sophistication needed to discount or interpret what they see.

Sir Gerald Beadle, formerly director of BBC-Television, tells of Africans who are convinced that the United States is not really advanced, since so many programs show men on horseback.

One by one the emerging nations have said that their greatest need and hunger is for education. What help do they find in our radio and television? What they do find is that our profit—not their education—comes first. Consequently, many of these countries are turning to other sources for educational programs; these sources frequently include Eastern nations. This is a great blow not only to the income of United States broadcasters and film companies, but also to the prestige and image of the United States. It is a great tragedy to thus contribute to their demand for Soviet, Yugoslav, Polish, Czech, and even Red Chinese educational materials. It is a bitter irony indeed that those allegedly profiting most from the American way unwittingly contribute most to its undoing.

Despite the difficulty and painfulness of seeing ourselves as others see us, we must look hard and honestly at the impression the United States is creating abroad via its television, radio, and films. If the democratic system is to win adherents, it must do so not on the basis of what it *says* it stands for, but on the basis of its demonstrated accomplishments. Our survival as *the* democratic example will be decided much more by what we are seen and heard to do, through the windows of our television and radio, than by what we profess. Moreover, these media must provide the windows through which we may ourselves fearlessly look outward.

Perhaps the most tragic aspect of the present problem of the United States image abroad lies in what we are *not* doing. While giving lip service to many United Nations objectives, we too often violate and ignore them. That United States broadcasting has not taken an overwhelming, worldwide editorial position in favor of the United Nations and its subsidiary organizations is regrettably conspicuous to the rest of the world. The

United Nations was, after all, created at San Francisco and is now housed in New York, both in the United States. In the free choice it enjoys of what to show and what to ignore, United States broadcasting has chosen largely to ignore world order rather than to promote it, and to promote the pursuit of profits above almost all other considerations. Mankind must become one family or destroy itself—and nothing less than the full mobilization of all media can make us one family. What nation could take the lead better than the United States?

International law need not await internationally directed force. It is the growth of respect for international law that makes an international police force possible. That United States mass media are not more positively pressing for world order and world peace is a great tragedy. There is much conjecture abroad regarding the extent to which our large communications firms find world tensions, which give them profitable defense contracts, more profitable than promoting peace. As Einstein has said, the problems of peace and security are the most vital ones we have to cope with, far more important than problems of economics. Can the United States system, as now organized, meet this changed need? Wars quite literally begin in the minds of men. The electronic mass media, which have access to the minds of the world's citizens as no other media have, lie almost unused for this purpose; they are too often used for selfish, trivial, or contrary objectives.

If United States broadcasting would care to be remembered for an act of world leadership, deserving of our democratic tradition, the opportunity is here and now. If the objectives of world order were really inconsistent with those of the United States, or of free broadcasters, present tendencies to ignore and repress such points of view would be understandable. But the interests of both basically coincide.

Does the United States really want universal disarmament and world peace? If so, let our media be used as the anvils and forums of the world on which to achieve them. Speaking in the United States in 1961, Sir Gerald Beadle described how television might be the greatest unifying force the world has ever had for communication among men of all colors, races, and creeds. Transcending literacy and language, it can provide, as he said, "that sense of world citizenship without which the human race is doomed."

American television could probably do more than the

United Nations to lay the foundations of peace. United States broadcasting with its great potential could lead all the rest of the world in such a crusade. It should; it must. Even now United States television is making history. For history records the failures of nations and leaderships as unremittingly as their successes.

9

An Agenda for Change: Some Proposals and Recommendations

In previous pages, some of the most important weaknesses and failures of United States broadcasting have been analyzed. There are many others. Enough trouble spots have been noted, however, to justify some recommendations.

The recommendations presented here are necessarily of various kinds. If a single grand design cannot be achieved, various intermediate types of improvements are still possible. Some of the suggestions given here can be implemented under certain conditions; some will be possible only under other circumstances. Some have international implications; some have implications for the federal government, some for state governments, some for the industry leadership itself, and some for the general public.

A National Study

Although many changes are suggested here which can be made without delay, the very basic changes needed will require immediate and careful top-level study. This must precede the most fundamental of the changes in broadcast structure, policy, leadership, and goals, which the nation requires. Such a study can be approached in any of a number of different ways. One is the creation of a special presidential commission to study the problem and bring in recommendations. Another is a joint effort of the House and Senate to set up a special commission to carry out a study. A third might involve a special privately endowed or foundation-financed study, perhaps in collaboration with government.

Such a commission would have a mandate to recommend and devise the best possible broadcasting structure or combination of systems for the United States, regardless of what we have had to date. Such an examination would study the role of commercial broadcasting; the desirability and role of pay television; the greatly increased development of educational broadcasting; and ways in which a public-service network, providing federal-state-local services which are not now available to the public via broadcasting, might be established, financed, controlled, and operated.

The make-up of such a commission would have to be very carefully balanced. The commissions found useful in England, Canada, Australia, Italy, Sweden, Japan, and various other European, African, and Asian countries are recommended as possible models; foreign experts, in addition to qualified Americans, might serve on the commission. A suggestion for the make-up of such a commission might be found in such other United States commissions and study groups as the Hoover Commission, the Rockefeller Brothers Fund Study, or the President's Commission on National Goals.

Since industry representatives have generally dominated previous studies, safeguards against undue influence by existing networks, associations, agencies, and other vested interests would be necessary. Such a study would require outstanding men from education, business, labor, economics, psychology, medicine, law, science, and the arts. In case a few representatives from broadcasting are included, stress should be placed on representation from smaller, independent stations, who have been little consulted to date. It might be preferable, however, to exclude industry representatives from the commission proper and to use them only as witnesses, along with others who have a stake in communications.

Such a commission might find it useful, through assigned subcommittees, to study the broadcast systems in other countries, as well as conduct hearings in various parts of the United States where labor, business, education, agriculture, religion, women's and youth groups, and the medical and legal professions might be heard. The practice of holding hearings only or principally in Washington has often resulted in ignoring the fact that the grass roots of the nation are too often dominated by a few large firms and associations. The hearings and study held, in various parts of the United States and abroad, should be conducted quietly and calmly over a period long enough to complete a thorough study. The reports of the special study committees might then be turned over to the full commission for the preparation of recommendations, which would then be submitted in proper form to the President and the Congress for implementation.

The commission would not be starting from scratch, since over a score of excellent studies and reports are available, though they are kept in inactive files by steady industry pressure, largely through friendly congressmen. The recommendations of the Barrow Report, the Jones Report, the Plotkin Report, Network Study Committees, the Hoover Commission, the Landis Report, Justice Department reports, the Report of the President's Communications Policy Board, and the reports of several House and Senate committees and subcommittees are already available. In the present situation, whereby no one committee in either the House or Senate has primary or continuing responsibility for broadcasting, there are a large number of congressional reports which have never been collated. One of the first tasks of the commission would be the collation of the principal reports made to date in the United States, extracting their salient results. The same would need to be done for the best of the twenty or so excellent foreign studies which have been made.

Perhaps one of the first tasks which such a commission might undertake is to provide for a continuing review of broadcasting after its own job is done. Many nations have distinguished broadcast advisory councils with members selected from the highest levels of science, the arts, education, labor, business, religion, and the professions. In the United States such a permanent commission might report to the President, the Congress, and the people and engage in periodic reviews and studies to see that necessary revisions are made in the structure of broadcasting—and to ensure against the present division of jurisdiction among executive, legislative, and industry representatives and conflicting operational responsibilities (such as those which currently divide the attentions of the present FCC). Special provisions for public hearings should be included in such a commission, if it is to be alert to changing problems, moods, and public needs. The commission might carry on review functions virtually continuously into matters related to broadcasting, inviting witnesses and securing and issuing reports and recommendations. It would have no enforcement or operational authority or functions.

In planning a balanced, mixed system of broadcasting for the United States, providing for a fair blend of business, educational, and general public interests, a national study commission would have to explore the problems we have discussed earlier: the increasing perversion of the broadcast media toward sales uses and away from other services; the deterioration of the news services provided by radio and television; public-relations uses of broadcasting by candidates with the most money; joint ownerships of the various media which reduce cross-media criticism; adverse cultural effects of New York and Hollywood concentrations of the networks; apparent anti-educational effects and pressures in broadcasting; the proper role of the manufacturing and publishing corporation in broadcasting; the problem of America's tarnished TV image abroad; the proper function and control of networks; and the validity of present practices and laws regarding political broadcasts.

Such are some of the difficult problems a national commission would have to cope with. Congress has never been able to solve them—since all congressmen and senators need access to broadcast facilities, and since virtually each one owes, or believes he owes, his election to present facilities and their managers. Being appointed, rather than elected, a national commission should be a better mechanism than Congress for finding solutions for this problem and other problems.

A National Public-service Radio and Television Network

One of the principal functions of a special commission study of broadcasting in the United States would be to explore the feasibility and possible organization of a publicly owned and financed public-service network, in both radio and television. Such a network would serve in the electronic area the same purpose that the *Congressional Record* and government publications at the federal, state, county, and city levels now serve in printed form.

The idea of such a Federal public-service broadcast system is not new, and public ownership and operation in broadcasting already exist in the United States. One of the best-known municipally owned radio stations in the nation is WNYC, owned and operated by the city of New York. WNYC's record in the arts and in the international and UN areas is particularly exemplary.

Samuel Morse in 1845 tried to persuade government to take over and operate telegraphic communications. He was supported by the postmaster general at that time. The Woodrow Wilson victory in 1912 was followed by a recommendation from a special committee, requested by the Senate, for government ownership and operation of radio. Secretary of the Navy Josephus Daniels, during and after World War I, favored government ownership of radio. He was supported by Postmaster General A. S. Burleson. Secretary Daniels's bills died in the congressional committees to which they were referred. His plea that the Congress at least conduct a careful study of the alternatives before deciding was ignored.

On January 12, 1932, Senator James Couzens, chairman of the Committee on Interstate Commerce, introduced Senate Resolution 129 into the United States Senate; it was passed with little difficulty and it called upon the Federal Radio Commission to look into the feasibility of government ownership and operation of broadcasting facilities. The FRC, like the FCC today, sensitive to the many pressures promptly brought to bear on it, recommended continuance of the private system then developing.

The Commission on the Freedom of the Press (some twenty years ago) recommended the establishment of government-owned and -operated facilities if the commercial media were unwilling to supply the people with adequate information on a number of problems about which they needed to make intelligent and crucial decisions. The proposals of this distinguished commission would be useful for the new study proposed here.

In more recent years, several specific proposals have been published. Walter Lippmann made one such proposal in his New York *Herald Tribune* column on October 27, 1959. This proposal is included as Appendix D of this book, with Mr. Lippmann's kind permission and that of the *Herald Tribune*.

In June of 1961, TV pioneer Allen Du Mont in a speech suggested that FCC Chairman Newton N. Minow "start swinging an axe within the FCC to grind out the necessary channels to add a fourth, noncommercial, government-sponsored network which will reach every possible community in the United States." Emergency and civil-defense uses alone could justify the existence of such public-service radio and television networks, giving priority to noncommercial rather than commercial commitments. By present commercial standards the number of listeners and viewers at most hours of the day might be small. But on the basis of need, they could well make the difference between survival and nonsurvival in case of national emergency or tragedy.

Present television networks spend millions to discover and develop the best show talent in the United States. A public-service network would allow the best *minds* in our nation to analyze our many problems. On such programs, all our national congressmen, senators, and cabinet members would at some time appear in fireside chats or discussions. At local levels, the same would be true of state and local officials, trustees and board members of educational institutions, and others. The public would be brought closer to the government and would gradually become better informed. Commercial networks could carry such programs if they wished, but they would not be required to do so. Such a network would also serve as a standard against which the operations of the privately owned media could be judged. The nation has a number of private laboratories; yet an official Bureau of Standards is found useful. There are many medical and health institutions; yet the National Institute of Health is found useful. There are many educational, university, and school libraries; yet the Library of Congress is indispensable.

A publicly operated communications system would be no less free and no less in keeping with American traditions than present public control of schools, libraries, floods, health, highways, air and water pollution, conservation, and a score of other services handled by government. At present, the government has no voice for broadcasting; a perusal of what government does on paper, adapted to broadcasting, would suggest many of the informational uses which a public governmental network would have.

It should be noted that what is suggested here is not government or public-service networks to *replace* the present commercial structure, but to coexist with it, along with pay television and educational broadcasting. Just as millions of people find government publications useful for an understanding of issues and problems, so too will millions undoubtedly use the publicly owned and operated broadcast system. Just as public schools or libraries are not expected to make a profit, neither would such a network. But, like them, it would be an indispensable social agency.

The so-called "mixed" systems which many other countries already have suggest the greater flexibility and variety of services which are possible as compared with those of our business-managed system. Such a system would have to be maintained politically independent of government. But this problem has successfully been met in England, Canada, and a score of other countries.

Abundant examples are available as models for the public corporation which might be one possible mechanism for operating this network. The ABC, CBC, and BBC in Australia, Canada, and Britain, respectively, represent carefully devised systems which might be studied with profit. The type of public institution represented by the British Broadcasting Corporation is a unique type of social institution, one of the most significant inventions or developments of the twentieth century. The legal ownership of BBC properties is vested in the corporation itself; they are not the property of the state. The respects in which the government and the political parties are prevented from meddling in BBC broadcast affairs also deserve careful study. Similarly independent systems, in some cases devised with the assistance of United States consultants, are also to be found in Germany, Japan, and other nations of both the Western world and the Far East. In recent years the United States has developed variations of this same approach in the form of such public corporations as the RAND and Aerospace Corporations, chartered to perform quasigovernmental functions.

The public corporation approach to many problems is established in the United States. Examples are numerous, beginning with the United States ownership and operation of the Panama Railroad Company in 1904. This company has been operated in recent years under the U.S. Department of Defense. The Federal Reserve System, dating from 1913, is another illustration of an early government agency found essential as a balance wheel and standard-setter for the commercial bank structure of the United States. A plethora of public corporations came into existence during World War I: the United States Shipping Board Emergency Fleet Corporation, which recognized the need for the United States government's participation in transportation; the United States Grain Corporation; the War Finance Corporation; and the United States Housing Corporation. These and many others illustrate early efforts in this area.

A federal network might well be controlled by a board of distinguished citizens. Employees would be professionals operating on a merit basis similar to recent Civil Service arrangements. Just as Edward R. Murrow and other distinguished Americans found government service compatible, it is likely that distinguished professionals would be attracted to a service in which tenure and security do not depend on the whims of single individuals, as is so generally the case in commercial broadcasting. It might well be financed principally by license fees paid by commercial stations, which would be relieved of primary responsibility for political broadcast time, presidential speeches, and other public services which they find financially burdensome. (Networks and stations claim that cancellations for political and public affairs programs now cost them many millions of dollars each year.) Present fees would have to be increased. In 1962, a proposal for modest license fees, to go into effect in 1964, was approved. These fees, however, neither are related to the ability of each station to pay, nor will they return significant income. The $100 maximum for a television station and $50 maximum for a radio station are a fraction of the assessment needed, and would bring in less than 4 million dollars a year. Additional funds could be secured through a tax on commercial stations. A rate-card or profit-based tax would not be difficult to devise or administer. It would equalize the competition between VHF and UHF stations until that time when all television is transferred to what is now called UHF. Funds could be used to defray most or all regulatory agency expenses and other federal costs on behalf of broadcasting, including the operation of a federal service, much as income from automobiles and gasoline taxes is used to defray governmental and highway expense.

In view of the experience of other nations with variations of mixed ownership, outright public ownership and operation might be considered as a preferred alternative, although the RAND and Aerospace-type corporations mentioned above would seem to offer many advantages. It is not here recommended that a receiving-set tax be used to finance such a system. Since the average family already pays perhaps $150 per year in hidden taxes of one type or another for television, to make the public service appear to be responsible for the only *visible* tax seems undesirable. A percentage of the income of the commercial stations of the nation, as suggested earlier, should be more than adequate to cover necessary expenses. If not, it might be supported by the same type of appropriations that any other essential government agency has.

In Canada, where public and private ownership coexist, Alphonse Ouimet, president of the Canadian Broadcasting Corporation, late in 1959 noted with appreciation the cooperative arrangement between the government-chartered CBC and the commercial stations: "It is a good relationship and a good working partnership of private and public enterprise," he said. Wherever such mixed systems are in operation, there seem to be greater satisfaction and better service than where either government or private enterprise is the sole or dominant operator.

The securing of frequencies would have to be worked out equitably. A public agency or corporation could take over, with appropriate compensation, the physical plants of selected existing private stations, much as public-domain proceedings now make such reclamation of land and other national resources possible in other respects. Since the frequencies already belong to the public, no compensation beyond that for physical assets should be necessary. Fortunately, one valuable provision of the Radio Act of 1927 and the Communications Act of 1934 still stands; it is the one which makes clear that the frequency channels used by stations are not, and may not become, the property of private stations. Each station licensee signs a statement which recognizes this fact, and agrees that use of this frequency may have to be surrendered whenever the public interest so justifies.

Television and Radio as Electronic Instruments of Democracy

Present mass uses of television and radio might be compared with direct current (DC) concepts and uses of electricity. It was not until alternating current (AC) was put into use that maximum usefulness of electricity was possible. Similarly, reciprocal (back and forth) communication uses are essential if broadcasting's full and potential values are to be realized. Communication is or should be a two-way process; democratic communication must provide for the *back* as well as the *forth* part of the process; the better balanced the two parts, and the more adequate the feed from people to leaders, the better balanced will democratic communication be.

At a time when leaders influence people with all the speed and engulfing power of the electronic media, such devices as the ballot box, the letter to the senator, and the election are woefully anachronistic. The political dialogue, like the other uses of the mass media, has become a monologue.

The flow to people from centers such as New York, Hollywood, and Washington is highly developed. The media do not provide for the flow from people to Washington, New York, and Hollywood, or even to local and state capitals. If the people want to talk to leaders or government today, they must do so via nineteenth-century media; the broadcasters monopolize the twentieth-century electronic instruments. Such feedback as broadcasters urge is, as we have discussed, usually a perversion of what used to be public opinion—inspired telegrams, dictated letters, deluges of threats against reelection, and similar pressure tactics rather than considered suggestions for representatives. Yet true democracy demands the active response of every citizen. Feedback uses of electronic media would permit citizens to react and respond with the speed and directness of the media themselves. With feedback the nature of the media themselves and our concept of communication would change drastically in democracy's favor. The devices now being used by rating firms, whereby viewers may react instantaneously to programs, would make such feedback a reality. The messages or reactions are relayed to a center where they are compiled. Educational broadcasters today use procedures whereby student suggestions or questions, winnowed by responsible staff members, can be handed to professors in studios while they are still engaged in their lesson. Audience study devices now exist, whereby the speaker can see the reaction of people before television sets. The possibilities of these devices have scarcely been explored.

Since most present leaders are sensitive only to market cues, whatever feedback now exists is not heard, or is misunderstood, *or mistranslated into market terms.* But democratic uses do not even need to await new inventions or feedback circuits. One of the simplest ways to begin to establish this service is to establish small, local, publicly owned radio and television stations as part of the federal system proposed. It would be hard to overestimate the opportunity for democratic discussion afforded by a small station—which (like schools and parks) the public of a community knew belonged to *it*. In the exchange of political, social, and economic information, the small radio or television station could reinstitute the function of the town meeting. Sufficient frequencies should be shaken loose from the grip of corporate, sales, and other types of business control to make this public, democratic dialogue a reality. In this dialogue, it is not important who speaks, or how radical or conservative he may be. What *is* essential is the full use of the electronic instruments to arouse and engage the intelligence of the nation.

Feedback would require not only better channels and better use of them, but also individuals in the media and in political leadership positions who are professionally trained to decode and use the messages transmitted. For the cues which will be generated with such "open" uses of television and radio will need to be decoded instantaneously and relayed without delay to the proper men and places.

A public-operated service would try to involve the public as participants instead of audience. Programs would be designed to stimulate the individuals they reach. Viewing television would be a means, not an end in itself as it has now become. It would drive people to *do* rather than to *watch*. And it would provide channels and opportunities for the best of the locally stimulated talent and ideas to find their way into the mainstream of the nation's leadership and decision making. All other purposes of these new electronic frequencies would be subservient to this feedback function.

In many nations provision has been made for feedback service to racial, linguistic, and cultural minorities. Germans, Armenians, Swedes, Italians, Negroes, Hungarians, Indians, and many other minorities in the United States have proud traditions that are now nearly lost. At the local and state levels, a new type of broadcast service could encourage such diversity as still exists in our land in ways which are now ignored by the media. The diversified services of the Canadian Broadcasting Corporation, with its French network, and its four national and seven regional services, illustrate an approach that might be used in this country.

The Creation of a Profession

Basic to any adequate use of the broadcast media, regardless of the system which prevails, is the need to establish a profession, with professional standards, attitudes, and safeguards against violations.

Presently only the engineer of broadcast stations needs to meet specific qualifications: a license from the FCC, based on demonstrated technical knowledge. But qualifications are even more essential for station managers, writers, producers, and other policy and creative individuals who make up and determine what the engineers shall deliver. High professional, character, moral, and educational standards, avoiding only violation of genuine freedom of expression considerations, should be established without delay for all who work in the creative areas of broadcasting. Licenses of stations engaged in overseas broadcasting already presently specify that "competent personnel" will be used. Similar provisions, with equally specific definitions of qualifications, would seem indicated for networks and film companies, much of whose material is exported in film or tape form. Provision for the establishment of a code of ethics for personnel practices, to eliminate the type of record compiled by the networks in blacklisting would also seem desirable.

In probably no other field are specialists overruled by the owners and entrepreneurs to the extent the professionals are in broadcasting. Until a profession is established from within, it appears that the public must establish, through government, minimum protection for the exercise of professional integrity by such individuals as newsmen. Such standards might prohibit the dismissal of a newsman or editor for refusal to violate those professional standards based on freedom of the press, or serving the public interest. Professionals, in this sense, deserve at least as much protection as labor union members. The relation of the owner of a drugstore to his pharmacists, or of a hospital director to the surgeons, is suggestive of the protection needed for professionals. As long as decisions can be made from profit, ownership, or other power motives, rather than from professional judgement alone, there can be no real profession in broadcasting. Newsmen, writers, editors, producers, and others do not enjoy the prerogatives of professionals as long as they can be fired for doing what professional standards require.

As long as network and agency officials, sponsors, or publishers of such publications as *Red Channels* or *Counterattack* may ruin a professional's career, for reasons other than his professional competence, or determine what he may or may not do, the position of the professional is jeopardized. As long as news decisions can be made by network presidents or station owners, there is no secure place for the real professional in broadcasting. At the management level itself certain principles might be laid down to aid in the creation of a profession of broadcasting. They might even be incorporated into the NAB Code. Under such principles management would recognize its lack of authority to dismiss professionals who do their professional duty well, unless there are *other* reasons for dismissal.

What can be done by state or federal government to create professional standards is exemplified in a bill introduced into the California legislature in 1962 for the accreditation of advertisers. It would amend the California business and professional code by establishing a six-member board made up of licensed advertising counselors. Licenses to practice advertising could be revoked, refused, or suspended upon conviction of a felony or for proved dishonesty, deceit, fraud, or gross negligence. License fees for the service would cover the cost of administering the written examinations involved and the other expenses.

Government could provide a very great impetus to professionalism by specifying professional qualifications and a merit basis for all employees of the public-service network recommended above. Codes of ethics for personnel practices, as well as for news and program personnel, would be established by law in such a network. Qualified professionals in creative posts would be required before a station could go on the air. This would be consistent with the present law which already forbids the operation of any transmitter unless supervised by an engineer who meets specific educational and performance standards, as well as providing that such a licensed engineer shall not be required to do anything which would violate his professional standard of ethics.

How far government could go in establishing minimum standards for all workers in broadcasting would need to be carefully considered. To what extent should broadcast organizations be required to provide safeguards, as other factory communities do, against dismissal of employees for arbitrary reasons? Does not regulation or standard-setting need to be extended into these human-rights areas, as well as into the technical and professional areas of engineering, news, writing, programming, and research?

Regulatory Changes Needed

A public-service network would balance the abuses found in commercial services, but it would not necessarily correct them. The slow creation of a profession would gradually establish a proud tradition of integrity in the news and creative fields of broadcasting, but this will take many years. Meanwhile, regulation by government on behalf of the people must be relied upon to keep abuses of the public's confidence and credulity to a minimum.

There is little hope that the present Federal Communications Commission, the Communications Law of 1934, and later amendments to the latter can do what is needed. The national commission study recommended will have a most difficult task: to suggest needed regulatory changes in view of the mounting evidence that the regulatory functions and agencies of government, as well as those related to broadcasting, are now in need of basic revision, if not replacement.

One alternative to the regulatory agency for the supervision and coordination of broadcasting is the creation of a cabinet post. Broadcasting appears to have reached an important enough phase of the nation's life and to present sufficiently continuous problems to deserve consideration for this status. The departmentalization necessary to separate broadcasting from telephone, telegraph, and other utility-type problems might also be simpler under such arrangement. The Department of Health, Education and Welfare provides an illustration of the creation of a government department to meet such new needs. Both the specific regulatory agency responsible for all broadcasting and the administrative agency responsible for the operation of the public network recommended would report to a Department of Communications. In this way a new element might be integrated with our present system and the regulatory function strengthened.

Another alternative is the creation of a single regulatory structure for broadcasting with qualifications and tenure of members similar to that of the Supreme Court. This status would, it is hoped, relieve commissioners of *ex parte* pressures and the political harassments and considerations which now prevail. The permanent status would prevent the sort of thing noted in regulatory agencies today: those commissioners whose terms approach expiration date who suspect or know they will not be reappointed begin to shop around for jobs for the future. Industry itself is the most convenient prospect. This new agency would have the full jurisdictions now held by the FCC, the IRAC, and FTC, and other agencies now involved in broadcasting; its creation would involve other major reorganizations within the Federal government.

One of the most practical specific suggestions for a revision of the present FCC was made in February, 1963, by Leonard Marks, the distinguished former president of the FCC Bar Association. Mr. Marks's report on behalf of the Association recommended "that the adjudicatory and administrative functions of the Federal Communications Commission should be reassigned to a Communications Court and a communications administrator respectively, and that a bipartisan Commission of at least five members should be retained for policy-making and rule-making functions." This proposal would go far toward removing many of the present obstacles which hamper the present FCC.

Currently the FCC works more closely with the FTC than it does, for example, with the United States Information Agency or the State Department. When asked for information on pirateship operation, for example, the FCC had none to offer. Yet the USIA was considerably disturbed, the Voice of America was affected, and the task of the State Department was made much more difficult by the activities of several United States broadcasters in this connection. Should the FCC not be interested in and aware of such activities? Do they not affect these individuals' qualifications as licensees of stations? As we enter a satellite age, is it not likely that the FCC (or the mechanism which succeeds it) may now be teamed most closely with the wrong departments of government, when it has liaison principally with agencies concerned only with advertising or education?

Through the years the FCC has been edged further and further out of policy and program matters into technical and detail matters. Safeguards against weakening of a successor agency would have to be built into the measures which create it.

When present station-license applications (which now deal so predominantly with irrelevant technical details) are replaced, more emphasis might be given to program and policy considerations. The following sample policy and operational questions suggest the reorientation which might be undertaken in license applications. These questions do not claim to be complete:

1. What is the operational and program philosophy of this station? What are the standards and qualifications of the staff which will implement this policy?

2. What steps will be taken to ensure adequate free service in prime time to the principal educational, social, religious, labor, and other community groups, including minority ones?

3. What research, experimentation, and development activities will be instituted, and what professional staff will be used for such efforts?

4. What checks and controls will be maintained over program content of all programs, including those received from syndicates and networks?

5. What use will the station make of its editorial power, and what editorial staff and research facilities are planned for this purpose?

6. How much local and nonlocal news will be broadcast? What criteria of significance will be used? What are the qualifications of the news personnel? What safeguards are proposed against management, sponsor, or other pressures which might affect the professional freedoms and civil rights of such personnel?

7. What specific time and content limitations will be placed on commercials? What pretesting for accuracy of advertising claims will be devised or used to protect the public against deception?

8. How will pressure groups be prevented from keeping fair and valid controversy off the air?

9. What time limitations will be placed on the use of films and other materials from outside sources, and on the amount of time which any one corporation or type of business may purchase or control?

10. For applications for renewal: Include a list of network public-service programs not carried during the past three years, with an explanation and a list of the programs which replaced them.

If regulation by either the FCC or any other agency is to be effective, it must be enforced. The penalty scale now in force is adequate to injure the poor or independent station, but does not significantly injure or deter the powerful offender. A $100-a-day fine, which a large company will write off as a "business expense," is hardly a deterrent to a firm or station making $1,000 or more per day from the censured practice. In some cases such profits have been found to amount to several thousand times the penalties levied. The entire penalty structure for proved fraudulent practices or statements or for misrepresentation should be revised to provide for mandatory imprisonment and loss of license by those listed as ultimately responsible in the license application. Fiscal penalties, where assessed, should be in realistic terms of percentages of income, on the basis of rate cards for the period of the violation, rather than on the basis of flat fees—which are unrealistic when some stations earn less than one hundred-thousandth as much as others.

The validity of suspension of station licenses as penalties should also be reinvestigated. The FCC has hesitated to use this penalty in the past because of the loss to the public of an essential service. With the number of stations now on the air, the FCC should be able to permit the carrying of the principal missed programs by substitute stations under a relaxation of affiliation exclusivity contracts (which are overdue for scrutiny in any case). In view of the duplication in television, radio, and newspaper service in most of the areas of the country, this would seem to be less serious a prospect than the FCC or industry has usually alleged.

What Congress Could Do

There are many steps which Congress could take immediately which would greatly alleviate present malpractices in broadcasting.

One of the first steps which could be taken, and undoubtedly would be if adequate public pressure were brought to bear, is the elimination of the conflict-of-interest problem which now exists in Congress. Those congressmen and senators who are owners, part-owners, or especial beneficiaries of certain stations, networks, and companies with a great stake in such stations or agencies should divest themselves before serving on committees supervising the FCC and broadcasting, or disqualify themselves from voting and participating in broadcast regulation.

A permanent broadcasting committee could be appointed in both the House and Senate to replace the *ad hoc,* sporadic and hit-or-miss, and frequently conflicting and overlapping jurisdictions which now prevail. Such a single, continuing broadcasting committee would have sole and exclusive jurisdiction over broadcasting problems. Members of such a committee could not be whole or part-owners of broadcast properties. Neither could they be whole or part-owners of newspapers and other communications or media firms either owning or operating broadcast properties or competing with them.

Further, Congress should in some manner bar itself from the constant overruling it has exerted to hamper, discredit, and render ineffective the present regulatory agencies. Once regulation is delegated, Congress should not be able to pass legislation which contradicts the regulatory agency.

In view of the way in which public opinion is manufactured by broadcasters, congressmen should weigh more carefully than in the past the petitions, letters, and wires they receive. When petitions of support or endorsement of a station's license renewal or other interests are presented, the station management or originator of the petition might be required to provide a certified explanation of how the signatures were solicited or secured, and whether provision for contrary expression was provided. If such signatures were secured in meetings, who was invited and who was present should also be indicated. Who did *not* sign, as well as who did, should be specified. If signatures or mail were secured in reply to on-the-air appeals, copies of the solicitation, together with evidence of equal time or other evidence of responsible behavior should be required before the station license could be extended or renewed. Such steps on the part of Congress itself would go far toward the restoration of fair evaluation of real public opinion as the basis of democratic government and regulation.

Just as there are certain things which the FCC and the Congress can do while awaiting the results of a national study leading to basic restructuring of American broadcasting, there are several things which the industry itself might do during this interim period.

Some Suggested Steps for Industry

In earlier pages there have been suggestions of steps which broadcasters might take to win back the confidence of the people. Primarily, these include removal of the pall of secrecy which surrounds the economics of broadcasting, divestiture by large industry of conflict-of-interest holdings, and the establishment of professional standards.

To illustrate the types of steps which might be taken in another area, the following are suggested as helpful steps toward ensuring better television for children. Such steps could include:

1. The inclusion of a simple lock on each set manufactured, so that parents could control what young children view.

2. The development of training in the creative and discriminating use of television and radio. This could be done in much the same way as driver training programs are handled in the schools. Manufacturers of equipment could make available to the schools the receivers and materials necessary to conduct such courses in television and radio analysis.

3. Labeling of the programs not appropriate for children's viewing just as warnings on the unfitness of certain drugs for children are included on the bottles.

4. The certification of fitness of films for different age groups; this is done now in most other countries.

5. The inclusion, with each set sold, of a copy of the NAB Code, clearly setting forth the provisions of the Code regarding length and number of commercials and types of unacceptable programs and advertising, together with steps the viewer could and should take when he discovers violations. The procedure used in Sweden might be found useful for study in this connection.

6. Provision for weekly on-the-air discussions of problems of broadcasting in a sort of "letters to the editor" self-criticism program.

7. The creation of a quality-control facility to precheck all programs shown. At the present time, station personnel and management do not see programs until the viewers do. This would involve specialists in various subject disciplines along with the station staff.

8. The publication in magazine form by the broadcast industry, network, or station of its most significant talks, discussions, or documentaries. The best foreign example of this is the *BBC Listener,* whose file includes the classics of the last twenty years. In the United States, WFMT's *Perspective,* published in Chicago, illustrates what one imaginative local station was able to do in magazine form.

The steps which industry could take are numerous. Many of them have already been adopted by enterprising local stations; many of their fine local activities deserve wider adoption—and many such steps might well be listed when regulatory revisions are made.

Effects Research Needed

The present generation was caught defenseless against television and radio. Experts in *offense* (salesmen and market-research people) have gotten ahead of the defense (the education and understanding of the consumer). In most cases when a responsible American industry found that its products or activities were creating serious social problems, at home or abroad, it has taken positive leadership in helping solve those problems. The firm which developed Thalidomide set up a program of $750,000 for additional research into its effects. The automobile industry has helped introduce and has heavily financed driver training courses. When Mrs. Grace Johnson of ABC testified before the Senate Committee to Investigate Juvenile Delinquency, she said that if it could be proved that certain programs were harmful to children they would be eliminated. The comment of the committee was that *the producer,* whether of programs or of food and drugs, has a moral obligation to withhold products from the market until every precaution has been taken to ensure their purity. Such precautions include careful, honest research.

A new basic research program into the long-range effects of television and radio, announced by the French Broadcasting System in late 1961, is an example of what United States broadcasters ought to be doing. Compared with such a program, the research projects of the broadcast industry in the United States are nothing more than token public-relations efforts, which often look suspiciously like efforts to cover up, rather than reveal, basic problems and facts. United States industry studies continue to prove that all is well, while mental-health and physical-fitness records and research in thirty or more countries prove the opposite. Most recent studies do not see the light of day if they are very critical. Portions of those studies which are published, like the British Himmelweit Studies, are carefully selected excerpts which conceal the critical or disturbing findings.

British film research scholar Mary Field has assisted in setting up research programs in numerous countries. She has suggested cooperation in international research. This would include research projects to be carried out nationally and internationally; studies with children, primitive peoples, and underdeveloped countries; and international exchanges of the results of such research. This international cooperation has already been started, and in many cases without including the United States. It is showing signs of success—at the Venice Conference in 1950 thirteen countries agreed to cooperate. The British film and broadcast industries promoted it most aggressively; much of the early expense was borne by the J. Arthur Rank Organisation. In this worldwide concern and effort, United States leadership has been notably absent.

In ten or more countries the film industry and the broadcast system, sometimes jointly, have provided full cooperation for studies of broadcasting's effects on children, by infrared photography, the measurement of pulse and respiration, tests and depth interviews, and scores of other approaches.

Research is essential if a station is to operate in the public interest. The ability to cary on such research should be a requirement for securing a station license, or at least a prerequisite to renewal. This requirement might best be made a condition required of networks, just as quality control and inspection measures are required of producers of food and drugs.

Research scholars have for years been calling on the industry for an adequate program of basic research into the long-range effects of the broadcast media. The sums spent on market research in the United States are already very large. The total has been estimated at between 10 and 20 million dollars per year. One of the broadcast research devices with associated equipment, the Nielsen Audimeter alone, is reported to have cost over 9 million dollars. In comparison with this, the $85,000 to $95,000 allocated to research by the National Association of Broadcasters is certainly inadequate.

Many congressional commitees have already called for such

research. The report of the Subcommittee to Investigate Juvenile Delinquency (of the Senate Committee on the Judiciary) in 1956 suggested that the National Science Foundation (or some such existing group) consider extending its activities into the area of broadcast-program effects, and noted the confusion resulting from the present uncoordinated efforts of industry and nonindustry studies. Such suggestions should provide useful material for consideration by the special national commission suggested. Perhaps a new National Communications Research Council needs to be created. In any case, several decisions need to be made: What research should be required by industry itself? What part of it, or its reporting, should be carried out by or on behalf of the government itself? And how might such a research effort best be organized and coordinated?

The relationship of television to crime, delinquency, and mental and physical fitness needs to be studied—also: What is television doing that should be left to radio, or that radio could do best? Should television and radio be separately owned and operated, and separately regulated? In what respects do their effects appear to be opposite? Is it true that radio is a "hot" medium, tending to *arouse* people, in the way Hitler and Mussolini used it, whereas television is a "cold" medium, likely to inactivate its audience? How can such unique qualities, if they exist, best be used and balanced? Should both media be governed by the same rules and regulations?

What is the effect of a medium like television on other media such as newspapers and magazines? What would this effect be if they were genuinely competitive?

What are the effects of broadcasting on the arts and humanities? This subject is a broad one: it would require analyses by qualified consultants in the areas of music, the graphic arts, poetry and fiction, and the other arts and humanities. What are some of the effects, for instance, of the millions of dollars devoted to the composition, orchestration, and performance of singing commercials?

It is possible that cooperative studies of broadcasting in the arts might well be launched by the recently organized National Cultural Center. Such a study might well be commissioned by the national commission type of study recommended here. This cooperative approach, using existing organizations, might well be used also in the study and development of other needed research in the broadcast media.

Even such matters as maximum recommended dosages of television should be investigated. Is it in the overall public interest for television to operate full time? And what proportion of the time should be allowed for advertising as balanced against other uses? The FCC already limits the *minimum* hours a station may operate and still retain its license. It also limits the hours of operation of limited-time, shared-time, and daytime-only radio stations, specifying maximum limits for them. Considering the number of hours television now fills, Eric Sevareid once said: "It's surprising there's even enough mediocrity to go around." Should quality as well as quantity standards be set? As discussed earlier, other nations have limited the number of acts of violence that may be shown on television, or the frequency and kind of weapons and techniques permitted to be shown. How can an exchange of research with other countries be facilitated? Such are some of the many other questions which need to be investigated. A massive effort is needed.

The Radio Act of 1927 and the Communications Act of 1934 charged the Federal Radio Commission, and the Federal Communications Commission, with the development and encouragement of techniques that would result in greater competition and variety in the uses of the frequency spectrum. How much use should be made of the spectrum for broadcasting, and how much for point-to-point and people-to-leaders communication, or for narrowcasting (the use of radio and TV for minority services)?

Jerome B. Wisner, former director of MIT's electronic research laboratory, who has also served as special science adviser to the President, has pointed out that only in the UHF bands can enough frequencies be found for an adequate national service. Ways of making this shift as painlessly as possible need to be devised. More recently, Dr. Wisner and others have noted that the development of the UHF band, and the continuance of study into present bands, is not enough. Lasers and masers as alternatives to present frequency uses need to be considered; and their introduction should not be determined solely on the basis of how profitable they will be to those who control patents on them. The reassessment needed must take into account all the developments of the past twenty or so years, which certain vested interests have often found it most profitable not to promote. With its own engineering staff, the FCC or its successor agency, should be investigating the uses of higher-powered transmitting tubes; better circuitry and components; the redesign of transmitters and receivers in terms of such new developments as transistors; and the development of the equipment, frequency uses, and techniques necessary to implement the instantaneous feedback suggested earlier.

Attention should be given also to the desirability and means of creating *small* communications systems: low-cost printing presses and facsimile printers, low-power and low-cost transmitters, and low-cost wire communications. For it is in small clusters of low-power facilities that the democratic uses of these media will find maximum realization. In such uses, facsimile and other currently neglected techniques could be applied.

With access to lasers, satellites, low-power transmission, and the score of other new developments now available, what technological breakthroughs are not now possible? Surely all the present technical possibilities pose many new uses of broadcasting; the people may *participate* in radio and television rather than merely view or listen; criticism, mutual respect, and the necessary (and democratic) give and take will be possible as never before. After years of "flying blind" we need to know—instead of conjecture about—the many kinds of narrow and specific as well as broad services which electronic media can provide.

Conclusion

The solution to America's broadcasting problems will be arduous and complex. Many of the suggestions offered here are made as an agenda for national discussion, rather than as definitive proposals. Hopefully, the drastic changes necessary in broadcasting can be made before the full effects of satellite and color broadcasting are added to the present ones. The anachronistic and obsolete structure, controls, leadership, orientation, and techniques of today are inadequate in our atomic and space age. Their wise replacement, urgent as it is, will require a careful and responsible national effort.

So far broadcasting has been controlled instead of released. It needs to be unshackled and used in other new ways by scores of different kinds of groups. No country should be better able than the United States to show how the instruments of television and radio can help man adjust to the machine age and cope with the many tyrannies which technology imposes. Since the United States bears a heavy responsibility for the spread of technology around the world, it has an obligation to lead also in making sure that human values survive under it. Broadcast instruments, wisely used, can create a forum of the nations. There are certain forces in any given culture which must be controlled. Broadcasting, it is increasingly evident, is such a force. Like education, which is too important to leave only to the educators, broadcasting must become a subject of *national* interest and constructive thinking. At various times in history the American people have seen the need for establishing countervailing forces by government on behalf of the total or larger welfare, opposed to the welfare of only specialized segments of our society. It is hoped that once the need is recognized for such an effort in broadcasting, it will be supported and approved, not as an act of retaliation or anger against present or past leadership, but as a cooperative act of public responsibility. These recommendations are submitted in that spirit.

Over three hundred years ago John Milton said that the print media must be freed from oppressive controls by either the church or the state, which were then the only institutions large enough to threaten freedom. In November of 1644 he wrote in his *Areopagitica:* "Methinks I see in my mind a noble and puissant nation rousing herself like a strong man after sleep, and shaking her invincible locks." [1] Will America arouse herself about broadcasting in time?

A

Edward R. Murrow Address to the Radio and Television
News Directors' Association Convention,
Chicago, Illinois, October 15, 1958
(Reprinted here with Mr. Murrow's permission)

This just might do nobody any good. At the end of this dis-
course a few people may accuse this reporter of fouling his own
comfortable nest; and your organization may be accused of having given hospitality to heretical and even dangerous thoughts.

But the elaborate structure of networks, advertising agencies
and sponsors will not be shaken or altered. It is my desire if not
my duty to try to talk to you journeymen with some candor about
what is happening to radio and television in this generous and
capacious land.

I have no technical advice or counsel to offer those of you
who labor in this vineyard that produces words and pictures. You
will forgive me for not telling you that the instruments with
which you work are miraculous; that your responsibility is un-
precedented; or that your aspirations are frequently frustrated.
It is not necessary to remind you of the fact that your voice is
amplified to the degree where it reaches from one end of the
country to the other does not confer upon you greater wisdom or
understanding than you possessed when your voice reached only
from one end of the bar to the other. All of these things you
know.

You should also know at the outset that, in the manner of witnesses before Congressional Committees, I appear here voluntarily—by invitation—that I am an employee of the Columbia Broadcasting System—that I am neither an officer nor a director of that Corporation—and that these remarks are of a "do-it-yourself" nature. If what I have to say is responsible, then I alone am responsible for the saying of it. Seeking neither approbation from my employers, nor new sponsors, nor acclaim from the critics of radio and television, I cannot well be disappointed. Believing that potentially the commercial system of broadcasting as practiced in this country is the best and freest yet devised, I have decided to express my concern about what I believe to be happening to radio and television. These instruments have been good to me beyond my due. There exists in my mind no reasonable grounds for personal complaint. I have no feud, either with my employers, any sponsors, or with the professional critics of radio and television. But I am seized with an abiding fear regarding what these two instruments are doing to our society, our culture and our heritage.

Our history will be what we make it. And if there are any historians about fifty or a hundred years from now, and there should be preserved the kinescopes for one week of all three networks, they will there find recorded in black-and-white, or color, evidence of decadence, escapism and insulation from the realities of the world in which we live. I invite your attention to the television schedules of all networks between the hours of eight and eleven p.m. Eastern Time. Here you will find only fleeting and spasmodic reference to the fact that this nation is in mortal danger. There are, it is true, occasional informative programs presented in that intellectual ghetto on Sunday afternoons. But during the daily peak viewing periods, television in the main insulates us from the realities of the world in which we live. If this state of affairs continues, we may alter an advertising slogan to read: "Look Now, Pay Later." For surely we shall pay for using this most powerful instrument of communication to insulate the citizenry from the hard and demanding realities which must be faced if we are to survive. I mean the word—survive—literally. If there were to be a competition in indifference, or perhaps in insulation from reality, then Nero and his fiddle, Chamberlain and his umbrella, could not find a place on an early-afternoon sustaining show. If Hollywood were to run out of Indians, the program schedules would be mangled beyond all recognition. Then, some courageous soul with a small budget might be able to do a documentary telling what, in fact, we have done—and are still doing—to the Indians in this country. But that would be unpleasant. And we must at all costs shield the sensitive citizens from anything that is unpleasant.

I am entirely persuaded that the American public is more reasonable, restrained and more mature than most of our industry's program planners believe. Their fear of controversy is not warranted by the evidence. I have reason to know, as do many of you, that when the evidence on a controversial subject is fairly and calmly presented, the public recognizes it for what it is—an effort to illuminate rather than to agitate.

Several years ago, when we undertook to do a program on Egypt and Israel, well-meaning, experienced and intelligent friends shook their heads and said: "This you cannot do—you will be handed your head—it is an emotion-packed controversy, and there is no room for reason in it." We did the program. Zionists, anti-Zionists, the friends of the Middle East, Egyptian and Israeli officials said, with a faint note of surprise: "It was a fair count. The information was there. We have no complaints."

Our experience was similar with two half-hour programs dealing with cigarette smoking and lung cancer. Both the medical profession and the tobacco industry co-operated in a rather wary fashion. But in the end of the day they were both reasonably content. The subject of radio-active fall-out and the banning of nuclear tests was and is highly controversial. But according to what little evidence there is, viewers were prepared to listen to both sides with reason and restraint. This is not said to claim any special or unusual competence in the presentation of controversial subjects, but rather to indicate that timidity in these areas is not warranted—by the evidence.

Recently, network spokesmen have been disposed to complain that the professional critics of television have been "rather beastly." There have been hints that somehow competition for the advertising dollar has caused the critics of print to gang up on television and radio. This reporter has no desire to defend the critics. They have space in which to do that on their own behalf. But it remains a fact that the newspapers and magazines are the only instruments of mass communication which remain free from sustained and regular critical comment. If the network spokesmen are so anguished about what appears in print, let them come forth and engage in a little sustained and regular

comment regarding newspapers and magazines. It is an ancient
and sad fact that most people in network television, and radio,
have an exaggerated regard for what appears in print. And there
have been cases where executives have refused to make even
private comment on a program for which they were responsible,
until they had read the reviews in print. This is hardly an exhibition of confidence.

The oldest excuse of the networks for their timidity is their
youth. Their spokesmen say: "We are young; we have not developed the traditions, nor acquired the experience of the older
media." If they but knew it, they are building those traditions,
creating those precedents every day. Each time they yield to a
voice from Washington or any political pressure, each time they
eliminate something that might offend some section of the community, they are creating their own body of precedent and tradition. They are, in fact, not content to be "half safe."

Nowhere is this better illustrated than by the fact that the
Chairman of the Federal Communications Commission publicly
prods broadcasters to engage in their legal right to editorialize.
Of course, to undertake an editorial policy, overt and clearly
labelled, and obviously unsponsored, requires a station or a network to be responsible. Most stations today probably do not have
the manpower to assume this responsibility, but the manpower
could be recruited. Editorials would not be profitable; if they
had a cutting edge they might even offend. It is much easier,
much less troublesome to use the money-making machine of television and radio merely as a conduit through which to channel
anything that is not libelous, obscene or defamatory. In that
way one has the illusion of power without responsibility.

So far as radio—that most satisfying and rewarding instrument—is concerned, the diagnosis of its difficulties is rather easy.
And obviously I speak only of news and information. In order
to progress it need only go backward. To the time when singing
commercials were not allowed on news reports, when there was
no middle commercial in a fifteen-minute news report; when
radio was rather proud, alert and fast. I recently asked a network
official: Why this great rash of five-minute news reports (including
three commercials) on week ends? He replied: "Because that
seems to be the only thing we can sell."

In this kind of complex and confusing world, you can't tell
very much about the *why* of the news in broadcast where only
three minutes is available for news. The only man who could do

that was Elmer Davis, and his kind aren't about any more. If radio news is to be regarded as a commodity, only acceptable when saleable, and only when packaged to fit the advertising appropriation of a sponsor, then I don't care what you call it—I say it isn't news.

My memory also goes back to the time when the fear of a slight reduction in business did not result in an immediate cutback in bodies in the News and Public Affairs Department, at a time when network profits had just reached an all-time high. We would all agree, I think, that whether on a station or a network, the stapling machine is a poor substitute for a newsroom typewriter.

One of the minor tragedies of television news and information is that the networks will not even defend their vital interests. When my employer, C.B.S., through a combination of enterprise and good luck, did an interview with Nikita Khrushchev, the President uttered a few ill-chosen, uninformed words on the subject, and the network practically apologized. This produced a rarity. Many newspapers defended the C.B.S. right to produce the program and commended it for initiative. But the other networks remained silent.

Likewise, when John Foster Dulles, by personal decree, banned American journalists from going to Communist China, and subsequently offered contradictory explanations. For his fiat the networks entered only a mild protest. Then they apparently forgot the unpleasantness. Can it be that this national industry is content to serve the public interest only with the trickle of news that comes out of Hong Kong? To leave its viewers in ignorance of the cataclysmic changes that are occurring in a nation of six hundred million people? I have no illusions about the difficulties of reporting from a dictatorship; but our British and French allies have been better served—in their public interest —with some very useful information from their reporters in Communist China.

One of the basic troubles with radio and television news is that both instruments have grown up as an incompatible combination of show business, advertising and news. Each of the three is a rather bizarre and demanding profession. And when you get all three under one roof, the dust never settles. The top management of the networks, with a few notable exceptions, has been trained in advertising, research, sales or show business. But by the nature of the corporate structure, they also make the final and crucial decisions having to do with news and public affairs. Frequently they have neither the time nor the competence to do this. It is not easy for the same small group of men to decide whether to buy a new station for millions of dollars, build a new building, alter the rate card, buy a new Western, sell a soap opera, decide what defensive line to take in connection with the latest Congressional inquiry, how much money to spend on promoting a new program, what addition or deletions should be made in the existing covey or clutch of vice presidents, and at the same time—frequently on the same long day—to give mature, thoughtful consideration to the manifold problems that confront those who are charged with the responsibility for news and public affairs.

Sometimes there is a clash between the public interest and the corporate interest. A telephone call, or a letter from the proper quarter in Washington is treated rather more seriously than a communication from an irate but not politically potent viewer. It is tempting enough to give away a little air time for frequently irresponsible and unwarranted utterances, in an effort to temper the wind of criticism.

Upon occasion, economics and editorial judgment are in conflict. And there is no law which says that dollars will be defeated by duty. Not so long ago the President of the United States delivered a television address to the nation. He was discoursing on the possibility or probability of war between this nation and the Soviet Union and Communist China—a reasonably compelling subject. Two networks—C.B.S. and N.B.C.—delayed that broadcast for an hour and fifteen minutes. If this decision was dictated by anything other than financial reasons, the networks didn't deign to explain those reasons. That hour-and-fifteen-minute delay, by the way, is about twice the time required for an I.C.B.M. to travel from the Soviet Union to major targets in the United States. It is difficult to believe that this decision was made by men who love, respect and understand news.

So far I have been dealing largely with the deficit side of the ledger, and the items could be expanded. But I have said, and I believe, that potentially, we have in this country a free enterprise system of radio and television which is superior to any other. But to achieve its promise, it must be both free and enterprising. There is no suggestion here that networks or individual stations should operate as philanthropies. But I can find nothing in the Bill of Rights or the Communications Act which says that they must increase their net profits each year, lest the republic collapse. I do not suggest that news and information should be subsidized by foundations or private subscriptions. I am aware that the networks have expended, and are expending very considerable sums of money on public affairs programs from which they cannot hope to receive any financial reward. I have had the privilege at C.B.S. of presiding over a considerable number of such programs. I testify, and am able to stand here and say that I have never had a program turned down by my superiors because of the money it would cost.

But we all know that you cannot reach the potential maximum audience in marginal time, with a sustaining program. This is so because so many stations on the network—any network—will decline to carry it. Every licensee who applies for a grant to operate in the public interest, convenience and necessity, makes certain promises as to what he will do in terms of program content. Many recipients of licenses have, in blunt language, welshed on those promises. The money-making machine somehow blunts their memories. The only remedy for this is closer inspection and punitive action by the F.C.C. But in view of many this would come perilously close to supervision of program content by a federal agency.

So it seems that we cannot rely on philanthropic support or Foundation subsidies, we cannot follow the "sustaining route," the networks cannot pay all the freight, and the F.C.C. cannot or will not discipline those who abuse the facilities that belong to the public.

What, then, is the answer? Do we merely stay in our comfortable nests, concluding that the obligation of these instruments has been discharged when we work at the job of informing the public for a minimum of time? Or do we believe that the preservation of the republic is a seven-day-a-week job, demanding more awareness, better skills, and more perseverance than we have yet contemplated?

I am frightened by the imbalance, the constant striving to reach the largest possible audience for everything; by the absence of a sustained study of the state of the nation. Heywood Broun once said: "No body politic is healthy until it begins to itch." I would like television to produce some itching pills rather than this endless outpouring of tranquilizers. It can be done. Maybe it won't be, but it could. Let us not shoot the wrong piano player. Do not be deluded into believing that the titular heads of the networks control what appears on their networks. They all have better taste. All are responsible to stockholders, and in my experience all are honorable men. But they must schedule what they can sell in the public market. And this brings us to the nub of the question.

In one sense it rather revolves around the phrase heard frequently along Madison Avenue: "The Corporate Image." I am not precisely sure what this phrase means, but I would imagine that it reflects a desire on the part of the corporations who pay the advertising bills, to have the public imagine, or believe, that they are not merely bodies with no souls, panting in pursuit of elusive dollars. They would like us to believe that they can distinguish between the public good and the private or corporate gain. So the question is this: Are the big corporations who pay the freight for radio and television programs wise to use that time *exclusively* for the sale of goods and services? Is it in their own interest and that of the stockholders so to do? The sponsor of an hour's television program is not buying merely the six minutes devoted to his commercial message. He is determining, within broad limits, the sum total of the impact of the entire hour. If he always, invariably, reaches for the largest possible audience then this process of insulation, of escape from reality, will continue to be massively financed, and its apologists will continue to make winsome speeches about giving the public what it wants, or "letting the public decide."

I refuse to believe that the presidents and chairman of the boards of these big corporations want their "corporate image" to consist exclusively of a solemn voice in an echo chamber, or a pretty girl opening the door of a refrigerator, or a horse that talks. They want something better, and on occasion some of them have demonstrated it. But most of the men whose legal and moral responsibility it is to spend the stockholders' money for advertising, are removed from the realities of the mass media by five, six, or a dozen contraceptive layers of vice presidents, public relations counsel and advertising agencies. Their business is to sell goods, and the competition is pretty tough.

But this nation is now in competition with malignant forces of evil who are using every instrument at their command to empty the minds of their subjects, and fill those minds with slogans, determination, and faith in the future. If we go on as we are, we are protecting the mind of the American public from any real contact with the menacing world that squeezes in upon us. We are engaged in a great experiment to discover whether a free public opinion can devise and direct methods of managing the affairs of the nation. We may fail. But we are handicapping ourselves needlessly. Let us have a little competition. Not only in selling soap, cigarettes and automobiles, but in informing a troubled, apprehensive but receptive public. Why should not each of the twenty or thirty big corporations which dominate radio and television, decide that they will give us one or two of their regularly scheduled programs each year, turn the time over to the networks, and say in effect: "This is a tiny tithe, just a little bit of our profits. On this particular night we aren't going to try to sell cigarettes or automobiles; this is merely a gesture to indicate our belief in the importance of ideas." The networks should, and I think would, pay for the cost of producing the program. The advertiser, the sponsor, would get name credit, but would have nothing to do with the content of the program. Would this blemish the corporate image? Would the stockholders object? I think not. For if the premise upon which our pluralistic society rests—which as I understand it is, that if the people are given sufficient undiluted information, they will then somehow, even after long, sober second thoughts reach the right decision. If that premise is wrong, then not only the corporate image but the corporations are done for.

There used to be an old phrase in this country, employed when someone talked too much. It was: "Go hire a hall." Under this proposal the sponsor would have hired the hall; he has bought the time; the local station operator, no matter how indifferent, is going to carry the program—he has to. Then it's up to the networks to fill the hall. I am not here talking about editorializing, but about straightaway exposition as direct, unadorned and impartial, as fallible human beings can make it. Just once in a while let us exalt the importance of ideas and information. Let us dream to the extent of saying that on a given Sunday night the time normally occupied by Ed Sullivan is given over to a clinical survey of the state of American education, and a week or two later the time normally used by Steve Allen is devoted to a thorough-going study of American policy in the Middle East. Would the corporate image of their respective sponsors be damaged? Would the stockholders rise up in their wrath and com-

plain? Would anything happen other than that a few million
people would have received a little illumination on subjects that
may well determine the future of this country, and therefore the
future of the corporations? This method would also provide real
competition between the networks as to which could outdo the
others in the palatable presentation of information. It would
provide an outlet for the young men of skill, and there are some
even of dedication, who would like to do something other than
devise methods of insulating while selling.

There may be other and simpler methods of utilizing these
instruments of radio and television in the interests of a free society. But I know of none that could be so easily accomplished
inside the framework of the existing commercial system. I don't
know how you would measure the success or failure of a given
program. And it would be hard to prove the magnitude of the
benefit accruing to the corporation which gave up one night of a
variety or quiz show in order that the network might marshal its
skills to do a thorough-going job on the present status of NATO,
or plans for controlling nuclear tests. But I would reckon that
the president, and indeed the majority of shareholders of the
corporation who sponsored such a venture would feel just a little
bit better about the corporation and the country.

It may be that the present system, with no modifications and
no experiments, can survive. Perhaps the money-making machine
has some kind of built-in perpetual motion, but I do not think
so. To a very considerable extent the media of mass communications in a given country reflects the political, economic and
social climate in which it flourishes. That is the reason ours
differs from the British and French, or the Russian and Chinese.
We are currently wealthy, fat, comfortable and complacent. We
have currently a built-in allergy to unpleasant or disturbing information. Our mass media reflect this. But unless we get up
off our fat surpluses and recognize that television in the main is
being used to distract, delude, amuse and insulate us, then television and those who finance it, those who look at it and those
who work at it, may see a totally different picture too late.

I do not advocate that we turn the television into a twenty-
seven-inch wailing wall, where long-hairs constantly moan about
the state of our culture and our defense. But I would just like
to see it reflect occasionally—the hard, unyielding realities of the
world in which we live. I would like to see it done inside the

exciting framework, and I would like to see the doing of it redound to the credit of those who finance and program it. Measure the results by Nielsen, Trendex or Silex—it doesn't matter, the main thing is to try. The responsibility can be easily placed, in spite of all the mouthings about giving the public what it wants. It rests on big business, and on big television, and it rests at the top. Responsibility is not something that can be assigned or delegated. And it promises its own reward: good business and good television.

Perhaps no one will do anything about it. I have ventured to outline it against a background of citicism that may have been too harsh, only because I could think of nothing better.

Someone once said—I think it was Max Eastman—that: "That publisher serves his advertiser best who best serves his readers." I cannot believe that radio and television, or the corporations that finance the programs, are serving well or truly their viewers or listeners, or themselves.

I began by saying that our history will be what we make it. If we go on as we are, then history will take its revenge, and retribution will not limp in catching up with us.

We are to a large extent an imitative society. If one or two or three corporations would undertake to devote just a small fraction of their advertising appropriation along the lines that I have suggested, the procedure would grow by contagion, the economic burden would be bearable, and there might ensue a most exciting adventure—exposure to ideas, and the bringing of reality into the homes of the nation.

To those who say: People wouldn't look, they wouldn't be interested, they're too complacent, indifferent and insulated— I can only reply: There is, in one reporter's opinion, considerable evidence against that contention. But even if they are right, what have they got to lose? Because if they are right, and this instrument is good for nothing but to entertain, amuse and insulate, then the tube is flickering now and we will soon see that the whole struggle is lost.

This instrument can teach, it can illuminate; yes, and it can even inspire. But it can do so only to the extent that humans are determined to use it to those ends. Otherwise it is merely wires and lights in a box. There is a great and perhaps decisive battle to be fought against ignorance, intolerance and indifference. This weapon of television could be useful.

Stonewall Jackson, who knew something about the use of weapons, is reported to have said: "When war comes, you must draw the sword and throw away the scabbard." The trouble with television is that it is rusting in the scabbard—during a battle for survival.

B

Excerpts from *Congressional Record* for Saturday, June 9, 1934

[AFTER SENATE AND HOUSE CONFERENCES ON SENATE BILL S.3285 (THE SO-CALLED DILL BILL) AND HOUSE BILL HR. #7716 (THE SO-CALLED RAYBURN BILL), THE RESULTING COMPROMISE BILL WAS BROUGHT TO THE FLOOR OF THE HOUSE. THE MANAGERS ON THE PART OF THE HOUSE (SAM RAYBURN, CLARENCE LEA, CARL E. MAPES AND CHARLES A. WOLVERTON) BRIEFLY EXPLAINED THE COMPROMISE MADE IN RECONCILING SENATE AND HOUSE VERSIONS OF THE LEGISLATION REQUESTED BY PRESIDENT F. D. ROOSEVELT FOR THE CREATION OF A NEW REGULATORY AGENCY, REPLACING EARLIER PROVISIONS DATING FROM 1927. THE FOLLOWING EX-CERPTS ARE TAKEN FROM THE CONGRES-SIONAL RECORD OF HOUSE DEBATES FROM JUNE 9, 1934, 73RD CONGRESS, SECOND SESSION, PP. 10988–10995.]

MR. (Schuyler O.) BLAND (Democrat, Virginia): . . . The Senate has undertaken to repeal the Radio Act of 1927. . . . They

239

do the useless or futile thing, so far as radio is concerned, of repealing the law and then reenacting the same law. Now, the question might arise, What difference does it make? It may make a most material difference in a new set-up. . . . I mean no reflection on the distinguished gentlemen of the Interstate and Foreign Commerce Committee but they conceded themselves upon this floor one week ago that they knew nothing about radio, and they said that they believed the wise thing to do—and it was a wise judgment on their part . . . was to set up a communications commission which could study the law and find out just what ought to be done. . . . I submit that in as delicate an art as the radio art, and with its effect upon the public and the public interests involved, the conference report ought to be rejected. . . . They did not have the time to go to the bottom of this matter; they had most important matters to consider. . . .

MR. (Frederick R.) LEHLBACH (Republican, New Jersey): Mr. Speaker, we have a situation where we are passing most important legislation on the say-so of the Senate which has never been considered by the House of Representatives. We have been called rubber stamps of the Government, but we have never passed twenty pages of a radio act, repealing the existing radio law on the recommendation of the Senate without a single Member of the House who knows anything about radio giving the slightest consideration to it. . . . Why is the House asked to accept the Senate say-so in this radio legislation? Why should not the House . . . send back the conference report and eliminate the substantive radio act; as my chairman from Virginia says, let the Communications Committee study the law and recommend changes in the law that are desirable to be made, and let the House committee having jurisdiction consider that question and report with respect thereto and, after debate on the floor, enact the law as the House in its dignity ought to do? (Applause.). . . .

MR. (Louis T.) McFADDEN (Republican, Pennsylvania): Mr. Speaker, this legislation comes as a result of a message by the President to the Congress. Simultaneously with the delivery of that message there was delivered to the Committee on Interstate and Foreign Commerce, of the House, and a similar committee of the Senate, a draft of the particular legislation which was recommended in the message. The Interstate and Foreign Commerce Committee of the House had never had jurisdiction over the question of radio. The Merchant Marine, Radio, and Fisheries Committee had, and has grown up with the growth of radio in the United States. Under this direction in the message of the President, jurisdiction for the consideration of this message was transferred to the Interstate and Foreign Commerce Committee, who were engaged to the full limit in the consideration of other measures that were being forced through the House under great pressure—the securities bill, railroad legislation, and stock-exchange control legislation. It is only fair to say that which we all know, and the members of that committee know, that they did not have time to fairly consider this bill. . . .

. . . So here we find ourselves in the predicament of considering one of the most important bills that could possibly come before this House, without any consideration on the part of the House, putting it through here in a few minutes. It is a fair example of what we may expect under the administration of this communications law, where we have consolidated all matters of communication in one commission. That applies to telephone and telegraph, radio, national and international, one of the most important parts of government. I say to the House that which I believe: that this bill was written, or at least the controlling and important part of it, in conformity with the wishes of the people who control this industry, and propose to control it as a monopoly, to control public sentiment in the United States, to control it now immediately for political purposes. . . .

MR. LEHLBACH: That is what we are complaining about. We are enacting a law dictated by the chairman which we have never considered. . . .

MR. (Robert) RAMSPECK (Democrat, Georgia): . . . Mr. Speaker, I join with my colleague from Virginia (Mr. Bland) and my colleague from New Jersey (Mr. Lehlbach) in opposition to this conference report. Every Member of this House, perhaps, has in his district a radio station or several of them. Millions of dollars have been invested in those plants and we are proposing here in this conference report to wipe out the law under which those stations have been established, or to wipe out everything that has gone heretofore and reenact it under an act which we are asked to pass here in a few minutes and which we have had no opportunity to examine. No committee of the House which has given study or thought to radio legislation has had an opportunity to consider this matter.

It seems to me it is unwise, it is unjust to our people back home, to enact legislation of such far-reaching effect in this matter. . . . I think if we are going to reenact the radio law, which

I think is unnecessary, it ought to be considered by the committee of this House which has jurisdiction of it, upon which committee there are Members who have given years of study to that subject. For that reason I expect to vote against the adoption of this conference report, and I hope it will be rejected. (Applause). . . .

MR. LEHLBACH: . . . Has any Member of the House conference committee examined the old law and the new law that is proposed in order to ascertain just what differences there may be, and if they have not, has any other Member of the House who knows anything about it had that opportunity?

MR. (Carl E.) MAPES (Republican, Michigan): Of course, the conferees went over every provision of this new matter and passed upon it, exercising their best judgment in regard to it. Our judgment may not have been as good as the judgment of the members of the Radio Committee would have been, but we were confronted with this legislation and had to exercise such judgment as we had.

MR. LEHLBACH: How could reading a new bill give you any idea how it changed the old law that you did not know and had not read?

THE SPEAKER (Henry T. Rainey, Democrat, Illinois): The time of the gentleman from Michigan [Mr. Mapes] has again expired.

MR. (Albert C.) WILLFORD (Democrat, Iowa): Mr. Speaker, as a member of the Committee on Merchant Marine, Radio, and Fisheries, I have listened while this bill has been both cussed and discussed over quite a period of time. . . . I believe . . . that more time should be given to a thorough study and consideration of this subject. We had before the committee men who had spent their entire time since its discovery in the study of radio . . .

MR. LEHLBACH: Does not the gentleman (Mr. Blanton) realize that a revision of existing radio laws in the next Congress, desirable as it may be, will be precluded if we enact a new radio law by accepting this conference report?

MR. (Thomas L.) BLANTON (Democrat, Texas): Nothing will be precluded, and everything will be possible, if a majority of the Members of this House in the next Congress set their heads and concertedly work together with a determined purpose to fairly and justly distribute and reallocate stations, wave lengths, channels and power. All obstacles can be overcome, and anything they want done can be done by a determined majority. . . . Some of the big monopoly-controlled radio stations persecute men in public life, whose actions they cannot control, just as monopoly-controlled newspapers persecute them. If it were not for the *Congressional Record* the big radio and the big press could ruin any man in Congress. They could misrepresent his every act. Were it not for the *Congressional Record,* the big press would defeat and put out of Congress every man it could not control. . . .

MR. (Sam) RAYBURN (Democrat, Texas): Mr. Speaker, I move the previous question on the adoption of the conference report.

(The previous question was ordered.)

THE SPEAKER: The question is on the adoption of the conference report.

(The question was taken; and on a division [demanded by Mr. Ramspeck and Mr. Lehlbach] there were—ayes 58, noes 40.)

MR. RAMSPECK: Mr. Speaker, I object to the vote on the ground there is not a quorum present, and I make the point of order that a quorum is not present.

MR. (Joseph W.) MARTIN (Republican) of Massachusetts: May I ask the majority leader if this is the last bill we are to take up today?

MR. RAMSPECK: Mr. Speaker, I withdraw the point of no quorum.

(So the conference report was agreed to. A motion to reconsider was laid on the table.)

C

J. Edgar Hoover's May 1, 1958 message "To All Law Enforcement Officials." This was published as Mr. Hoover's introductory statement to the May 1, 1958, *FBI Law Enforcement Bulletin* (Used with Mr. Hoover's kind permission).

As a law enforcement officer and as an American citizen, I feel duty-bound to speak out against a dangerous trend which is manifesting itself in the field of film and television entertainment. In the face of the Nation's terrifying juvenile crime wave, we are threatened with a flood of movies and television presentations which flaunt indecency and applaud lawlessness. Not since the days when thousands filed past the bier of the infamous John Dillinger and made his home a virtual shrine have we witnessed such a brazen affront to our national conscience.

As an illustration, two brothers, aged 10 and 12, who a few weeks ago terrorized a town in Oklahoma in a shooting spree that left one man dead and two others wounded, told the police they got the idea from watching television and movie crime stories.

There are, of course, many responsible leaders in the motion picture and television industries who dedicate their efforts to producing wholesome entertainment and to upholding the worthwhile principles of established production codes of ethics. Again and again, they serve the best interests of law enforcement and the public welfare by genuine portrayals of criminals in their true light—wretched, unglamorous leeches who bring nothing but deg-

244

radation to themselves and human suffering to their fellow men. Regrettably, however, there are some unscrupulous individuals who value money above morals, and whose actions should be exposed in the searching klieg light of public opinion. In their lust for bigger and bigger profits, they glorify violence, glamorize corruption, and picture criminals as heroes for youth to idolize.

One movie code official recently declared that the number of murders in a film is not particularly important—only the reason why the criminal committed a murder is of concern. He said he would not permit a wanton killing to be depicted but indicated that the killer first had to be "wronged." What kind of double moral stand is this? This same official, in describing a film, said there were *only* twelve murders—not an excessive number according to his interpretation of the production code. What kind of rationalization is this?

I deplore censorship—and certainly law enforcement officials have no right to dictate what should or should not be shown on the rectangular screens. They do have, however, the obligation to insist on the observance of the moral law which binds men in all matters. They also have the right to speak out when law enforcement is held up to ridicule and the criminal is elevated to heroic proportions.

No standard of decency or code of operations can justify portraying vile gangsters as modern-day Robin Hoods. Film trash mills, which persist in exalting violence and immorality, spew out celluloid poison which is destroying the impressionable minds of youth. In commenting on a current blood-drenched screenplay, one reviewer wrote, "If you enjoy turning over rocks to see what crawls out, you'll have a gay time. . . ."

Parental supervision over the entertainment fare of children, discretion on the part of movie and television viewers, fulfillment of community responsibility by film exhibitors and television station executives, and citizen protests to producers of offensive shows can solve this problem.

Unless the leaders in the television and motion picture industries take the initiative to correct this ominous trend of crime glorification, they may be assured it can be accomplished by the strong pressure of public opinion. Time after time, the voice of the citizen has brought action, and it can be done again.

D

"The Problem of Television" by Walter Lippmann, as published in the New York *Herald Tribune*, October 27, 1959 at the time of the quiz and payola scandals (Used with the kind permission of Mr. Lippmann and the New York *Herald Tribune*.)

Television has been caught perpetrating a fraud which is so gigantic that it calls into question the foundations of the industry.

The fraud was not the work of a few cheats who had wormed their way into the company of honest men. The fraud was too big, too extensive, too well organized to be cured or atoned for by throwing a few conspicuous individuals to the wolves, and by putting on a pious show of scrupulosity about the details of the productions.

There has been, in fact, an enormous conspiracy to deceive the public in order to sell profitable advertising to the sponsors. It involves not merely this individual or that, but the industry as a whole. This is the judgment of the leading professional critics of television on both the New York *Herald Tribune* and The New York *Times*. Mr. John Crosby has said that the "moral squalor of the quiz mess reaches clear through the whole industry." Mr. Jack Gould has said that the fraud could not have been carried out without "the constant involvement of representatives of networks, advertising agencies, and sponsors."

The size of the fraud is a bitter reflection on the moral condition of our society. But it is also sure proof that there is something radically wrong with the fundamental national policy under which television operates. The principle of that policy is that for all practical purposes television shall be operated wholly for private profit. There is no competition in television except among competitors trying to sell the attention of their audiences for profit. As a result, while television is supposed to be "free," it has, in fact, become the creature, the servant, and indeed the prostitute, of merchandising.

Television is expensive and the available channels are few. These channels are possessed by a few companies who are in fierce competition among themselves. But what are they competing about? About how to capture the largest mass audience which can be made to look at and listen to the most profitable advertising.

In this competition, as in Gresham's famous law of money, the bad money drives out the good. In order to capture the largest mass audience the companies have resorted to fraud, as in the case of the quiz shows. But, reprehensible as it is to play the gullible public for suckers, that is not the worst of their offending. The worst things they do are, first, to poison the innocent by the exhibition of violence, degeneracy and crime, and second, to debase the public taste.

According to *Newsweek,* the television networks decided about a year ago that in the coming season, during the prime evening hours which draw the biggest audiences, they would devote to violence a total of 24 hours a week. "Heroes and villains crumple under the impact of blackjacks, whisky bottles, wrenches, and even gold-headed canes. A goggle-eyed public sits by while its fellow humans are pistol-whipped, stabbed, garrotted, mugged, and mussed up."

What to do about it? The great offense of the television industry is that it is misusing a superb scientific achievement, that it is monopolizing the air at the expense of effective news reporting, good art and civilized entertainment. The crux of the evil is that in seeking great mass audiences, the industry has decided from its experience that the taste of great masses is a low one, and that to succeed in the competition it must pander to this low taste.

Quite evidently, this is an evil which cannot be remedied by a regulating commission or by some form of government or self-constituted censorship. The alternative which is practiced in one form or another in almost every other civilized country, is competition—competition not for private profit but for public service. The best line for us to take is, I am convinced, to devise a way by which one network can be run as a public service, with its criterion not what will be most popular, but what is good.

No doubt, this network would not attract the largest mass audience. But if it enlisted the great talents which are available in the industry, but are now throttled and frustrated, it might well attract an audience which made up in influence what it lacked in numbers. The force of a good example is a great force, and should not be underrated.

We should not, I believe, shrink from the idea that such a network would have to be subsidized and endowed. Why not? Is there any doubt that television is a mighty instrument of education—education for good or education for evil? Why should it not be subsidized and endowed as are the universities and the public schools and the exploration of space and modern medical research, and indeed the churches—and so many other institutions which are essential to a good society, yet cannot be operated for profit?

They are unwise friends of our system of private capitalism who do not recognize the fact that the higher life of our society depends on respect for and support of non-commercial institutions. It is true that the best way for this country to produce wealth is by private enterprise for private profit. But there are a lot of other things that need to be done besides producing wealth and selling goods. One of them is to inform, instruct and entertain the people through the media of mass communications. And among these media there must be some which aim not at popularity and profit, but at excellence and the good life.

That it is possible to operate non-commercial institutions is attested by the fact that we do operate successfully schools, universities, hospitals, laboratories of research. Harvard and Yale and Princeton and Columbia and Dartmouth and so on are not operated for profit. Their trustees do not play politics. They are concerned with excellence and not with making money. Why should not people of this sort be able to find ways to operate a television network?

Chapter 1

1 Brock Chisholm, *Prescription for Survival*, New York, Columbia University Press, 1957, p. 88.

Chapter 2

1 *Michigan Reports: Cases Decided in the Supreme Court of Michigan*, vol. 204, p. 507, Chicago, Callaghan and Co., 1919. Emphasis added.

2 Richard Hofstadter, *Social Darwinism in American Thought*, Revised Edition, Boston, Beacon Press, 1958, p. 45.

3 Jack Levin, *Power Ethics: An Analysis of the Activities of the Public Utilities in the United States, Based on a Study of the United States Federal Trade Commission Records*, New York, Alfred A. Knopf, Inc., 1931.

4 Lawrence P. Lessing, *Man of High Fidelity: Edwin Howard Armstrong, A Biography*, Philadelphia, J. B. Lippincott Company, 1956.

5 United States House of Representatives, *Hearings before the Antitrust Subcommittee (Subcommittee No. 5) of the Committee on the Judiciary: Consent Decree Program of the Department of Justice: American Telephone and Telegraph Co.* 85th Congress, 2d Session, Part II, Vols. 1–3, Serial no. 9, U.S. Government Printing Office, 1958.

6 See Chap. 4 for additional examples.

7 Lawrence P. Lessing, "The Television Freeze," *Fortune*, vol. 40, part 2, no. 11, p. 123, November, 1949.

8 "Television and the Corporate Challenge," *Television Age*, vol. **V**, no. 9, p. 31, December 2, 1957.

9 *Ibid.*, p. 54.

10 Editorial, "Second Wind," *Broadcasting*, vol. 48, no. 8, p. 122, February 21, 1955.

11 Edward Hallett Carr, *The New Society*, Boston, Beacon Press, 1957.

12 John G. Fuller, *The Gentlemen Conspirators*, New York, Grove Press, Inc., 1962.

13 N. R. Danielian, *A.T.&T.: The Story of Industrial Conquest*, New York, Vanguard Press, Inc., 1939, pp. 398-399.

14 Quoted in Marquis W. Childs and Douglass Cater, *Ethics in a Business Society*, New York, Harper & Row, Publishers, Incorporated, 1954, p. 39.

Chapter 3

1 Federal Communications Commission, *Report on Chain Broadcasting*, Commission Order No. 37, Docket No. 5060, pp. 21-23, May, 1941, U.S. Government Printing Office.

2 With Mr. Murrow's kind permission, the entire text of this address is included as Appendix A of this book.

3 J. C. W. Reith, *Broadcast over Britain*, London, Hodder and Stoughton, Ltd., 1924, pp. 17, 25.

4 John Steinbeck, *The Wayward Bus*, New York, Bantam Books, 1950, p. 30.

5 *The Press*, Interviews by Donald McDonald with Mark Ethridge and C. D. Jackson, with a comment by John Cogley, Santa Barbara, Calif., Center for the Study of Democratic Institutions, 1961, p. 4.

6 United States Senate, *Juvenile Delinquency: Hearings before the Subcommittee to Investigate Juvenile Delinquency, of the Committee on the Judiciary, United States Senate, Eighty-seventh Congress: Part 10: Effects on Young People of Violence and Crime Portrayed on Television*, U.S. Government Printing Office, 1963, p. 2588.

7 Digests of the various positions filed by the networks and others were published by *Television Digest*, Washington, D.C., June 11, 1955. Later statements on pay television are to be found in United States House of Representatives, *Hearings before the Committee on Interstate and Foreign Commerce*, 85th Congress, U.S. Government Printing Office, 1958.

8 *Television*, an interview with Jack Gould, television critic of *The New York Times*, with a comment by Henry S. Ashmore, Santa Barbara, Calif., Center for the Study of Democratic Institutions, 1961, p. 28.

9 William T. Gossett, "The Role of the Corporation in Public Affairs: The Reality and the Opportunity," Brochure, containing the text of Mr. Gossett's remarks on a panel, August 25, 1959, at Miami Beach, Florida; reprinted from the November, 1959, issue of *The Business Lawyer*, p. 98.

10 John Bartlow Martin, "Television, U.S.A.," *The Saturday Evening Post*, Oct. 21 and 28, Nov. 4 and 11, 1961. The Oct. 28 article was sub-

titled: "Battle of the Big Three." Quotation is from this article (vol. 234, no. 43, p. 58).

11 Federal Communications Commission, *op. cit.*, p. 56.

12 Edward H. Carr, *The New Society*, Boston, Beacon Press, 1957, p. 26.

13 William S. Paley, "The American System of Broadcasting," address delivered before the Second Conference on Educational Broadcasting, Chicago, Nov. 29, 1937. Brochure, New York, CBS, p. 1.

14 Arthur Schlesinger, Jr., "Notes on a National Cultural Policy," *Daedalus*, vol. 89, no. 2., p. 395, Spring, 1960.

15 Barbara Ward, "A Direction for the West," *Saturday Review*, vol. 45, no. 4, p. 12, Jan. 27, 1962.

16 Meyer Weinberg, *TV and America: The Morality of Hard Cash*, New York, Ballantine Books, Inc., 1962, pp. 239–240.

17 William S. Paley, "Radio as a Cultural Force," Remarks, Oct. 17, 1934 before the FCC in its inquiry into proposals to allot fixed percentages of the nation's radio facilities to noncommercial broadcasting. Brochure, New York, CBS, 1934.

18 Frank Stanton, "The Right of Radio to Editorialize," Mar. 1, 1948. Brochure, New York, CBS, 1948.

19 Paul Goodman in Conversation with Studs Terkel, "What Is a Man's Work?" WFMT *Perspective*, vol. 11, no. 8, p. 31, Chicago, August, 1962.

20 Harold Mehling, *The Great Time-killer*, Cleveland, The World Publishing Company, 1962, p. 205.

21 John Cogley, *Report on Blacklisting*, vol. II: *Radio-Television*, New York, Fund for the Republic, 1956.

22 Weinberg, *op. cit.*, p. 142.

Chapter 4

1 *Broadcasting* magazine for Feb. 15, 1960 (vol. 58, no. 7, pp. 88, 91) listed the holdings of thirteen senators and seventeen representatives in thirty-six AM, twelve FM, and twenty-seven TV stations at that time. *The New York Times*, Jan. 26, 1958 (p. 1) also listed nine senators and seventeen representatives with such holdings.

Chapter 5

1 Harold E. Fellows, President and Chairman of the Board, National Association of Broadcasters, *"Pay" TV—"the Only Loser the Public."* Testimony before the Senate Committee on Interstate and Foreign Commerce, April 25, 1956. Published in brochure form by NAB.

2 Eugene Paul, *The Hungry Eye: An Inside Look at Television*. New York, Ballantine Books, 1962, p. 183.

3 Federal Communications Commission, *Report on Chain Broadcasting*, Commission Order No. 37, Docket No. 5060, May, 1941, U.S. Government Printing Office, p. 33.

4 Fred W. Hinickle, "What the Public Pays for Advertising," *Sponsor*, vol. 16, no. 43, p. 32, Oct. 22, 1962.
5 *Printers' Ink*, vol. 117, no. 2, pp. 90–96, Oct. 13, 1921 reports on the cranberry campaign. *Printers' Ink Monthly*, vol. 18, p. 45, May, 1929 reports on the Simcoe story.
6 133 NLRB No. 165. Decision and Order, Case No. 10-CC-452, Chattanooga, Tenn. (Local No. 662, Radio and TV Engineers, IBEW, AFL-CIO v. Middle South Broadcasting Co., Radio Station WAGC.)
7 *Telecommunications: A Program for Progress*, Report by the President's Communications Policy Board, U.S. Government Printing Office, 1951, p. 82.
8 Gunther Anders, "The Phantom World of TV," in Bernard Rosenberg and David Manning White (eds.), *Mass Culture*, New York, The Free Press of Glencoe, 1957, p. 359.
9 *Broadcasting*, "Networks Seek Profit Equalizer," vol. 61, no. 24, p. 52, Dec. 11, 1961.
10 Quoted in *Television Is Yours*, published by National Association for Better Radio and Television, 822 Victoria Avenue, Los Angeles 5, Calif., 1957, p. 11.
11 Clive Jenkins, *The Power behind the Screen: Ownership Control and Motivation in British Commercial Television*. London, MacGibbon and Kee, 1961. See especially pp. 169, 201, 255.
12 Paul, *op. cit.*, p. 40.
13 *Ibid.*, p. 173.

Chapter 6

1 Alan Thomas, *Audience, Market, Public: An Evaluation of Canadian Broadcasting*, Occasional Paper no. 7, University of British Columbia, Department of University Extension, April, 1960, 24 pages.
2 United States House of Representatives, *Evaluation of Statistical Methods Used in Obtaining Broadcast Ratings:* Report of the Committee on Interstate and Foreign Commerce, Oren Harris, Chairman. House Report no. 193, 87th Congress, 1st Session. U.S. Government Printing Office, 1961. (This is commonly referred to as The Madow Report, after William G. Madow, of Stanford University, who served as chairman of the professional group set up to study ratings and report on them to the House Committee.)
3 Quoted in *Newsweek* magazine, vol. 61, no. 14, p. 80, April 8, 1963.
4 *Newsweek*, vol. 61, no. 12, p. 71, March 25, 1963.
5 Harold Mehling, *The Great Time Killer*, Cleveland, The World Publishing Company, 1962, p. 235.
6 J. C. W. Reith, *Broadcast over Britain*, London, Hodder and Stoughton, Ltd., 1924, p. 34.

Chapter 7

1 UNESCO (United Nations Educational, Scientific and Cultural Organization), Reports and Papers on Mass Communication, no. 31: *The*

Influence of the Cinema on Children and Adolescents: An Annotated International Bibliography, Paris, UNESCO, 1961. 106 pages, 491 abstracts.

2 The *UNESCO Courier*, Paris, March, 1961, vol. 14 (14th year), no. 3, p. 28.

3 W. W. Charters, *Motion Pictures and Youth: A Summary* (of the Payne Fund Studies). New York, Macmillan Company, 1934, pp. 54–55. (1st ed., 1933.)
Other studies in the Payne Fund series, published by The Macmillan Company by 1935 include:
Getting Ideas from the Movies, by P. W. Holaday, Indianapolis Public Schools, and George D. Stoddard, Director, Iowa Child Welfare Research Station, 1933.
Motion Pictures and the Social Attitudes of Children, by Ruth C. Peterson and L. L. Thurstone, Department of Psychology, University of Chicago, 1933.
The Social Conduct and Attitudes of Movie Fans, by Frank K. Shuttleworth and Mark A. May, Institute of Human Relations, Yale University, 1933.
The Emotional Responses of Children to the Motion Picture Situation, by W. S. Dysinger and Christian A. Ruckmick, Department of Psychology, State University of Iowa, 1933.
Motion Pictures and Standards of Morality, by Charles C. Peters, Professor of Education, Pennsylvania State College.
Children's Sleep, by Samuel Renshaw, Vernon L. Miller and Dorothy Marquis, Department of Psychology, Ohio State University, 1933.
Movies and Conduct, by Herbert Blumer, Department of Sociology, University of Chicago, 1933.
The Content of Motion Pictures, by Edgar Dale, Research Associate, Bureau of Educational Research, Ohio State University, 1935.
Children's Attendance at Motion Pictures, by Edgar Dale, 1933.
Movies, Delinquency, and Crime, by Herbert Blumer and Philip M. Hauser, Department of Sociology, University of Chicago, 1933.
Boys, Movies, and City Streets, by Paul G. Cressey and Frederick M. Thrasher, New York University, 1933.
How to Appreciate Motion Pictures, by Edgar Dale, Research Associate, Bureau of Educational Research, Ohio State University, 1935.
Our Movie-made Children, by H. J. Forman, 1933.

4 *Ibid.*, pp. 49–50.

5 Martin Keilhäcker, "Results of Recent Psychological and Pedagogical Research on the Protection of Youth and the Cinema" (in German). *Jugend und Film*, Munich, 1958, pp. 13–30. Dr. Keilhäcker has also published some twenty other studies on the effects of films on children. See UNESCO, *op. cit.*, pp. 11, 14, 43–44, 56–57, 75.

6 Elisabeth Würth, "Films for Children" (in German), Special issue of *Zeitschrift für Theologie und Geistesleben*, vol. 8, no. 1, pp. 53–60, Vienna, 1953. See also UNESCO, *op. cit.*, p. 254.

7 K. Taggart, "Symposium: Moral and Spiritual Values in TV," in *This Is Television*, Report of Provincial Conference, Regina, Saskatchewan, Canada, Apr. 27–28, 1956, p. 56.

8   Randall Jarrell, "A Sad Heart at the Supermarket," *Daedalus*, vol. 89, no. 2, p. 366, Spring, 1960.

9   David Martin, *Television Tension Programs*, A study based on a content analysis of western, crime, and adventure programs televised by Melbourne stations, 1960–1961. Melbourne, Australian Broadcasting Control Board, 1963, pp. 25, 35, 38. Emphasis added.

10   Robert Warshow, "The Gunfighter as a Moral Hero," WFMT *Perspective*, vol. 11, no. 1, p. 23, January, 1962.

11   Edgar Dale, *The Content of the Motion Pictures*, Payne Fund Study, New York, The Macmillan Company, 1935, pp. 171, 173.

12   Fredric Wertham, M.D., "How Movie and Television Violence Affects Children," *Ladies' Home Journal*, vol. 77, no. 2, p. 58, February, 1960.

13   Stephen White, "Television: Culture in the Wee Hours," *Horizon*, vol. 4, no. 1, pp. 113–114, September, 1961.

14   S. I. Hayakawa, "Advertising versus Proper Evaluation: A review of *Reality in Advertising* by Rosser Reeves (New York, Knopf, 1961)," *ETC: A Review of General Semantics*, vol. 18, no. 3, pp. 367–374, October, 1961.

15   W. W. Charters, *op. cit.*, pp. 11–12.

16   Wilbur Schramm, Jack Lyle, and Edwin Parker, *Television in the Lives of Our Children*, Stanford, Calif., Stanford University Press, 1961, p. 91.

17   Paul W. Merrill, "The Principles of Poor Writing," *The Scientific Monthly*, vol. 44, no. 1, pp. 72–74, January, 1947.

18   UNESCO, *op. cit.*, p. 50.

19   *Ibid.*, pp. 13, 20, 54, 68, 84.

20   *Ibid.*, p. 52.

21   James Baldwin, "Black Man in America," WFMT *Perspective*, vol. 10, no. 12, p. 30, December, 1961.

22   Hans Luxenburger, "Psychiatric and Mental Hygiene Problems of Films" Munich, no date. Reviewed in UNESCO, *op. cit.*, p. 58.

23   UNESCO, *op. cit.*, pp. 63, 71–72.

24   United States Senate, *Television and Juvenile Delinquency*, Report of the Committee on the Judiciary, Report No. 1466, U.S. Government Printing Office, 1956 (84th Congress, 1st Session, January, 1956), p. 30.

25   *Ibid.*, pp. 58–59.

26   UNESCO, *op. cit.*, p. 63.

27   United States Senate, *op. cit.*, p. 74.

28   Sherwood Ross, "Violence on the Air," *The Progressive*, vol. 25, no. 11, p. 28, November, 1961.

29   UNESCO, *op. cit.*, p. 65.

30   W. W. Charters, *op. cit.*, pp. 53–54.

31   United States Senate, *op. cit.*, p. 80.

32   *Ibid.*, p. 77.

33   Siegfried Kracauer, *From Caligari to Hitler*, Princeton, N.J., Princeton University Press, 1947.

34   Wertham, *op. cit.*, p. 168.

35   Leonard Berkowitz, "Violence in the Mass Media," in *Studies in*

Communication, University of Paris and Stanford University, Institute for Communication Research, Stanford, 1962, pp. 117, 119.

36 *Ibid.,* p. 133.

37 Yosal, Rogat, *The Eichmann Trial and the Rule of Law,* Santa Barbara, Calif., Center for the Study of Democratic Institutions, 1961, p. 15.

38 United States Senate, *op. cit.,* p. 76.

39 Eugene David Glynn, M.D., "Television and the American Character: A Psychiatrist Looks at Television," in *Television's Impact on American Culture,* Edited by William Y. Elliott, East Lansing, Michigan, Michigan State University Press, 1956, p. 182.

40 Barbara Ward, "A Direction for the West," *Saturday Review,* vol. 45, no. 4, p. 59, Jan. 27, 1962.

Chapter 8

1 *Broadcasting,* "Editorial: The 'American Plan' Prevails," vol. 48, no. 21, p. 27, May 23, 1955.

2 *Advertising Age,* "Commercial Television Booms Overseas . . ." vol. 30, no. 45, p. 91, Nov. 9, 1959.

3 H. H. Wilson, *Pressure Group: The Campaign for Commercial Television,* London, Martin Secker and Warburg, Ltd., 1961, p. 215.

4 *Ibid.,* p. 14.

5 *Ibid.,* p. 129.

6 *Ibid.,* p. 147.

7 *Ibid.,* p. 139.

8 *Broadcasting,* Editorial, vol. 45, no. 22, p. 132, Nov. 30, 1953.

9 Jens Evensen, *Certain Aspects of International Law Concerning the Operation of Pirate Stations from Ships and Airplanes,* Oslo, Norwegian Broadcasting System (for the European Broadcasting Union), 1960.

10 John Tebbel, "U.S. Television Abroad: Big New Business," *Saturday Review,* vol. 45, no. 27, pp. 44–45, July 14, 1962.

11 Hugh Carleton Greene, "The Broadcaster's Responsibility," Address at Alfred I. Du Pont Awards Foundation Dinner, Mayflower Hotel, Washington, D.C., Mar. 26, 1962.

12 John Osborne, "Sex and Failure," in *The Beat Generation and the Angry Young Men,* Edited by Gene Feldman and Max Gartenberg, New York, The Citadel Press, 1958, pp. 316–319.

13 C. James Proud, Address to Shoe Service Institute of America, New York, July 17, 1961.

14 Brock Chisholm, *Prescription for Survival,* New York, Columbia University Press, 1957, p. 86.

15 Ashley Montagu, *Man: His First Million Years,* Cleveland, The World Publishing Company, 1957, p. 132.

16 Brock Chisholm, *op. cit.,* p. 88.

17 Mr. Murrow's address was quoted in numerous publications including *Broadcasting* magazine, vol. 62, no. 15, p. 76, Apr. 9, 1962.

18 Asa Briggs, *The History of Broadcasting in the United Kingdom,*

vol. I: *The Birth of Broadcasting*, London, Oxford University Press, 1961, p. 67.

19   Royal Commission on Broadcasting, *Report*, Mar. 15, 1957.   Ottawa, Canada, Edmond Cloutier, 1957, pp. 8–9.

Chapter 9

1   Douglas Bush, Ed., *The Portable Milton*, New York, The Viking Press, Inc., 1962, p. 196.

"Abbott and Costello," 190
ABC, in foreign countries, 187, 189
    stations owned by, 112*n*.
ABC-Paramount, 20, 36, 37
    in foreign countries, 187
    management, 43, 44
    military contracts, 19
    profits, 110, 111
ABC-TV, 36, 43, 44
    programs, 147
ABC-TV News, 44
Actors (actresses), ratings, 135
    salaries, 117
Adams, Sherman, 85
Advertising, contradictory, 102
    cost of, 95-98, 104
    deceptive, 104, 107
    effect, on behavior, 108, 109, 155,
        168
        on prices, 99-102
    information and misinformation
        in, 103, 104, 158
    in international broadcasts, 184
    rigged quiz shows and, 101
    small businesses in, 104
    time used by, 108, 109
    (*See also* Commercials)
Advertising Age, 181

Advertising agencies, executives, 44
    in international broadcasting, 183,
        188
Advertising tax, 91, 95-98
Aerospace Corporation, 208, 209
AFL-CIO Committee on Political Ac-
    tion, 51
Air pollution, 87, 106
Allen, Charles, 131
Allen, Steve, 135
Alsop, Joseph, 43
Altavilla, Enrico, 166
American Broadcasting Company
    (*see* ABC)
American Home Products, 107
American Research Bureau, 127, 133
American Telephone and Telegraph
    Corporation (*see* AT&T)
American Tobacco Company, 184
Anders, Gunther, 109
Antitrust law violation, 27-29, 33, 86,
    107, 116
Arab-American Oil Company
    (ARAMCO), 188
Argentina, 187
Aristotle, 175
Armstrong, Edwin H., 26, 34
Arnaz, Desi, 117

Ashmore, Harry S., 55
Associated Television (ATV), 186, 187
AT&T, 21, 25, 26, 32, 34, 37
    antitrust suit, 27, 28
    FCC investigation, 83
    profits, 31
Aubrey, James T., 44, 51, 57
Audience (*see* Public)
Audience research, 122, 123, 127-131
    Audimeter, 127-129, 133, 222
    diary type, 130
    interviews, 130, 134
    telephone surveys, 130, 133
Audimeter, 127-129, 133, 222
Australia, broadcasting in, 187, 208
    programs in, 153, 187, 190
Austria, broadcasting in, 8, 188
Automobiles, advertising tax on, 96
    in crime films, 153
    regulation of, 87
Autry, Gene, 117
AVCO Rule, 83
Aviation Corporation of America, 83
Aylesworth, Merlin H., 52

Baldwin, James, 167
Ball, Lucille, 117
Banay, Ralph Steven, 168
Bangkok, 187
Barber, John H., 170
Barron's, 111
Barrow Report, 204
Barry, Jack, 48
Bartley, Robert, 81
"Bat Masterson," 189
Bates, Ted, and Company, 188
Baxter and Whitaker, 178
BBC, 9, 208
    American influence on, 186
    origin of, 20
BBC Listener, 221
Beadle, Sir Gerald, 199, 200
Bell, Alexander Graham, 45
Bell Telephone Company, 23, 25
Bennett, James V., 170, 171
Benton and Bowles, 188
Berkowitz, Leonard, 174, 175
Berle, Milton, 117, 135
Beveridge Commission, 137
Beville, Hugh M., 53, 54
"The Big Party," 57
"Big Surprise," 48
Blacklisting, 66, 124
Blumer, Herbert, *Movies, Delinquency, and Crime*, 155, 169, 173

Bok, Curtis, 170
"Bonanza," 189
Bonjour (ship), 184, 185
Brennan, Walter, 117
Bricker, John W., 112
Briggs, Asa, *The Birth of Broadcasting*, 197
Britain (*see* Great Britain)
British Broadcasting Corporation (*see* BBC)
Broadcasting, commercial vs. noncommercial, 7-8
    as common carrier, 78, 79
    controlled by corporations, 17-38, 45-48, 73, 74
    (*See also* Corporations)
    costs of, 89-90, 93-95
    economic aspects of, 89-119
    faults of present system, 9-16
    government regulation of (*see* Government regulation)
    improvements suggested, 220, 221
    international (*see* International broadcasting)
    investments and income in, 93-95, 110
    as product, 100
    as profession, 213, 214
    study of, recommended, 118, 202-205
    as young industry, 56
Broadcasting (magazine), 31, 40, 51, 105, 110, 181, 183
Broadcasting Yearbook, 90
Broun, Heywood, 233
Brown, Cecil, 66
Bruel, Oluf, 167
Bruno–New York, Inc., 40
"Bugs Bunny," 133
Bureau of Broadcast Measurement, 127
Bureau of the Budget, 82
Bureau of the Census, 134
Burleson, A. S., 70, 206
Burnett, Carol, 117
Burns, John, 35
Burns and Allen, 117

"Camera Three," 124
Canada, American programs in, 190, 198
    broadcasting in, 7, 122, 208, 210, 212
    manufacturers in, 93
    television tax, 98

Carr, Edward H., *The New Society,* 32, 59, 60
Case, Nelson, 117
Catharsis, 174, 175
Catholic Association for Radio and Television, 149, 198
Catton, Bruce, 75
CBS, 36, 37, 43, 66, 71, 78
    editorialized news, 63
    executive salaries, 116
    in foreign countries, 187, 189
    investments and income, 93, 94
    management, 43, 52-54, 58, 61
    military contracts, 19
    origin, 41
    profits, 110, 111, 113, 115
    programs, 125, 135, 147
    quiz shows, 49
    sale of stations, 114
    stations owned by, 112*n.*
    stock ownership in, 41
    Television City, 113
    time for public services, 62, 71
CBS-TV, 44, 147
Celler, Emanuel, 28, 94
Censorship, 14, 87
Central America, television in, 187
"The Challenge," 48
Charters, W. W., 146, 158, 171
Chayevsky, Paddy, 66
Children, better television for, 220
    effects of television on, 143-146, 149, 157-159, 164, 167, 175, 192
    programs for, 126, 133, 149
    television habits of, 157, 177
    (*See also* Juvenile delinquency)
Children's Neuro-Psychiatric Center, Paris, 144
China, news from, 193, 231
Chisholm, Brock, 12, 13
Christian Science Monitor, 76
Cigarettes, advertising of, 97
    cancer and, 97, 106
    smoking on television, 154, 155
    teenage smoking, 106
"Cisco Kid," 189
Civil Aeronautics Board, 76
Civil defense, 207
Civil rights, 13
Closterman, Gerhard, *Artistic Education through Films,* 167
Code, NAB (*see* National Association of Broadcasters)
Colgate-Palmolive, 107
Colin, Ralph F., 51
Collins, LeRoy, 63, 76, 120
Collins, Norman, 115, 182, 183

Color television, 123
    cost of, 92, 95
    profits from, 35, 115
Columbia Broadcasting System (*see* CBS)
Commercials, cost of, 117, 118
    inattention as protection against, 159, 160
    irritation, 125, 126, 166
    language of, 161
    in news broadcasts, 58
    salaries of performers, 117
    singing, 162
    time used for, 109
    (*See also* Advertising)
Commission, proposed, for regulation of broadcasting, 215, 216
    for study of broadcasting, 202-205
Commission on the Freedom of the Press, 206
Commissions on broadcasting in foreign countries, 203, 204
Common carrier, broadcasting as, 78, 79
Communications Act of 1934, 10, 37, 70, 71, 210, 215, 224
    debate on, from *Congressional Record,* 239-243
    Wagner-Hatfield amendment, 71
Communications Research Council proposed, 223
Como, Perry, 189
Cone, Fairfax, 125, 135
Congress, action on broadcasting, 10, 37, 70-73
    recommended changes for, 203-205, 218, 219
    debate on Communications Act, 239-243
    and FCC, 81, 82, 84, 85
    hearings on television finance, 91, 94
    House Committee on Interstate and Foreign Commerce, 54, 128
    House Committee on the Judiciary, 28, 169
    House Special Subcommittee on Investigations, 133
    lobbying in (*see* Lobbying)
    Senate Subcommittee to Investigate Juvenile Delinquency, 51, 145, 221, 223
Congress Cigar Company, 34, 39, 41, 42, 52
Conlan, Robert S., rating service, 127, 133
Consolidated Cigar Company, 39

Contests, 109
Coolidge, Calvin, 70
Cordiner, Ralph, 30
Corporate citizenship, 21
Corporate image, 234, 235
Corporations, control of broadcasting
    by, 17-38, 45-47, 73, 74
  decision making in, 43, 44
  democracy in, 22, 23, 34, 37, 51
  education influenced by, 25-27, 35
  in international broadcasting, 21,
    186-188
  investments and income of, 93-95
  in politics, 50, 51
  profits of, 109-113, 118
  public, 208, 209
  in quiz scandals, 47-50, 53
  regulation of (*see* Government regu-
    lation)
  staff, morale of, 65, 66
  stockholders in, 18, 23, 24, 41
  (*See also* Managers; Networks)
Cosmetics, advertising of, 96, 101
Coughlin, Father, 140
Couzens, James, 206
Cowan, Louis, 44
Coyle, Donald, 187
Crime in television, 146, 152, 153, 166-
    174, 244, 245
  (*See also* Violence on television)
Crosby, Bing, 117
Crosby, John, 67, 112, 246
Crossley, S. D., rating service, 127
Cuba, news from, 193
Cullen, Bill, 117
Culpepper, Garland L., Jr., 47
Cummings, Bob, 117
Czechoslovak State Cinema, 144

Dale, Edgar, *The Content of Motion
    Pictures*, 154, 155
Danielian, N. R., 37
Daniels, Josephus, 69, 206
Davis, Elmer, 231
Deceit (*see* Rigging)
Defense contracts (*see* Military con-
    tracts)
De Forest, Lee, 26
Democracy, in corporations, 22, 23,
    34, 37, 51
  mass media and, 138-141, 179, 180
  public opinion in, 136
  television and radio as instruments
    of, 210-212
Dentifrices, advertising of, 96, 97
Department of Commerce, 80

Department of Communications pro-
    posed, 215
Department of Defense, 28, 80, 208
Department of Health, Education,
    and Welfare, 215
Department of Justice, 28, 107, 204
Department of State, 136, 188, 216
DeSales Realty Company, 40
Dill, Clarence C., 70, 71
Dill-White Radio Act (*see* Radio Act,
    of 1927)
"Ding Dong School," 54
Distribution and production costs,
    103
Dodd, Thomas J., 51, 145
Dodge, John F., 18
Doerfer, John C., 72, 81
Dominican Republic, propaganda for,
    47
"Douglas Fairbanks, Jr., Presents,"
    189
Dreier, Alex, 117
Dulles, John Foster, 231
Du Mont, Allen, 207
Durocher, Leo, 117
Dyna-Fota-Chron, 131

Eastman, Max, 237
Economic concepts of executives, 55,
    56, 99
Economics of broadcasting, 89-119
  study of, recommended, 118, 202-
    205
Editorializing in broadcasts, 53, 62,
    63, 230
Education, corporations influencing,
    25-27, 35
  effect of television on, 156-160
Educational broadcasting, 73, 137
  opposition to, 35, 43, 53, 61, 62
  in underdeveloped countries, 199
Educational television, 35, 141
  ratings, 132
Eichmann trial, 175
Einstein, Albert, 192, 200
Eisenhower, Dwight D., 73
Election campaigns, 105, 178, 179
Electronic Industries Association, 90
Emerick, Lucille, 169
England (*see* Great Britain)
Engstrom, Elmer W., 35
Ethridge, Mark, 50
European Broadcasting Union, 186
Evensen, Jens, 186
Executives (*see* Managers)

Families in corporations, 33, 39-42
Family, effect of television on, 149,
  150
Federal Communications Commission
  (FCC), 28, 36, 53, 71, 72, 90, 94,
  107, 112, 115, 118, 119, 170, 224
  changes proposed, 215-218, 233
  creation of, 70
  faults of, 76, 80-86
  investigations by, 83, 91, 104
  opposition to, 60, 76, 80, 81
  radio authorizations, 82, 83
  Report on Chain Broadcasting, 41,
    59, 93
  rules, 62
Federal Maritime Board, 76
Federal Radio Commission, 29, 70,
  206, 224
Federal Reserve System, 208
Federal Trade Commission, 29, 80,
  107, 216
  investigations by, 25, 48, 52, 58
  on misleading advertising, 58
Feedback, 139-141
  as instrument of democracy, 211,
    212
  as testing device, 131
Field, Mary, 134, 144, 222
Film companies, executives, 44
Films, 146-148
  as art form, 148, 149
  crime and violence in, 146, 147,
    152-154
  effects of, on children, 143, 144,
    147, 149
    on juvenile delinquency, 166,
      167, 169-174
  excessive use of, 10, 11, 61
  in foreign broadcasts, 189, 190
  old, 146, 147, 189
  sex in, 154-156
Fisher, Eddie, 117
Fly, James L., 10
FM, 32
Food-Drug-Cosmetics Reports, 40
Ford Motor Company, 18, 96, 184
Foreign countries (*see* International
  broadcasting)
Fortune, 29
France, American programs in, 190
  research program, 221
  television tax, 98
  violence on television forbidden,
    197
Frankfurter, Felix, 75
"Free" broadcasting, 89-119
Freedom in broadcasting, 74, 75

Freud, Sigmund, 175
Fulchignoni, Enrico, 144
Fuller, John, *The Gentleman Con-
  spirators*, 33
"Fury," 189

Galbraith, John K., 75
"Gale Storm Show," 190
Gallup Poll, 130, 134
Gambrill, Michael Lee, 174n.
Garroway, Dave, 132
General Electric Company, 20, 26, 30,
  33, 86, 107, 188
General Foods, 103
General Motors Corporation, 32, 96
Germany, broadcasting in, 8, 140,
  187, 188, 208
  juvenile delinquency in, 144, 170
  Nazis in, 172, 178, 179
  time limitation for television pro-
    posed, 198
  West German Television Com-
    mittee, 149, 198
Giraud, Jean, 166
Gleason, Jackie, 117
Glynn, Eugene David, 177
Goldenson, Leonard, 20, 36, 190
  career of, 39, 42
  as executive, 44
Goodman, Paul, 64, 65
Gossett, William T., 56
Gould, Jack, 124, 246
Government, corporations influencing, 27-29
Government ownership of broadcasting, 205-210
Government regulation, 10-16, 28, 29,
  36, 37, 69-88
  changes proposed, 215-218
  opposition to, 60, 71, 72
  of quiz shows, 49
  of radio, 69-72
  taxes used in, 107
Great Britain, American programs in,
  190, 196, 197
  broadcasting in, 7, 8, 79, 208
  commercial television in, 115, 126,
    127, 182, 183
  "pirate" ship broadcasts to, 185
  quiz show in, 49
  research programs, 222
  television tax, 98
  time limitations proposed, 197
  United States influence, 182, 183
Greene, Sir Hugh Carleton, 9, 12, 190

Grotjahn, Martin, 176, 177
"Gunsmoke," 187, 189
Guterma, Alexander L., 47

Hagerty, James C., 43, 44
Hailsham, Lord, 182, 183
Hand, Learned, 142
Hansen-Rubensohn agency, 188
Harris, Oren, 133
Harris, Phil, 117
"The Hathaways," 187
Hauser, Philip M., 169
Hausman, Louis, 49, 50
"Have Gun Will Travel," 189
Hawthorne Effect, 129
Hayakawa, S. I., 156
Hazel Bishop cosmetics, 101
Henry, E. William, 72
Herald Tribune, New York, 206, 246
"Highway Patrol," 189
Hilgemeier, Edward, 48
Hill, George Washington, 125
Himmelweit Studies, 222
Hinickle, Fred W., 96
Hofstadter, Richard, *Social Darwinism in American Thought*, 24
Hogan, Frank, 48
Holland, broadcasting in, 73
Hollenbeck, Don, 66
Hong Kong, 191
Hooper, C. E., rating service, 127, 133
Hoover, Herbert, 47, 69-71, 74
Hoover, J. Edgar, 170
  statement by, 244, 245
Hoover Commission, 203, 204
Hope, Bob, 117
Hurleigh, Robert, 120
Hurwitz, William, 134
Hyde, Rosel, 82, 86

Iglehart, Joseph A. W., 51
Illinois Bell Telephone Company, 25
Image, corporate, 234, 235
  of intellectuals and artists, 194
  of labor unions, 194
  racial bias in, 193, 194
  of United States, 12, 13, 21, 190-196, 198-201
Intellectuals, contempt for, 194
Interdepartmental Radio Advisory Committee (IRAC), 80, 216
Internal Revenue Service, 119
International broadcasting, 11, 12, 181-201

International broadcasting, commercial, introduced by United States, 181-184
  corporations in, 21, 186-188
  criticism of, 190-194, 196-198
  "pirate" ships, 184-186, 216
International research programs, 222
International Telemeter Corporation, 91
International Television Corporation, 189
Interstate Commerce Commission, 76
Inventors, neglect of, 45
Iran, 188
Isobe, Yuji, 193
Italians, image of, 194
Italy, broadcasting in, 8, 140

Japan, American programs in, 190
  broadcasting in, 8, 140, 188, 208
  violence on television forbidden, 144, 196
Jarrell, Randall, 151
Jenkins, Clive, *The Power behind the Screen*, 115
Jobson, John, and Partners, 188
Johnson, Grace, 221
Johnson, Laurence A., 124
Johnson, Lyndon B., 105
Johnson, Samuel, 160
Jolar Corporation, 40
Jones, Robert F., 31
Jones Report, 204
Journalists in broadcasting, 66
Jung, Carl, 137, 176
Juvenile delinquency, television and, 13, 63, 155, 156, 166-174, 244, 245

Kaye, Danny, 117
KDWB, 84
Keilhäcker, Martin, 149
Keller, Father, 116
Kennedy, Edward, 105
Kennedy, John F., 72, 86, 105, 116, 164, 170
Kerr, Robert, 105
Khrushchev, Nikita, 58, 67, 231
Kimble Glass Company, 91
Kintner, Robert, 31
  as executive, 43, 44, 48, 51, 54, 68
Kohler strike, hearings on, 124
KOMA, 84
Kotschack, Jack S., 184, 185
KPFA, 139
Kracauer, Siegfried, 172

"Kraft Theatre," 68
Kronenberg, Frank J., 170
Kupperman, Bert, 185

Labor, management and, 18, 34
Labor unions, 23, 34, 37, 73
  corporations and, 51
  image of, 194
  televised hearings, 124
Lambe and Robinson, 188
Landis, James, 86
Landis Report, 204
Language, effect of television on, 160, 161
Laos, 193
La Palina Cigar Company, 39, 52
Lasers, 224
"Lassie," 189
Latin America, television in, 187
Laurent, Lawrence, 147
Lavies, Hans Wilhelm, 170
Lazarsfeld, Paul, 21
Lee, Robert E. (FCC commissioner), 81, 83
Lescoulie, Frank, 117
Lessing, Lawrence, 29
  Man of High Fidelity, 26
Levathes, Peter, 67
Lever Brothers, 107, 184
Levin, Jack, *Power Ethics*, 25
Levy, Isaac D., 41
Levy, Leon, 41
Lewis, Jerry, 117
Licensing, 60, 78, 79
  and antitrust law violations, 86
  by FCC, 82, 86
  of FCC, 80
  policy questions proposed, 216, 217
  for public-service network, 209
  of radio, 82
  suspension of, 218
  "trafficking in licenses," 114
"Lifetime Unlimited," 58
Lippmann, Walter, 180
  article by, 206, 246-248
Lobbying, by corporations, 27-29
  in FCC, 85
  on government regulation, 70, 71
Loews's Theatres, 114
"The Lone Ranger," 189
Long, Huey, 140
Look, 48
Louchheim, Jerome H., 41
Luxemberger, Hans, *Psychiatric and Mental Hygiene Problems of Films*, 167
Lyle, Jack, 159, 177

McCann-Erickson agency, 44, 188
McClellan hearings on Kohler strike, 124
McConnaughey, George G., 81
McCoy, Wayne, 84
McFarland, Bill, 84
McGill, Ralph, 164
McLendon, Gordon, 185
Macquarie (firm), 187
Madow Report, 128, 130
Magazines, television, proposed, 221
Majority, will of, 136
Managers, 39-68
  economic concepts of, 55, 56, 99
  families of, 33, 39-42
  salaries of, 115, 116
Mansfield, Frank, 91
Marks, Leonard, 216
Martin, David, 152, 153
Martin, John Bartlow, 57
Masers, 224
Mass medium, television as, 139-141, 145
"Maverick," 187
Mayer, J. P., 144
Mayer, Martin, *Madison Avenue, U.S.A.*, 24
MCA (Revue), 189
Meade, Julia, 117
"Meet the Press," 125
Mellon Institute, 106
Mental health, advertising as influence on, 108
  television and, 13, 108, 109, 146, 153, 159, 163, 165-168
Merrill, Paul, 160
Mexicans, image of, 193, 194
Mexico, radio network, 187
  violence on television forbidden, 197
"Mike Hammer," 191
Militarism in broadcasting, 192
Military contracts, 11, 19, 36
Millington, Leonora, 49
Milton, John, 226
Minow, Newton, 14, 62, 123
  as chairman of FCC, 72, 207
Mirams, Gordon, 144
"Mr. Lucky," 187
Montagu, Ashley, 192
Moore, Thomas W., 43, 44
Morgan, Edward P., 66
Morse, Samuel, 69, 206
Murrow, Edward R., 45, 46, 66, 195, 209
  address by, 227-238
Music, effect of television on, 162, 163

Music Corporation of America, 84, 115, 116
Mutual Broadcasting System, 124
Dominican Republic propaganda, 47
profits, 111
Muzak, 186, 187
"My Little Margie," 190
Mycalex Corporation of America, 40

National Association of Broadcasters (NAB), 48, 60, 63, 71, 80, 89, 220, 222
codes, radio, 76
television, 61, 63, 76, 154, 161
National Association of Educational Broadcasters, 35
National Association of Manufacturers, 25, 124
National Broadcasting Company (*see* NBC)
National City Bank, 77
National Cultural Center, 223
National Electric Light Association, 25, 52
National Labor Relations Board, 100
National Science Foundation, 223
Nazis, 172, 173, 178, 179
NBC, 54, 71, 78, 79
advertising costs, 103
in foreign countries, 187, 189
investments and income, 93, 94
management, 52
organization, 34, 35, 37
profits, 31, 110
programs, 125, 147
in quiz show rigging, 48, 49
sale of stations, 114
stations owned by, 112*n.*
Negroes, image of, 193
Network Study Committees, 204
Networks, ethics, 59, 60
profits, 31, 35, 58, 59, 94, 109-113, 118
public relations, 113, 114
public-service, proposed, 205-210
sale of stations, 114, 115
stations owned by, 112*n.*
Neuberger, Richard, 157
"The New Breed," 187
New York Post, 48
New York Times, 184, 185, 246
New York Transit Authority, 168, 169
New York World-Telegram and Sun, 48
News broadcasts, commercials in, 58
distortion and secrecy in, 192, 193

News broadcasts,
editorializing in (*see* Editorializing)
individual freedom in, 66
violence in, 174
Newspapers, founders of, 20, 42
profits of, 113
stations owned by, 34, 113
Newsweek, 133, 147, 247
Nielsen, A. C., rating service, 127-129, 133, 136, 222
Nigeria, 187, 193
Nixon, Richard, 50, 136
Norway, "pirate" ship broadcasts to, 185, 186

Office of Education, United States, 156
"Omnibus," 68
Opera, 134, 135
"Opinion," 58
Ortega y Gasset, José, 179
Osborne, John, 190
Ouimet, Alphonse, 210

Packard, Vance, 109
Page, Patti, 113
Paley, Jacob, 39
Paley, Samuel, 39, 41, 42
Paley, William S., 30*n.*, 34, 60-62, 65, 71, 111, 135
career of, 39, 41-42, 52
as executive, 48, 51, 53, 57, 115, 116
Paley family, 20, 23, 41
Panama Railroad Company, 208
Parker, Edwin, 159, 177
Passivity, 176-178
indifference and, 159, 160, 177, 178
in sports, 125, 164, 165
Patents, control of, 32, 35
Patterson, George, 190
Patterson, George L., Inc., 40
Paul, Eugene, *The Hungry Eye,* 91, 115
Pay television, films on, 146
opposition to, 54, 55, 113
Payne Fund Studies, 143, 146, 152, 154, 155, 158, 164, 169, 173
Payola, 21, 23, 28, 31, 50, 53, 135, 246
Peace, efforts toward, 11, 19, 192, 200, 201
Pease, H. M., 186
Pepsi-Cola, 188
"The Perfect Crime," 173
"Perry Mason," 189
Pharmaceuticals, Incorporated, 101
Philco-Ford, 20
Philharmonic broadcasts, 57, 135
Philippines, television in, 187

Physical fitness, effect of television on, 163-165
Pickard, Sam, 52
"Pirate" ships, broadcasting by, 184-186, 216
Pittsburgh, air pollution in, 106
"Playhouse 90," 57, 61
Plotkin Report, 204
Politics, in broadcasting, 105, 106, 178-180
corporation executives in, 50, 51
Polls, 61, 130, 131, 136
presidential preference, 134
(*see also* Audience research)
Presidential elections, 105
Presidential preference polls, 134
President's Commission on National Goals, 203
President's Communications Policy Board, 103, 204
Prices, effect of advertising on, 99-102
Printers' Ink, 97
Procter & Gamble, 96, 97, 101, 102
Production and distribution costs, 103
Profession of broadcasting, 213, 214
Profits of networks (*see* Networks)
Programs, control of, 74, 124
cultural vs. mass-audience, 141
dropped by management, 57
juggling of, 67
quality of, and ratings, 67, 68
(*See also* Ratings)
Proud, C. James, 191
Public, as audience, 121, 122
as citizens, 122
as market, 121, 122
tastes of, 57, 135, 137
wants and needs of, 121-123, 133, 135, 136
Public interest, representation of, 73
Public opinion, manufacturing of, 74, 75, 179
Public relations, of corporations, 29, 30, 54
in elections, 178
of networks, 113, 114
Public-service network proposed, 205-210
Public services, time for, 62, 65

Quiz shows, 135
rigging of, 21, 23, 47-50, 53, 101, 246

Radio, advertising tax, 95, 96
authorizations, 82, 83

Radio, effects of, 143, 148, 157, 196
research on, 221-225
in foreign countries, 187
government regulation of, 69-72
"pirate" ship broadcasts, 184-186, 216
public-service network proposed, 205-210
separation from television, 223
Radio Act, of 1912, 69
of 1927, 29, 69, 70, 210, 224
(*See also* Communications Act)
Radio Andorra, 183
Radio Atlanta, 184, 185
Radio Caroline, 184, 185
Radio Corporation of America (*see* RCA)
Radio Eulenspiegel, 184
Radio Luxembourg, 183
Radio Mercur, 184
Radio Nord, 184, 185
Radio sets, cost of, 92, 93
manufacturers of, 93
number of, in use, 92
production of, 91
Radio Syd, 184
Radio Veronica, 184
"Ramar of the Jungle," 190
RAND corporation, 208, 209
Rank, J. Arthur, Organisation, 222
Ratings, 53, 54, 58, 120-142
audience research and, 122, 123, 127-131
averages in, 137
vs. favorite programs, 133
Nielsen Audimeter, 127-129
quality of program and, 67, 68
rigging of, 57, 131, 132
Rayburn, Gene, 117
Rayburn, Samuel, 70, 71, 81
RCA, 20, 26, 32, 34, 35, 37, 79, 123
antitrust suits, 29, 107
electronic data-processing branch, 35
executive salaries, 116
finances, 93-95
in foreign countries, 188
military contracts, 19
profits, 31, 35, 110, 111
in research, 32
"The Rebel," 187
Regulation, by government (*see* Government regulation)
self-, 76-78
Reith, J. C., Lord, 139, 142
Broadcast over Britain, 46, 47
Religious groups, 73

Religious programs, 58, 137
Research, by corporations, 31, 32
    on effect of television, 143, 144, 221-225
    international programs, 222
    (*See also* Audience research)
"Restless Gun," 187
Reston, James, 67
Reuther, Walter, 124
Revlon cosmetics, 101
"Ride with Terror," 168, 169
Rigging, 47, 61
    of quiz shows, 21, 23, 31, 47-50, 53, 101, 246, 247
    of ratings, 57, 131, 132
Roach, Hal, Jr., 47
Rockefeller, John D., 24
Rockefeller, Nelson, 105
Rockefeller Brothers Fund Study, 203
Rodgers, John, M.P., 182
Rogat, Yosal, 175
Rogers, Attorney General, 73
Rome, University of, Psychological Institute, 149
Roosevelt, Franklin Delano, 70, 71
Roper polls, 130, 134
Ross, Sherwood, 170
Russia, 189, 191-193, 199

Sabit, Habib, 188
St. Louis Post-Dispatch, 49
Salaries, of executives, 115, 116
    of performers, 116, 117
Sarnoff, David, 11, 34, 35, 99, 110, 115, 120
    career of, 39, 40, 42, 52
    as executive, 53-55
Sarnoff, Irving, 40
Sarnoff, Robert, 31, 40, 43, 54, 56, 64, 72, 91, 99, 110, 139, 195
Sarnoff, Thomas, 40
Sarnoff family, 20, 39, 40
Schlesinger, Arthur, Jr., 60
Schools (*see* Education)
Schramm, Wilbur, 159, 177
Schweitzer, Albert, 192
Schwerin (firm), 122, 123
Scott, Walter D., 58, 104
Screen Gems (Columbia), 189
"Sea Hunt," 189
Secrecy, in broadcasting, 30, 31
    in news broadcasts, 192, 193
Securities and Exchange Commission, 90, 116
Self-regulation, 76-78

Senate (*see* Congress)
"Sergeant Preston," 190
Serling, Rod, 66
Sevareid, Eric, 33, 224
"77 Sunset Strip," 187
Sex on television, 145, 146, 154-156
"Sheena, Queen of the Jungle," 189
Ships, "pirate," broadcasting from, 184-186, 216
Shore, Dinah, 117
Silvers, Phil, 113, 135
Sinatra, Frank, 117
Sindlinger and Company, 133
Smith, Adam, 37
Smith, Howard K., 66
Smoking on television, 154, 155
    (*See also* Cigarettes)
Soviet Union (*see* Russia)
Spanish Guardianship Tribunals, 144, 169
Splawn, W. W., 89
Sports broadcasts, 125, 164, 165
    wrestling, 47, 164
Standard Brands, 107
Standard and Poor, 111
Stanton, Frank, 36, 42, 62, 64, 113, 136, 138, 139
    as executive, 43, 48, 51-54, 56, 57, 61
Stations, licensing (*see* Licensing)
    network control of, 59, 60
    in networks, 112*n.*
    sale of, 114, 115
Stein, Jules, 115, 116
Steinbeck, John, *The Wayward Bus,* 50
Sterling Radio and Electric Company, 40
Stisser, Frank, 133
Stockholders in corporations, 18, 23, 24, 41, 111
    congressmen as, 85
Storck, Henri, 144
Storer Broadcasting Company, 113, 114
Storm, Gale, 117, 190
Streisand, Barbra, 117
"Studio One," 124
Study of broadcasting recommended, 118, 202-205
Sullivan, Ed, 42, 58, 135
Supreme Court, 118
"Surfside 6," 187
"Susie," 147
Sweden, American "pirate" broadcasts to, 184, 185
    broadcasting in, 220

Taggart, K., 149, 150
Taishoff, B. T., 41
Taishoff, Jerome, 40
Taishoff, Lawrence B., 41
Taishoff, Sol, 39-42
Taishoff, Mrs. Sol, 41
Talent (*see* Television performers)
Taxes, advertising, 91, 95-98
  broadcasting supported by, 98
  excess profits, 118
  federal, used for broadcasting, 106, 107
  for public-service network, 209, 210
  television, per family, 110, 119
Tebbel, John, 189
Telecommunications Coordinating Committee (TCC), 80
Telephone coincidental surveys, 130, 133
Telephone participation, 141
Television, as art form, 148, 149, 162, 163
  economic aspects of, 89-119
  effects of, 143-180
    catharsis, 174, 175
    on children, 143-146, 149, 157-159, 164, 167, 175, 192
    on education, 156-160
    emotional, 149
    on family, 149, 150
    on juvenile delinquency, 13, 63, 155, 156, 166-174
    on language, 160, 161
    on mental health, 13, 108, 109, 146, 153, 159, 163, 165-168
    on music, 162, 163
    passivity, 176-178
    on physical fitness, 163-165
    on politics, 105, 106, 178-180
    research needed, 221-225
  as mass medium, 138-141, 145
  proposals and recommendations on, 202-226
    congressional action, 218, 219
    improvements by industry, 220, 221
    as instrument of democracy, 210-212
    national study, 118, 202-205
    profession of broadcasting, 213, 214
    public-service network, 205-210
    regulatory changes, 215-218
    research, 221-225
  time spent in watching, 108, 109
  values promoted by, 150-156, 158, 165, 166

Television (Fund for the Republic brochure), 55
Television (magazine), 40, 41
Television Age, 29, 30
Television Factbook, 90
Television industry (*see* Broadcasting; Corporations)
Television performers, as celebrities, 117, 152
  ratings, 135
  salaries, 116, 117
Television sets, cost of, 90-93
  number of, in United States, 90
Telstar, 21
Terkel, Studs, 64
Testing (*see* Audience research)
Textbooks, corporations influencing, 25, 26
Thomas, Alan, 121
Thomas, Danny, 117
Thompson, J. Walter, agency, 126, 183, 188
Thompson, Robert F., 185
Thomson, Roy, 99, 112
"Three Musketeers," 189
Time, as cost of television, 108, 109
  limitations proposed, 197, 198, 224
  for public services, 62, 65, 71
  sales of, 95
  in watching television, 108, 109
Time (magazine), 48, 54, 110, 168
Time-Life Broadcast, Inc., 187
Times, London, 67
Tobacco (*see* Cigarettes)
Totalitarianism, 139, 140, 172
Trendex, 136
Treyz, Oliver, 36, 44, 51, 187
"Tugboat Annie," 190
Twentieth Century Fund, 103
"Twenty-one," 48, 49, 101
"Twenty-six Men," 189

UHF stations, 94, 112n., 209
UHF television, 32, 95, 123, 224
Underdeveloped nations, broadcasts to, 12, 13, 190-193, 199
UNESCO, 143, 144, 166, 170
Unions (*see* Labor unions)
United Nations, broadcasts, 124, 206
  Declaration of Rights of the Child, 192
  Food and Agriculture Organization, 192
  neglected in news broadcasts, 199, 200

United States, government (*see* Congress; Government; names of bureaus and departments)
image of, 12, 13, 21, 190-196, 198-201
United States Grain Corporation, 209
United States Housing Corporation, 209
United States Information Agency, 45, 188, 195, 216
United States Shipping Board, 209
United States Steel Corporation, 30
"The Untouchables," 171, 187, 191

Values on television, 150-156, 158, 165, 166
conformity, 152
prestige, 152
spending, 151
Variety, 71
Vaughan Williams, Ralph, 148
Venice Conference, 1950, 222
VHF, 32, 209
Videodex, Inc., 133
Violence on television, 145, 146, 152-154, 166-174
forbidden in Japan, 144, 196
French and Mexican regulations on, 197
Voice of America, 13, 195, 196, 216

Wachuku, Jaja, 193
Wage and Hours Act, 87
Wallander, Arthur W., 171
War Finance Corporation, 209
Ward, Barbara, 61, 180
Warner Brothers, 44, 187
Warshow, Robert, 154
Warwick, John P., 65
Wasem, Erich, 144
Wasey, Erwin, agency, 183
Wasserman, Lew R., 116
Watts, W. Walter, 35
WBNY, 124

WCBS-TV, 61, 112, 146, 147
Weaver, Pat, 44
Weinberg, Meyer, *TV and America*, 61
Wertham, Fredric, 156, 172, 173
West Germany (*see* Germany)
Western Electric, 27, 31
Westerns, Indians in, 157
women in, 154
Westinghouse, 20, 33, 86
WFMT, 64, 139
Perspective, 221
Wheeler, Bill, 72
"Whirlybirds," 189
White, Stephen, 156
"White Paper," 125
Whyte, William H., *The Organization Man*, 24
"Wide Wide World," 68
Wiener, Norbert, 166
Wilkey, Gene, 91
Wilson, Charles, 28, 29
Wilson, W. W., *Pressure Group*, 182, 183
Wilson, Woodrow, 206
Wireless Ship Act of 1912, 69
Wiskari, Werner, 184
Wisner, Jerome B., 224
WNYC, 206
Women as television characters, 154, 155
World War II, 140
WPIX, 146
Wrather, Jack, Organization, 187, 189
Wrestling matches, 47, 164
Wright, Robert, 117
Writers in television, 66, 67
Würth, Elisabeth, 149
"Wyatt Earp," 187

Young, Loretta, 117

Ziferstein, Isidore, 175
ZIV (United Artists), 189